1994

The Victimization and Exploitation
of Women and Children

The Victimization and Exploitation of Women and Children

A Study of Physical, Mental and Sexual Maltreatment in the United States

by R. Barri Flowers

McFarland & Company, Inc., Publishers
Jefferson, North Carolina, and London

British Library Cataloguing-in-Publication data are available

Library of Congress Cataloguing-in-Publication Data

Flowers, Ronald B.
    The victimization and exploitation of women and children : a study
of physical, mental and sexual maltreatment in the United States /
by R. Barri Flowers.
      p. cm.
    Includes bibliographical references and index.
    ISBN 0-89950-978-9 (lib. bdg. : 50# alk. paper) ∞
    1. Women—Crimes against—United States.   2. Children—Crimes
against—United States.   3. Abused women—United States.   4. Child
abuse—United States.   5. Wife abuse—United States.   I. Title.
HV6250.W65F55   1994
362.82'92—dc20   94-16362
                                               CIP

Manufactured in the United States of America

McFarland & Company, Inc., Publishers
 Box 611, Jefferson, North Carolina 28640

To my mermaid and dream girl
come to life as Audra, Angelique, and Cinderella...rolled into one

And my longtime friends Tanya, Leslie, Maria, and Marcy,
who represent the best in life and camaraderie

Contents

Part IV : The Violent Victimization of Women

Part V : The Sexploitation of Women

Part VI : Protecting Women and Children
from Violence and Exploitation

Figures and Tables

FIGURES

TABLES

ix

Preface

The 1980s and 1990s have seen a surge in the incidence of violence and aggression against women and children in the United States. Many believe this to be a product of a nation with easy access to guns. Others blame the rampant sexual exploitation of women and children in pornographic materials. Yet others see the victimization as being caused by an increase in domestic violence.

Very likely each of these is partly responsible for crimes of violence against millions of women and children each year. Perhaps equally culpable is the breakdown of the traditional family, the dysfunction of many families, and what appears to be a societal epidemic of selfishness, immorality, and lack of human and family values.

Child abuse, wife battering, domestic violence, sexual assault, pornography, prostitution, school violence, and sexual harassment have received more attention than ever before in the past few years as the nation and its legislators seek to deal with these serious issues and find ways to protect women and children from victimization. Solving these societal ills, each rooted in historical tradition, will not happen overnight. The complexities of hidden victimization, nonuniform laws, gaps in criminal justice, racial and sexual discrimination, victim and offender rights, and a fast changing technological society impede progress in the task ahead.

This book seeks to bring closer attention to the victimization and exploitation of children and women by examining the ways in which they are most susceptible in today's society, including domestic, sexual, and violent vulnerability and victimization. Understanding the dynamics of victimized and exploited women and children will help us to better understand the most effective means to approach the issue of victimization and to find solutions that will ensure the safety of victims or potential victims and treatment or prosecution and detention of perpetrators.

This section would not be complete if I did not express my appreciation to my administrative secretary, Loraine, without whose tireless devotion to painstakingly preparing tables and figures and typing the manuscript, this book would never have seen publication.

R. Barri Flowers is also the author of The Adolescent Criminal: An Examination of Today's Juvenile Offender *(McFarland, 1990).*

Introduction

Recent years have seen highly publicized cases of women and children who have been victimized by violence and exploitation. These have sadly served to dramatize a problem affecting countless children and women (whose voices are often never heard nor their faces seen by the public). Despite this greater recognition of the victimized and exploited woman and child and new laws designed to halt or prevent victimization, in reality, many women and children are more vulnerable to crime and violence than ever before.

Escaping violent homes, environments, or circumstances is hard for some and nearly impossible for others. The result is that no woman or child in the United States can be presumed to be safe from violence or exploitative victimization as long as *any* are unsafe or at risk.

The Victimization and Exploitation of Women and Children will explore the various means by which women and children are most often victimized today. The text concentrates on the incidence, dimensions, nature, correlates, causation, and legal avenues in responding to such victimization.

The book is divided into six parts. Part I examines family issues and child victimization including child abuse, domestic violence, runaways and "throwaways," and missing and abducted children.

Part II looks at the sexual exploitation and victimization of children in America, including sexual abuse, incest and child molestation, statutory rape and other sex crimes, child prostitution, and child pornography.

Part III explores violent crimes against children, such as murder, rape, and assault, as well as school crime and violence.

1

Part IV examines the violent criminal victimization of women, including murder, assault, rape, and battering.

Part V studies the sexual exploitation of women in American society, including the prostitution of women, pornography, sexual harassment, and stalking.

Part VI addresses legislative responses to the victimization and exploitation of women and children in the form of new and amended laws, as well as national and local agencies established to prevent victimization and protect victims.

PART I

Family Dynamics and Child Victimization

1. Child Abuse and Neglect

One of the greatest human tragedies occurs daily in homes across the United States. The victimization of children through abuse and neglect affects millions of American families. It is but part of the larger epidemic of domestic violence and family dysfunction. The last decade has seen significant strides in the understanding, recognition, and prevention of child abuse and neglect. This, in turn, has resulted in more effective intervention by social service agencies, learning institutions, and community organizations. Yet the dimension and severity of the problem remain.

DEFINING CHILD ABUSE AND NEGLECT

Definitions of child abuse and neglect have varied greatly, depending upon the source and parameters used. C. Henry Kempe's battered child syndrome defined the physical injuries of abused children.[1] Vincent Fontana's "maltreatment syndrome" broadened the definition to include neglect.[2] "Emotional neglect" was defined by a group of professionals as the "parent's refusal to recognize and take action to ameliorate a child's identified emotional disturbance."[3] David Mrazek and Patricia Mrazek defined child sexual abuse as the sexual misuse of a child for an adult's own gratification without proper concern for the child's psychosexual development.[4]

The Child Abuse Prevention and Treatment Act (Public Law 100-294) defines child abuse and neglect as

> the physical or mental injury, sexual abuse or exploitation, negligent treatment, or maltreatment of a child by a person who is responsible

5

for the child's welfare, under circumstances which indicate that the child's health or welfare is harmed or threatened thereby.[5]

The Child Abuse Amendments of 1984 (Public Law 98-457) expanded the definition of child abuse and neglect to include the withholding of medical treatment to an infant with a life threatening health condition or complication.[6]

Consistent with the broad based legal definition of child abuse and neglect is one adopted by the National Association of Public Child Welfare Administrators (NAPCWA), which defines child abuse and neglect as

> any recent act or failure to act on the part of a parent or caretaker, which results in death or serious physical, sexual, or emotional harm or presents an imminent risk of serious harm to a person under age 18.[7]

Because of the many dimensions child abuse and neglect can take, four general categories have been established: physical abuse, child neglect, sexual abuse, and psychological or emotional abuse.

Physical abuse refers to physical injury such as beating, punching, kicking, bruising, burning, etc., perpetrated upon a child by a caretaker. The degree of such abuse, the age of the abused, and the harm to the child as a result are all considered in defining the act as physical abuse (as opposed, for example, to acceptable physical punishment or discipline).

Child neglect refers to the failure of the parent or caretaker to provide adequately for the basic needs of the child. The National Incidence Study (NIS) subdivides child neglect into three types of neglect:

- Physical neglect—such as abandonment, inadequate health care, nonsupervision, and forcing the child to leave home (the child then becomes what is known colloquially as a "throwaway").
- Educational neglect—such as condoning truancy or failure to see to the child's educational needs.
- Emotional neglect—includes failure to meet the child's psychological needs, allowing the child to witness domestic violence (such as wife battering), condoning drug use by the minor.

Sexual abuse refers to sexual acts perpetrated upon a child by a parent or caretaker, such as fondling, intercourse, incest, sodomy, and sexual exploitation. This is differentiated from sexual violations of a child by a stranger or non-caretaker which would fall under the criminal laws as sexual assault. Both types of sexual victimization will be examined more closely in Part II.

Emotional or psychological abuse refers to acts or injury by the parent, guardian, or caretaker that cause or could potentially cause serious behavioral, emotional, cognitive, or mental disorders to the child.

Experts agree that although these types of child abuse and neglect can occur independently of one another, in many instances, they tend to go hand in hand. In nearly all cases, two or more categories are present in the child's victimization.

WHAT IS THE EXTENT OF THE PROBLEM?

Most estimates indicate that the problem of child abuse and neglect is severe in the United States.[7] In an April 1993 report of its annual fifty state survey, the National Committee for Prevention of Child Abuse (NCPCA) estimated that 2,936,000 children were reported for child abuse and/or neglect to child protective services or public social service agencies in the U.S. in 1992.[8] Of these cases, approximately 1,160,400 children were substantiated as victims of abuse and/or neglect for an overall substantiation rate of 40 percent.

The NCPCA survey found that over half the reported cases involved abuse in one form or another, with physical abuse accounting for slightly more than one in every four cases of abuse, followed by sexual abuse in nearly one-fifth of the cases, and emotional abuse reported in less than 10 percent of the cases.

Neglected children accounted for nearly half the cases of the child abuse and neglect reported in the 1992 survey, with other forms of neglect/abuse such as abandonment accounting for under 10 percent of the cases.

The National Child Abuse and Neglect Data System (NCANDS) also collects national data on child abuse and neglect. In its *Working Paper #2: 1991 Summary Data Component* (SDC), NCANDS estimated that 2.7 million children were reported as abused or neglected in the United States in 1991, with approximately 862,639 of the cases substantiated following an investigation. The substantiation rate of 39.3 percent increased 3.7 percent over the data from the 1990 SDC.[9]

8

TABLE 1-1

Substantiated Child Maltreatment, by Type, 1991 Study

	Totals[a]	Percentage
Total Maltreatment	838,232	100%
Neglect	367,200	44%
Physical Abuse	204,404	24%
Sexual Abuse	129,697	15%
Other/Unknown	70,541	9%
Emotional Maltreatment	49,124	6%
Medical Neglect	17,266	2%

[a] Based on forty-five states reporting.

Source: National Center on Child Abuse and Neglect, *National Child Abuse and Neglect Data System: Working Paper #2—1991 Summary Data Component* (Washington, D.C.: Government Printing Office, 1993), p. 29.

TABLE 1-2

Comparison of National Estimates of Reported Child Abuse and Neglect

Year	Source	Estimates of Children Reported
1986	National Incidence Study (NIS-2)	1,424,400
1987	American Humane	2,178,000
1988	National Committee for Prevention of Child Abuse (NCPCA)	2,265,000
1989	NCPCA	2,435,000
1990	NCPCA	2,557,000
1990	Summary Data Component (SDC)	2,600,000
1991	SDC	2,700,000
1991	NCPCA	2,723,000
1992	NCPCA	2,936,000

Source: *Child Abuse and Neglect Data: AHA Fact Sheet #1* (Englewood, Co.: American Humane Association, 1994), p. 1; National Center on Child Abuse and Neglect, *National Incidence and Prevalence of Child Abuse and Neglect: 1988* (NIS-2) (Rockville, MD: Westat, 1991).

The breakdown of substantiated maltreatment in the NCANDS findings for 1991 are shown in Table 1-1. Nearly twice as many victims of maltreatment were found to be neglected as physically abused. Over 40 percent of the substantiated cases of child maltreatment were classified as neglect, compared to just under one-fourth physical abuse, and 15 percent sexual abuse. Emotional maltreatment and medical neglect constituted less than 10 percent of the substantiated cases.

Table 1-2 compares the estimates of national studies of reported child abuse and neglect between 1986 and 1992. The figures indicate that reported child maltreatment has risen steadily over the period, approaching 3 million by 1992. The estimates of children reported as abused or neglected more than doubled from the second National Incidence Study (NIS-2) conducted in 1986 to the 1992 NCPCA survey.

Other studies have given attention as well to the widespread problem of child abuse and neglect. David Gil estimated that between 2.5 and 4 million children are maltreated annually.[10] A study conducted by Murray Straus and his colleagues of 2,143 American families with children aged 3 to 17 during the year of the survey, found that in families where abuse had ever happened, 8 percent of the children were punched, kicked, or bitten approximately 9 times per year; 4 percent were abused around 6 times yearly; and 3 percent were the victims of a knife or gun.[11]

THE NATURE OF CHILD ABUSE AND NEGLECT

Of the four major types of child abuse and neglect (physical, sexual, emotional/psychological, and neglect) victimization is most likely to occur as a result of neglect of the child (see Figure 1.1). According to the NCPCA, 45 percent of all reported cases of child maltreatment in 1992 involved neglect; while physical abuse accounted for 27 percent of the cases; and sexual abuse, 17 percent. Emotional abuse cases made up only 7 percent of reported child abuse and neglect, with the remainder of cases including abandonment and dependency.

The NIS-2 broke down the incidence of neglect by type (see Figure 1.2). More than half the cases of child neglect were defined as physical neglect. Nearly 29 percent involved educational neglect, with just over 20 percent of the neglect described as emotional neglect.

Given that most instances of child abuse and neglect are believed to go unreported, the full extent and range of all child victimization may never be fully recognized.[12]

FIGURE 1-1

The Distribution of
Child Abuse and Neglect

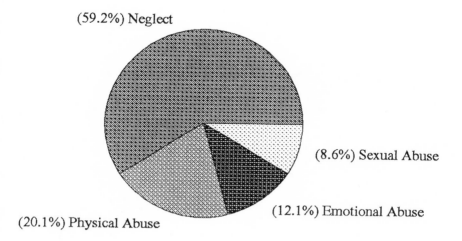

(59.2%) Neglect

(8.6%) Sexual Abuse

(12.1%) Emotional Abuse

(20.1%) Physical Abuse

Source: *Child Abuse and Neglect Data: AHA Fact Sheet #1.* (Englewood, CO: American Humane Association, 1994), p. 1.

FATALITIES AND CHILD ABUSE

Child abuse related fatalities are becoming more frequent. The NCPCA estimated that 1,261 children died in the United States in 1992 due to abuse and/or neglect. The rate of fatalities has risen 49% since 1985. Physical abuse accounts for 6 of every 10 deaths, while physical neglect causes 4 in 10 fatalities each year. Ray Helfer warned that unless the incidence of child abuse was curtailed, as many as 5,000 children a year could die due to abuse by parents or caretakers.[13]

The typical mother or father who kills their children are characterized as follows:

> Women who kill their infants or young children usually are severely disturbed, suffer from extreme bouts of depression, and may experience delusions. Before a woman kills her offspring, she is likely

FIGURE 1-2

The Distribution of Child Neglect

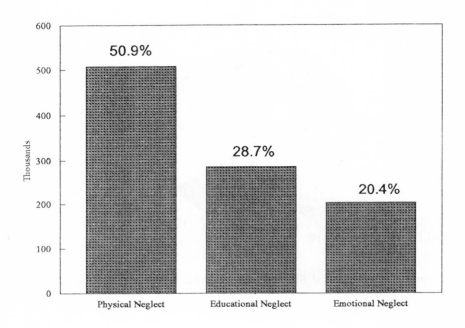

Source: *Child Abuse and Neglect: A Shared Community Concern* (Revised March 1992). (Washington, D.C.: U.S. Department of Health and Human Services, 1992), p. 4.

---

to go through a preliminary period when she thinks about how to commit the crime, visualizes the dead child and considers suicide. Fathers rarely kill their young children, but when they do, they also build up to the crime and often have a history of child abuse.

Fathers who murder are more likely to kill their teenage sons. These men are marginally adequate husbands and fathers who feel inferior and frustrated by life. Guns and alcohol play significant roles in their lives. Their criminal records, if any, usually involve drinking, drunk driving, and disorderly conduct. They rarely have any history of psychiatric illness. They simply are explosive individuals who kill impulsively.[14]

CHARACTERISTICS OF ABUSIVE
AND NEGLECTFUL PARENTS

Parents or guardians of abused and neglected children are often described as being impulsive, immature, dependent, self-centered, and rejecting of their children. They usually have limited nurturing and coping skills, a poor self-image, and a low level of tolerance. Violence is often a way of life.

Abusive or neglectful parents tend to be socially isolated and distrusting of others, often reside in high-risk neighborhoods for child maltreatment, have high stress levels, and display a general pattern of social impoverishment.[15]

Relationship to the Child

According to Gil's epidemiological study of child abuse in the United States, 86 percent of the perpetrators of child abuse were found to be parents or parent surrogates.[16] The mother or mother substitute was the abuser in 47.6 percent of the cases, compared to 39.2 of the cases in which the father or father substitute was the abuser.

A study by the American Humane Association (AHA) supported Gil's findings.[17] The AHA research on the perpetrator's relationship to the child by type of maltreatment reached the following conclusions:

- Physical abuse is more likely when a nonrelative or parent surrogate is the perpetrator.
- Sexual abuse is more often associated with parent surrogates or guardians than biological parents.
- Deprivation of necessities is greatest when the parent is directly responsible for the neglect.

Nearly half the children were living with a single, unemployed female caretaker receiving welfare during the year the AHA study was conducted.

Peggy Smith and Marvin Bohnstedt's study of child victimization found that mothers in single-parent households were guilty of the highest rate of neglect.[18] Abuse occurred more in homes with fewer children. When there were more children, neglect was more likely to take place.

Gender of the Parent

Much of the data indicates that female parents or caretakers are more likely than male parents or caretakers to maltreat their children. Richard Gelles found that 68 percent of the mothers versus 58 percent of the fathers in his study physically abused their children at least once.[19] Brandt Steele and C. Pollock's study of abuse revealed that the mother was the perpetrator in 50 of 57 cases examined.[20]

Other researchers suggest that the gender differences of abusive parents are not nearly as great. Blair Justice and Rita Justice's study indicates a more even split between female and male abusers.[21]

Age of the Parent

The majority of child abusers tend to fall within the 20 to 40 age group, the typical child-bearing and rearing years. Seventy-one percent of the mother or mother substitutes and 66 percent of the father or father substitutes in Gil's sample were between 20 and 40 years of age.[22] In the Justices' study, 75 percent of the abusive parents were found to be in this age range.[23]

Race-Ethnicity of the Parent

A strong correlation between race or ethnicity and child abuse and neglect has not been established in the literature. Child abusers are not overrepresented in any particular race or ethnicity; rather it is a problem that stretches across racial and ethnic lines. Official data suggest that child abuse is more prevalent among blacks than whites.[24] However, other research has found the incidence of child abuse to be lower in black families than white families.[25]

CHARACTERISTICS OF ABUSED AND NEGLECTED CHILDREN

At-Risk Factors

Certain children appear to be at risk or predisposed to conditions that lead to child abuse or neglect. F. J. Bishop identified six types of children that represent a "special" risk of maltreatment:

- Congenitally malformed babies.
- Premature babies.
- Illegitimate children.
- Children conceived during the mother's depressive illness.
- Twins.
- Children of mothers with frequent pregnancies and excessive work-loads.[26]

Unwanted pregnancies and pregnancy shortly after the birth of a previous child have also been shown to correlate with child abuse.[27] The size of the family may further place some children at greater risk for maltreatment. Gil reported that abused children were twice as likely to come from families with four or more children than was the case for the population as a whole.[28] Studies conducted in the United States, New Zealand, and England found that the average size for abusive families greatly exceeded the national average.[29]

In Ray Helfer's psychodynamic model of abuse, three events or circumstances had to be present for child abuse to occur: 1) a very special type of child, 2) a crisis or series of crises, 3) the parents' potential for abuse.[30] The Justices pointed towards situational and maturational crises as at risk factors for abuse.[31] Situational crises refer to "a rapid series of situational events." Maturational crises include marriage, pregnancy, a child leaving home, and retirement.

J. Milowe and R. Lourie referred to "difficult" children in their study and the relationship to abuse.[32] They found that some children's "difficult nature" or "irritable cry" predisposed them to child abuse. The literature suggests that even "normal" parents may resort to maltreating a particularly irritating or difficult child.

Age of the Child

The typical age of an abused or neglected child seems to vary with the type of maltreatment. The NIS found that the incidence of physical abuse was lowest for children aged two and under.[33] However, when such children were subjected to physical abuse, they were more likely than older children to be seriously or fatally injured. The study found that the incidence of neglect—emotional and educational—generally increased with age.

Gelles' study of physical violence against children age 3 and older found that abuse was greater the younger the age group.[34] Eighty-four percent of the children ages 3 to 4 were slapped or spanked the year of the survey, compared to 80 percent of the children 5 to 9, 48 percent aged 10 to 14, and 23 percent 15 to 17 years of age.

R. Galdston's study of abused children and their parents found the highest incidence of abuse to be amongst children 3 months to 3½ years old.[35] P. Resnick's examination of child murder perpetrated by parents indicated that most deaths occurred during the first year of life.[36]

The relationship between age and child abuse and neglect, by type, can be seen in Kentucky's 1991 annual report on child maltreatment (Table 1-3). Children aged 0 to 5 accounted for nearly 30 percent of the physical abuse reported and more than one-quarter of the sexual abuse. Nearly half the cases of neglect and dependency fell into this age group.

The highest percentage of physical and sexual abuse occurred amongst the 11 to 15 age group, accounting for more than one-third of the reports. Children aged 6 to 10 were maltreated in 28 percent of the cases. These patterns have proven to be fairly consistent in other states.

Gender of the Child

In general, the rate of child abuse and neglect by sex shows little difference between boys and girls. Justice and Justice found that over half the abused children in their study were female[37]; Gil reported just the opposite with more than half the victims of abuse being male.[38] The NIS found neglect of boys and girls to be relatively equal.[39]

The varying relationship between gender and child abuse and neglect is often associated with the age of the child and type of mistreatment. Murray Straus, Richard Gelles, and Suzanne Steinmetz found that maltreatment rates peaked at ages 3 to 4 and 15 to 17, with boys abused slightly more than girls.[40] Data of the NIS revealed that females are at greater risk for physical and sexual abuse.[41] The rate of sexual abuse for females was more than three times that for males.

Race of the Child

Race has not been shown to be a significant factor in child abuse and neglect overall. White children in lower income families tend to have a higher victimization rate than lower income children of other races.[42] However, reported cases of child maltreatment show a disproportionate rate of abuse among blacks. This is believed to be a reflection of greater ability by white and higher income families to seek private rather than public treatment for cases of abuse or neglect, where reporting is less likely.[43]

CORRELATES OF CHILD ABUSE AND NEGLECT

Socioeconomics

Although child maltreatment is reflected across the socioeconomic strata, children on the lower end of the social and economic classes face a higher susceptibility of being abused or neglected. The NIS found that children from families with an income below $15,000 had a rate of victimization nearly seven times that of children from higher income families.[44] In Bennie and Sclare's study eight of ten families experiencing child abuse were low income families.[45] In Gil's study, 77 percent of the fathers and 68 percent of the mothers were in skilled or semiskilled jobs.[46] The majority of the abusive parents did not finish high school, with 24 percent failing to surpass eighth grade.

Substance Abuse

In most cases of child maltreatment, alcohol or drugs have been shown to be a factor. Michael Martin and James Walters found a relationship between child sexual abuse and promiscuous, alcoholic fathers; and child abandonment and alcoholic mothers.[47] D. W. Behling's study of alcohol and child abuse found that 84 percent of the abused children had at least one alcoholic parent, while 64 percent of the suspected child abusers abused alcohol.[48]

In other studies, the correlation between drug abuse and child abuse has been well documented. Brandt Steele reported that chronic drug abuse can "cause severe distortions of mental functioning," which may lead to child abuse and other types of violent behavior.[49]

The Cycle of Child Abuse

There is solid support for an intergenerational cycle of child abuse. Most child abusers were themselves the victims of abuse. One study

TABLE 1-3

Reported Child Abuse and Neglect, in Kentucky, by Type and Age of Child, 1991

Type of Maltreatment

Age	Physical Abuse	Sexual Abuse	Neglect	Dependency	Total[a]
0-5	29.6%	25.8%	47.7%	48.8%	41.6%
6-10	27.3%	27.2%	28.6%	23.6%	27.9%
11-15	34.1%	36.9%	19.8%	20.4%	24.7%
16+	9.1%	10.0%	3.9%	7.2%	5.8%

[a]The percentages are for 51,465 children reported for abuse or neglect in the state of Kentucky.

Source: Division of Program Management, *Profile on Child Abuse and Neglect: Fiscal Year 1991* (Frankfurt, KY: Department for Social Services, 1991), p. 21.

found that 75 percent of the child sexual abusers were sexually abused during childhood.[50] Fontana contended that the childhoods of abusive parents were often unloving, cruel, and marked by brutality.[51] Christopher Ounsted and colleagues' study lends further evidence that child abuse reflects a family history of violence from generation to generation.[52] Norman Polansky and associates reached the same conclusions when examining the cycle of child neglect. The researchers noted "a lifestyle of neglect that comes from the sharing and passing on of family misfortunes."[53]

Juvenile Delinquency

Child maltreatment often leads to the maltreated becoming involved in juvenile delinquency and criminal behavior. Martin Haskell and Lewis Yablonsky advanced that juvenile detention facilities are filled with juveniles who were victims of child abuse and family violence.[54] Brandt Steele noted a study in which 82 percent of the juvenile offenders had a history of abuse and neglect; 43 percent of the sample admitted to being knocked unconscious by a parent.[55] H. E. Simmons postulated that "a brutal parent tends to produce a brutal child," who turns the hostility felt towards the parent into violence against others.[56]

A study of 653 delinquents by D. E. Adams and associates found that 43 percent of the sample had been abused, neglected, or abandoned.[57] In an examination of chronically violent juvenile offenders, Jeanne Cyriaque concluded that "violence-dominated lifestyles [of] . . . sexually and physically abusing families particularly characterize juvenile murders and sex offenders."[58] Other studies have linked excessive physical disciplinary practices with juvenile delinquency and violent aggression in children.[59]

CAUSES OF CHILD ABUSE AND NEGLECT

Clearly, child maltreatment is a reflection of many factors, often varying in degree and substance from family to family, type of abuse or neglect, and even society to society. In general, the following factors have been associated with creating, contributing to, or continuing abusive or neglectful practices:

- Vulnerability of the child.
- Habitual behavior by the parent/guardian.
- Unemployment/loss of income.
- Severe stress and strain.
- Extreme physical discipline.
- Learned behavior due to a cycle of maltreatment or environmental conditions.
- Cultural tolerance for abuse and/or neglect.
- Substance use/abuse.
- Mental instability of the parent/caretaker.

There are also more specific influences and conditions that can cause child abuse and neglect including a human history of child maltreatment, personality traits and family structure.

A Human History of Child Maltreatment

Perhaps it is the history of human existence itself and the historical mistreatment of children that is most to blame for child abuse and neglect. Children have, to some extent, always been viewed as unequal to parents and adults, subject to discipline at the parents' whim or choice of disciplinary manner, and personal property to be abused or exploited as the parent saw fit.[60] In the *Bibliotheca Scholastica* in 1633 was the dictum: "Spare the rod, spoil the child." The Bible itself has a number of references that encourage physical abuse of children. In Proverbs, for example, there is: "Discipline your son in his early years while there is hope... " (19:18) and "A youngster's heart is filled with rebellion, but punishment will drive it out of him" (22:15).

The right to property and the right to own children were often viewed as one and the same historically. Aristotle contended: "The justice of a master or a father is a different thing from that of a citizen, for a son or slave is property, and there can be no justice to one's own property."[61] In ancient Rome, the *patria potestas* empowered a father with the absolute right to sell, abandon, offer as sacrifice, murder, or determine what mode of mistreatment to perpetrate upon his child.[62]

Further historical precedent in permissive child maltreatment can be seen in such condoned or accepted practices as infanticide, child mutilation, abandonment, sexual exploitation of children, and child labor.[63] With this backdrop rooted in many customs, traditions, and beliefs, it is not surprising that child abuse and neglect continue as a sad way of life for many.

Personality Traits

This model of child abuse considers the underlying personality or character traits of the abuser as causal to abusive behavior, such as being immature, impulse-ridden, self-centered, highly frustrated, and habitually aggressive.[64] E. J. Merrill established four types of abusive parents in relation to personality traits:

- Chronically hostile and aggressive.
- Rigid, compulsive, lacking warmth and reason.
- A high degree of passivity and dependence.
- Extreme frustration.[65]

The major criticism with the personality trait model of child abuse is that while describing such traits, it fails to explain a cause and effect with respect to child abuse. Yet such limitations are mitigated when placed in context with the social environment the abuser and abusive live in.

Family Structure

The way in which the family is structured often plays an important role in the formation of child abuse and neglect as well as other family dysfunction. The establishment of certain alliances, coalitions, enmeshments, and disengagements among family members can create conditions conducive to child maltreatment. Although theories on family structure fail to focus directly on the problem of child abuse and neglect, they offer promise with regard to offering causal elements of child maltreatment and designing therapeutic intervention techniques.

Within the concept of coalitions are repeated findings that illegitimate and unwanted children face higher risks for abuse and neglect than other children.[66] Scapegoating by parents is also a behavior pattern attributed to family structure and often cited as a factor in abuse.[67]

THE EFFECTS OF CHILD ABUSE ON THE VICTIM

Child abuse can be devastating to its victims in many ways, both short- and long-term. Studies show that in addition to fractures and internal injuries, child physical abuse can result in mental retardation, cerebral palsy, seizures, hearing or visual damage, and learning difficulties.[68] Child neglect is also linked to physical problems for the child, such as malnutrition and inadequate medical care, which can have profound effects on the child's body and brain development.[69]

Abused and neglected children are also more susceptible to emotional distress than other children and are more likely to experience health problems such as poor weight gain, growth retardation, anemia, and neurological abnormalities.[70]

Psychological damage to the abused child has also been well documented. Common characteristics noted among abused children include "impaired capacity to enjoy life, withdrawal, low self-esteem, school learning problems, hypervigilance, and pseudomature behavior."[71] A study of emotional and behavioral problems experienced by abused children sometime after their original abuse found that the subjects displayed symptoms including hostility, social isolation, disruptive behavior, and violence.[72]

2. Domestic Violence

Domestic victimization of children does not end within the recognized parameters of child abuse and neglect. Family violence and dysfunction in the home are also cause for alarm with respect to child maltreatment. Children living in violent families face not only the risk of violence from parents, siblings or extended family members, but also may be subjected to emotional abuse and neglect as a result. In this chapter, we will explore the frightening problem of domestic violence.

THE SCOPE OF DOMESTIC VIOLENCE

Because of its family nature, domestic violence is often hidden from law enforcement, social service workers, victimization survey interviewers, and researchers. Consequently, it is difficult to assess accurately the magnitude of family violence. It is known that 11 to 52 percent of all assaults occur in domestic settings,[1] 12 to 18 percent of the murders in the United States annually are committed by spouses,[2] and domestic violence calls are among the most frequent and dangerous for police officers.[3]

Official data such as the Federal Bureau of Investigation's annual volume, *Crime in the United States: Uniform Crime Reports* (*UCR*) give only a glimpse of domestic violence in America, limiting its measurement to the number of persons arrested for "offenses against family and children" and homicide statistics.[4] In 1992, 66,423 people were arrested for offenses against family and children. This represented an 83.1 percent increase over the figures for 1983.[5] Of the 22,540 murders or nonnegligent manslaughters recorded by police agencies in 1992, 12 percent were perpetrated by family members of the victim. Another 35 percent of the victims were murdered by acquaintances.[6]

Victimization data indicate that the incidence of family violence is far greater than shown through official crime figures. The most comprehensive victimization survey is the U.S. Department of Justice's Bureau of Justice Statistics annual report, *Criminal Victimization in the United States: A National Crime Victimization Survey Report (NCVS)*. The report, based on interviews with persons aged 12 and over, estimates that approximately 456,000 cases of family violence occur each year.[7]

Between 1973 and 1981, the NCVS estimated that 4.1 million violent victimizations occurred in which the offender and victim were related.[8] In more than half the cases, the offender was a spouse or ex-spouse. Parents physically abusing children averaged 29,000 cases per year.

Another NCVS survey of female victims of violent crime between 1979 and 1987 showed that intimates—family members, ex-spouses, boyfriends, ex-boyfriends—committed 5.6 million victimizations against females over the nine year period.[9] This averaged out to nearly 626,000 violent victimizations yearly. Females were estimated to be the victims of parental violence nearly 21,000 times annually.

In 1991, 18.5 percent of the 2.2 million single-offender violent victimizations measured by the NCVS involved people who were related. As shown in Table 2-1, spouses and ex-spouses accounted for 11 percent of the total single-offender crimes of violence. However, 43.8 percent of victimizations involved persons unrelated but well known to the victim. We can reasonably assume that in the absence of a classification for intimates not married, a high percentage of the victimizations were committed by current or ex-lovers/mates. This further underscores the severity of domestic violence in the United States.

Multiple-offender victimizations in which at least one offender was known to the victim involved relatives in about 4 percent of the cases. Twenty-five percent of the victims were well associated with some or all of the perpetrators.[10]

Unreported Family Violence

There is strong reason to believe that most domestic violence goes unreported, making it much more difficult to assess its incidence and help victims. The NCVS found that the majority of crime victimizations it measured in 1991 were not reported to the police. Many victims of family violence are also reluctant to report their victimization to survey interviewers.

The main reasons for this underreporting can be seen in Table 2-2. The most common reason given by victims related to the offender was the belief that the victimization was a private or personal matter. Nearly 6 in 10 such violent victimizations went unreported. Fear of reprisal was the second most often reason cited for not reporting family violence, followed by fearing that nothing could be done, lack of proof, and the belief that police would not respond to the complaint.

THE NATURE
OF DOMESTIC VIOLENCE

Domestic violence spans the range of violent encounters and includes physical assaults, sexual assaults, verbal assaults, intimidation, threats, extreme emotional or psychological neglect, and death. The perpetrator-to-victim relationship also varies from situation to situation. Most commonly recognized is the parent-to-child violence (child abuse). Other patterns of domestic violence can be just as frequent and violent such as parent-to-parent violence (spouse abuse), child-to-parent violence (parent or grandparent abuse), and child-to-child violence (sibling abuse). Violence within the family setting knows no boundaries with respect to socioeconomics, race, ethnicity, or education. It can happen in any family and affects each member.

An NCVS nine year study of family violence produced the following key findings on the nature of domestic violence:

- Spouse-to-spouse violence occurred most frequently.
- Eighty-eight percent of the domestic violence involved assaults.
- One-third of the assaults involved use of a weapon or serious injury.
- Ten percent of the victimizations were robberies.
- Two percent were rape victimizations.
- One-quarter of the victims of spousal assaults had suffered at least three such victimizations within the previous six months.
- Fifteen percent of the parent-to-child violence occurred at least three times over six months.[11]

TABLE 2-1

Percent Distribution of Single-Offender Victimizations, by Type of Crime and Detailed Victim-Offender Relationship, 1991

Type of Crime	Number of Single-Offender Victimizations	Total	Related Total	Spouse	Ex-Spouse	Parent	Own Child	Brother or Sister	Other Relative	Well Known, Not Related[b]	Casual Acquaintance
Crimes of Violence	**2,198,390**	**100%**	**18.5%**	**7.7%**	**3.3%**	**0.6%[a]**	**2.1%**	**2.1%**	**2.8%**	**43.8%**	**37.7%**
Completed	837,630	100%	25.1	11.8	3.7	0.8a	1.3a	4.4	3.2	45.1	29.8
Attempted	1,360,760	100%	14.5	5.2	3.0	0.5a	2.6	0.6a	2.6	43.0	42.5
Rape	79,860	100%	16.5a	16.5a	0.0a	0.0a	0.0a	0.0a	0.0a	54.7	28.8a
Robbery	145,260	100%	12.0a	6.5a	1.4a	1.3a	0.0a	1.2a	1.5a	53.7	34.4
Completed	100,950	100%	9.1a	5.5a	0.0a	1.9a	0.0a	1.7a	0.0a	56.6	34.3
Attempted	44,300	100%	18.4a	8.8a	4.7a	0.0a	0.0a	0.0a	5.0a	47.0a	34.5a
Assault	1,973,270	100%	19.1	7.4	3.5	0.6a	2.4	2.2	3.0	42.6	38.3
Aggravated	479,160	100%	19.6	8.1	2.0a	0.5a	2.6a	3.3a	3.2a	45.2	35.2
Simple	1,494,100	100%	18.9	7.2	4.0	0.6a	2.3	1.8	3.0	41.8	39.3

Note: Detail may not add to total shown because of rounding.

[a] Estimate is based on about 10 or fewer samples.

[b] Includes data on offenders well known to the victim whose relationship could not be ascertained.

Source: U.S. Department of Justice, *Criminal Victimization in the United States, 1991: A National Crime Victimization Survey Report* (Washington, D.C.: Government Printing Office, 1992), p. 63.

TABLE 2-2

Percent of Violent Victimizations Not Reported to the Police, by Reasons for Not Reporting[a]

Reasons for Nonreporting	Related Offenders	Non-Related Offenders
Private or personal matter	59.0%	23.0%
Fear of reprisal	13.0%	5.0%
Nothing could be done, lack of proof	8.0%	19.0%
Police would not want to be bothered	8.0%	8.0%
Not important enough	7.0%	28.0%
Reported to someone else	5.0%	15.0%
Did not want to get involved	1.0%	3.0%
Too inconvenient or time consuming	1.0%	3.0%
Other reason	18.0%	21.0%

[a] Because some respondents provided more than one answer, the totals exceed 100%.

Source: U.S. Department of Justice, Bureau of Justice Statistics Special Report, *Family Violence* (Washington, D.C.: Government Printing Office, 1984), p. 4.

MURDER WITHIN THE FAMILY

At its worst, domestic violence can lead to murder. In 1992, 2,748 murders were attributed to family members, according to the UCR.[12] The circumstances by relationship of murder victims in 1992 can be seen in Table 2-3. Husbands or wives were the victims-offenders in most of the murders committed by relatives, accounting for nearly 1,300 murders in 1992. Other family members besides parents or children were responsible for the second highest percentage of domestic murders. Most murders committed by relatives involved arguments, felony circumstances or romantic triangles.

Other intimates—boyfriends or girlfriends—were responsible for

TABLE 2-3

Circumstances of Murder, by Victim Relationship to Offender, 1992

				Murder Circumstances				
Total[a]	Total[b]	Felony Type	Suspected Felony Type	Other Than Felony Type	Romantic Triangle	Brawl Related to Alcohol or Drugs	Argument Over Money or Property	Other Arguments
Total	22,540	4,887	280	11,152	335	675	481	6,027
Husband	383	22	0	323	5	17	6	240
Wife	913	37	4	762	34	10	12	480
Mother	121	4	1	97	0	1	8	64
Father	169	13	0	140	0	1	6	102
Son	325	31	0	276	1	4	4	69
Daughter	235	27	0	194	0	3	0	26
Brother	1675	0	146	0	16	17	96	
Sister	42	5	0	30	0	0	0	25
Other Family	393	44	0	307	5	13	27	199
Acquaintance	6,102	1,165	44	4,311	212	294	274	2,168
Friend	843	124	3	652	28	72	46	414
Boyfriend	240	6	0	214	3	5	5	182
Girlfriend	519	20	1	444	14	8	7	327
Neighbor	217	52	0	152	1	10	12	100
Stranger	3,053	1,374	29	1,323	25	104	38	699
Unknown Relationship	8,818	1,958	198	1,781	7	117	19	836

[a] Total number of murder victims for whom supplemental data was supplied.
[b] Includes victims for which circumstances of murder are not specified or unknown.

Source: U.S. Federal Bureau of Investigation, *Crime in the United States: Uniform Crime Reports 1992* (Washington, D.C.: Government Printing Office, 1993), p. 19.

759 murders in 1992 or 3.4 percent of the total murders in the country. Murders involving non-familial intimates were attributed largely to arguments and romantic conflicts.

Children Who Murder Family Members

Although most family homicides are spouse-to-spouse or spouse-to-child (see Chapter 1), children do kill members of the family. In 1992, 2.2 percent of the total murders or nonnegligent manslaughters were committed by children against their parents or siblings. In many instances, such killings come as the result of years of child abuse or neglect or other forms of parental culpability.

The *American Journal of Psychiatry* has advanced that homicidal tendencies among children are often related to extremely violent parents, a history of psychomotor seizures and suicidal behavior, and prior hospitalization of the mother in a psychiatric facility.[13] L. Bender and F. J. Curran contended that the most common factor in child homicide is "the child's tendency to identify himself with aggressive parents, and pattern after their behavior."[14] According to B. M. Cormier and colleagues:

> Amongst those adolescents who kill within the nuclear group, there is an inability to displace the problems encountered with the parents on to a broader group, such as their peers, where the problem can be defused and new gratifications experienced.[15]

Other studies suggest that children who kill are reflective of parental desires or psychological coercion. D. Sargeant postulated that in some cases child killers are the unwitting "lethal agents" of a parent who unconsciously incites them to kill so that the parent can vicariously enjoy the killing.[16] In a study of eight cases of adolescent aggravated assaults and murders, W. M. Easson and R. M. Steinhilber observed that all the adolescents came from normal homes. However, in each case "one or both parents had fostered and had condoned murderous assault."[17]

VIOLENCE BETWEEN SPOUSES

Violence involving a husband and wife has been given increased attention in recent years. This is due to more public awareness of the problem of spousal abuse, greater reporting, and frequent dramatization in movies and books of abusive relationships. Nevertheless, much of the violence between spouses remains hidden.

Estimates of marital abuse and violence reflect its severity. Murray Straus estimated that 65 percent of all married couples resort to some form of violent confrontation during the course of their relationship, 25 percent of the violence being of a serious nature.[18] Richard Gelles found that 55 percent of his sample of married couples had had at least one incident of violence.[19]

The typical offender-victim pattern of marital violence has the male as the aggressor. The assaultive nature of this aggression is often cited as the main factor in marital unhappiness, discord, and divorce.[20] According to official statistics, a woman is beaten or abused by her husband every 18 seconds in the United States.[21] Sociologists estimate that 2 million American women are battered each year.[22] R. Whitehurst theorized that increasing jealousy among husbands as a response to the trend toward social and economic equality for women was a strong factor in wife abuse.[23]

Only recently has husband abuse been taken seriously by researchers. Robert Langley and Richard Levy estimated that 12 million American men have been the victims of physical assaults by their wives during some point in their marriage.[24] Suzanne Steinmetz estimated that 280,000 men in this country are battered annually.[25] A nationwide study of marital violence found that approximately 2 million husbands compared to 1.8 million wives experienced at least one severe episode of spousal violence.

Despite these figures, most evidence indicates that men are more physically abusive and violent towards spouses than women. Police data show wife abuse complaints outnumber husband abuse complaints by a ratio of about 12 to 1.[26] A similar differential comes from NCVS findings which produced a female-to-male abused ratio of 13 to 1.[27]

After analyzing complaints of wives and husbands seeking divorce, G. Levinger wrote that wives' complaints included physical or verbal spousal abuse, neglect, lack of love, and mental cruelty; whereas husbands complained of emotional cruelty, neglect, sexual mismatching, and in-law interference.[28] The effects on children of spousal violence can be just as traumatic. Research shows that children living in violent families are emotionally and psychologically susceptible in adulthood to enacting the role of victim or batterer which they witnessed or experienced during childhood.[29]

The following true account illustrates how spousal violence can affect a child:

> A four-year-old child observed her father kill her mother. The child had been somewhat prepared for this event by her father's previous threats to her mother and, as a result, had to deal less with the unexpectedness of the murder than with the confirmation of her fears and anxieties.[30]

VIOLENCE BETWEEN SIBLINGS

Sibling abuse or violence may be the most underreported, least regarded form of domestic violence. Because society has often deemed wrestling, fighting, and arguing amongst siblings to be normal, expected, or harmless, little serious research has been conducted on violence involving brothers and sisters. Suzanne Steinmetz's study in the late 1970s of sibling violence was the first major empirical research on the subject.[31] The study involved college students at an urban university. Steinmetz's research found the following surprising results:

- Seventy percent used physical violence against siblings.
- Virtually all had been verbally abusive to siblings at some point.

A second study examined violence between 88 pairs of siblings from randomly selected families with two or more children who were between the ages of 3 and 17. Here are the findings:

- Seventy percent aged 8 and under resorted to physical violence to settle conflicts.
- Sixty-eight percent between ages 9 and 14 used violence against siblings.
- Seventy-three percent aged 14 and over perpetrated sibling violence to resolve conflicts.[32]

The conflicts involved:

- The youngest group: possessions such as toys.
- The middle group: infringement of personal space, touching, or looking "funny" at one another.
- The oldest group: responsibilities and social obligations.

Murray Straus and associates' study of family violence found that 75 percent of the families surveyed with children aged 3 to 17 reported some form of physical violence among siblings. Extrapolating the findings nationwide, based on "ever happened," it is estimated that 8.3 million children in this country have been "beaten up" by a brother or sister at some time, while 2.3 million have been victimized at least on one occasion by a sibling knife or gun assault.[33] Eighty-three percent of the male siblings engaged in sibling violence compared to 74 percent of the female siblings.

The message is clear—violence between siblings is no laughing matter. More studies are needed on this aspect of familial dysfunction and domestic violence.

PARENT BATTERING

Violence directed towards parents by children appears to be on the rise as broken homes, child abuse, family pressures, drug and alcohol abuse, and other stress factors of our times play an increasing role in family dynamics and unstable behavior. The "battered parent syndrome" has become so serious a problem that it prompted Richard Gelles to comment: "This is the next layer of family violence to be exposed. And if we were talking about some communicable disease, we'd be talking in terms of an epidemic."[34]

Researchers have estimated that 2.5 million parents in the United States are struck by their children each year.[35] Of these, approximately 900,000 are victims of severe violence, including being victimized by a knife or gun. The Straus and associates study found that nearly 1 in 10 parents reported being physically assaulted by a child during the survey year.[36]

Parent battering is being regarded as the next logical progression in the study of family pathologies. In a study of 15 adolescent psychiatric patients, Carol Warren found 3 main reasons for child violence directed toward parents:

- Violence as a response to the victim's use of alcohol.
- Violence in response to goals being blocked.
- Violence as a resource (such as status might be used).[37]

Other researchers blame children who abuse their parents as the recipients of poor models of social behavior and extremely stressful social circumstances.[38] A strong correlation has been established between parental abuse and child abuse. One study found that "parents who are not violent toward their children stand only a 1 in 400 chance of being on the receiving end. But if a parent is violent toward the child, the probability of attack goes up to 200 out of 400."[39]

The typical offender-victim profile of parental abuse is seen below:

- Teenage sons are most often the perpetrators.
- Most victims are mothers.
- Battered parents are often embarrassed, ashamed, and harbor feelings of guilt and failure.
- Middle-aged victims tend to be the most reluctant to seek help, usually out of fear.
- To keep the family unit intact, victims and parent abusers often hide behind a wall of secrecy and denial.

Child psychiatrist Rudolf Dreikurs postulated that with supportive parenting and encouragement, children can avoid violence towards parents or each other.[40]

GRANDPARENT ABUSE

Symptomatic of parental abuse is grandparent abuse. Often referred to as "granny bashing," the battering of elderly parents is thought by many to be the most neglected form of domestic violence. The relative ease in masking grandparent abuse due to fear, illness, misdiagnosis, and often isolation of the victim makes it difficult to assess its incidence.

Grandparent abuse is often perpetrated by adult children but can also include grandchildren offenders. The abuse can be physical or emotional and usually is a reflection of frustration due to the reversal of dependency roles, stress, socioeconomics, and weakening of the grandparents' power and influence in family decision making. A relationship between grandparent abuse and a cycle of domestic violence in which the grandparent or parent was once the abuser has been documented.[41]

WHAT CAUSES DOMESTIC VIOLENCE?

Family violence is generally a response to a number of familial factors, either individually or in relation to one another. These include a family history of domestic violence, substance abuse, external stresses placing strain on the family structure, and lack of adequate means or motivation to control violent impulses.

Theories of family violence have focused on three areas: (1) psychological theories, (2) social-structural theories, and (3) social-cultural theories.

Psychological Theories

Psychological theories of domestic violence concentrate largely on personality disorders. W. Goode hypothesized that "one reason intimates commit violence against one another is that they are in each other's presence a lot, and few others can anger one so much as those who are close."[42] S. Zalba associated child abuse with parents who exhibited impulse-ridden character disorders and violent or episodic schizophrenia.[43] Other studies have noted the relationship between aggressive children in violent families with the birth of another child, parents' indifference, and separation from parents.[44]

Social-Structural Theories

Social-structural theories relate family violence to the external and environmental factors that affect family life as well as the individual interactions between family members. The socialization of aggression is explored in the social-structural theory of family violence. It posits that children are more aggressive when parents punish them more severely, which perpetuates the cycle of violence.[45] Straus' general systems approach to family violence studies it in relation to family group characteristics such as organization, beliefs, values, and position in the social structure.[46]

Social-Cultural Theories

Social-cultural theories generally rely on factors outside the family as causing family violence. These include socially structured inequality and cultural norms related to abuse, violence, and family relations. David Gil examined the societal power struggles and the effect on domestic violence.[47] D. Abrahamsen noted cultural values and attitudes that sanctioned violence as a way of life.[48] Influential theories in this study of family violence are the structural-functional theory and the subculture-of-violence theory.[49]

THE HISTORICAL CONTEXT OF FAMILY VIOLENCE

The reality of domestic violence is that it is rooted in human history, which therefore must take some of the blame for the problem we face today within the family. Cain murdered his brother Abel long before family murders became almost commonplace. The Greek myth of Oedipus chronicles episodes of parricide, fratricide, filicide, and suicide spanning three generations in one family.[50] Novels written by Charles Dickens and others are replete with examples of domestic violence.[51]

M. A. Freeman once observed of domestic violence: "The home is a very dangerous place and we have more to fear from close members of our family than from total strangers."[52] Richard Gelles and Murray Straus put the problem of family violence in an even more dire perspective:

> With the exception of the police and the military, the family is perhaps the most violent social group, and the home the most violent social setting in our society. A person is more likely to be hit or killed in his or her own home by another family member than anywhere else or by anyone else.[53]

The solution to domestic violence may well lie in the teachings and mistakes of history which seem intent on repetition despite our best efforts to the contrary.

3. Runaways
and Throwaways

One of the saddest things we can imagine is a child living in the streets, with nowhere or no one to turn to for food, shelter, love, or compassion. In fact, this is a reality for thousands of children across America who have run away from home or were literally thrown out by their parents. A great many of these children are victims of dysfunctional and stressful families where there were often physical and sexual abuse, substance abuse, and other domestic crises. Homeless children are further subjected to many of the horrors of street life including AIDS, drugs, disease, prostitution, pornography, and deprivation of any semblance of a normal childhood.

A DIMENSIONAL COMPOSITE
OF THE RUNAWAY

Just how many runaways or throwaways there are at any given time varies from source to source. Most experts would agree that the figures are alarmingly high. Estimates have ranged from hundreds of thousands to millions who run away from home annually.[1] A recent report estimated that of the million plus youths who run away from home each year, more than half had run away at least three times.[2] Approximately 300,000 runaway children are believed to be "hard-core" street kids, who run away over and over.[3]

The best official barometer of runaways can be found in arrest

FIGURE 3-1

Arrests of Runaways by Sex, 1992

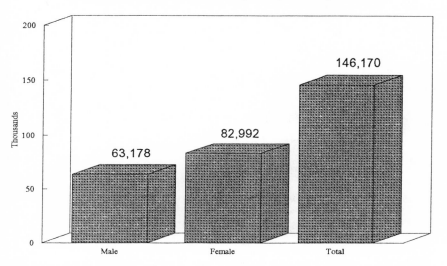

Source: U.S. Federal Bureau of Investigation, *Crime in the United States: Uniform Crime Reports 1992* (Washington, D.C.: Government Printing Office, 1993), pp. 229, 231.

statistics. While such data are inadequate in assessing true runaway figures, they do provide us with a composite of the runaway that seems consistent with other sources. In 1992, there were 146,170 persons arrested as runaways in the United States.[4] Most runaways are female. As shown in Figure 3-1, 82,992 females were arrested as runaways, accounting for 56.8 percent of all arrests for running away in 1992. However, when age and gender are considered, males aged 12 and under tend to run away at a greater rate than females in the same age category.[5]

Arrest of juveniles in 1992 for running away by age is broken down in Figure 3-2. Although ages 13 to 14 represented the highest number of arrests by age group, most arrests for running away occurred to persons aged 15, followed by 16. A noticeable decline in arrests can be seen by age 17.

J. A. Bechtel's examination of the age and sex of runaways found that most runaways fell into the 13 to 15 age group.[6] Males aged 14 and under had a higher rate of running away than females 14 and under.

FIGURE 3-2

Arrests of Runaways by Age, 1992

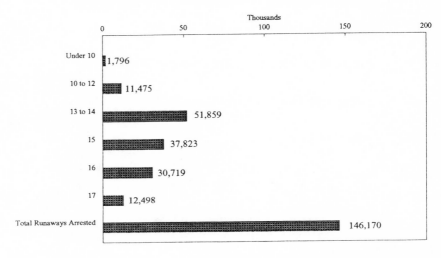

Source: U.S. Federal Bureau of Investigation, *Crime in the United States: Uniform Crime Reports 1992* (Washington, D.C.: Government Printing Office, 1993), p. 227.

However, beginning at age 15, female runaways outnumbered males. Runaways of both genders decreased at age 17. This is believed to reflect a loosening of parental control as children approach adulthood.

The vast majority of runaways are white. Nearly 80 percent of the arrestees for running away in 1992 were white (see Figure 3-3). Black runaways accounted for just over 17 percent of the arrests. Nevertheless, blacks are overrepresented as runaways relative to their juvenile population figures. Other racial groups comprise a relatively low percentage of runaways. Among ethnic groups, Hispanics tend to be disproportionately represented as runaways.[7]

Most runaways come from cities and suburbs. Table 3-1 shows arrests and rate of arrests of runaways in 1990 by size of the community they ran away from. The highest rate of arrests came in cities with populations between 50,000 and 99,999. Runaways from cities were arrested at a rate twice as high as runaways from rural counties. Suburban runaways were arrested more often within metropolitan areas than suburban counties.

FIGURE 3-3

Arrests of Runaways by Race, 1992

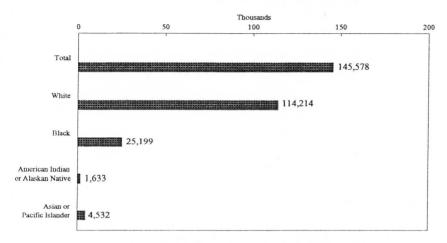

Source: U.S. Federal Bureau of Investigation, *Crime in the United States: Uniform Crime Reports 1992* (Washington, D.C.: Government Printing Office, 1993), p. 236.

Social class appears to play an important role in running away from home. James Hildebrand found that the majority of runaways he sampled came from the middle class.[8] Louise Homer's study of runaway females reflected mostly girls from the lower and middle classes.[9] Seventy percent of the runaways' families were on welfare. Robert Shellow found that only 28 percent of the runaways in his study were from lower class families, an even lower 15 percent from the upper middle class, with the bulk coming from middle and working class homes.[10]

WHY DO CHILDREN RUN AWAY?

Children elect to leave home for any number of reasons. Sexual or physical abuse at the hands of parents or other family members seems to be the primary motivating factor for a high percentage of children who run away. The National Network of Runaway and Youth Services estimated that 70 percent of the runaways who come to emergency shelters have been severely molested or physically abused.[11] However,

TABLE 3-1

Number and Rate[a] of Runaways Arrested, by Size of Place, 1990

		CITIES							COUNTIES		
	Total (10,206 agencies; population 193,507,000)[b]	Total city arrests (7,126 cities; population 132,247,000)	Group I (53 cities, 250,000 and over; population 37,095,000)	Group II (112 cities, 100,000 to 249,999; population 16,189,000)	Group III (298 cities, 50,000 to 99,999; population 20,291,000)	Group IV (581 cities, 25,000 to 49,999; population 20,156,000)	Group V (1,313 cities, 10,000 to 24,999; population 20,837,000)	Group VI (4,769 cities, under 10,000; population 17,680,000)	Suburban counties[c] (926 agencies; population 37,953,000)	Rural counties (2,154 agencies; population 23,306,000)	Suburban areas[d] (4,821 agencies; population 79,878,000)
Runaways	138,155	109,953	29,825	13,263	20,559	18,958	16,250	11,098	18,454	9,748	47,567
Rate	71.4	83.1	80.4	81.9	101.3	94.1	78.0	62.8	48.6	41.8	59.5

[a] Rate is for per 100,000 inhabitants.

[b] Population figures represent U.S. Bureau of the Census 1990 decennial census counts for individual agencies.

[c] Includes only suburban county law enforcement agencies.

[d] Includes suburban city and county law enforcement agencies within metropolitan areas. Excludes central cities. Suburban cities and counties are also included in other groups.

Source: Federal Bureau of Investigation, *Crime in the United States: Uniform Crime Reports 1990* (Washington, D.C.: Government Printing Office, 1991), pp. 176–177.

other reasons for running away have been found to be prominent as well, including:

- A poor home environment.
- Family problems.
- Rebellion.
- School difficulties.
- Sex-related issues (such as boyfriend or pregnancy).
- Boredom.
- Mental illness.
- Emotional problems.
- Divorce.
- Attraction to drugs and/or alcohol.

In Hildebrand's study, poor home environment and school problems were the primary reasons for running away.[12] In the article "Leaving Home: A Typology of Runaways," C. J. English identified four types of runaways based on the commitment to stay away from home and the precipitating factors for running away:

- *Floaters*: Children who run away for a brief period of time, usually returning when things "cool off."
- *Runaways*: Children who leave home for weeks or months, often due to an explosive family situation or a problem too difficult to share.
- *Splitters*: Children who are pleasure seekers—they seek to gain status among their peers.
- *Hard-Road Freaks*: Children who leave home for good, choosing to abandon family life for life on the streets. This is generally due to severe family problems or dysfunction.[13]

Young runaways have been typically characterized as often adolescent adventurers who run away to seek some form of action or excitement. Older runaways are often seen as leaving home as a way to establish their independence or adulthood. Studies show that female runaways may outnumber their male counterparts due to more severe family problems, such as sexual abuse or neglect, and a greater willingness to run away for action or adventure.[14]

A typical story of a 15-year-old runaway turned homeless teenage prostitute was recently described in an article titled, "Teen Sex for Sale":

> "What's your name?" he asks her.
> "What do you want it to be?" she asks back.
> "Sandi."
> "Then it's Sandi."
> Sandi grew up in New Jersey. When she was 11, her mother left her with a friend and never returned. The friend then turned her over to the police who, in turn, placed her in a foster home. The following year, her foster grandfather broke into her bedroom and molested her. She left home the next day for New York City—just one month after her 12th birthday.[15]

THROWAWAY CHILDREN

Not all children who leave home do so voluntarily. Many are forced out by parents or guardians. These children are often referred to as "throwaways" or "push-outs." Throwaway children reflect a hidden population of runaways, as they are rarely reported as missing. The number of children believed to be throwaways is staggering. The Youth Development Bureau estimated that 30 to 35 percent of the runaways in the United States were in fact thrown out of their homes.[16] The National Network of Runaway and Youth Services made a similar observation, estimating recently that 40 percent of the nation's 1.5 million homeless youth were throwaways.[17] Even these statistics may be underestimated. Carolyn Males and Julie Raskin argued that since throwaways "crash" wherever they can, it is virtually impossible to know how many there are.[18]

Throwaway children are typically suburban youths who are made to leave home due to family financial problems, incorrigibility, sexual identity issues, inability to relate to parental authority, and/or parent-child disagreements. K. C. Brown noted that while national attention is focused on missing children taken from loving homes, throwaway children are especially vulnerable to prostitution, pornography, and substance abuse.

> These are the children most preyed upon and exploited, the children most likely to be lying in John and Jane Doe graves all over the United States, unidentified because no one has reported them missing.[19]

RAT PACKERS

Many runaways are described as "rat packers," a growing number of incorrigible teens who have banned together and taken control of their lives outside the home. Rat packers often substitute peers for family, tend to be rebellious, resentful of authority figures (such as parents or the school), and against the "establishment." Some have been abused, others are abusive. Some are highly intelligent, others suffer from learning disabilities. Many of these youths leave home for weeks or months, supported by friends, neighbors, and even unknowing other family members.

Rat packers primarily run away from the suburbs of America. It is estimated that more than 30,000 troubled adolescents from the middle, upper middle, and upper classes become rat packers annually.[20] Noted one observer, these teens "glory in anarchy and destruction," often stealing what they need, indulging in alcohol and drugs, and committing petty crimes and vandalism.[21]

LIFE ON THE STREETS
FOR THE RUNAWAY

Whether a child runs away or is tossed out of the home, he or she faces a bleak existence as a homeless person on the streets. What often awaits them is a life of prostitution, crime, drugs, and virtually anything for survival. (See Part II for discussion of runaways and sexual exploitation.) "As a group, runaway children have a high mortality rate," says June Bucy, executive director of the National Network of Runaway and Youth Services. "They suffer from malnutrition, venereal disease, a high incidence of suicide, and they are frequently sexually exploited."[22]

A large number of runaways are also victims of severe emotional problems. In a study of runaways in youth shelters, David Shaffer and Carol Caton of the New York Psychiatric Institute found that 41 percent were categorized as depressed and antisocial, 30 percent as depressed, and 18 percent as antisocial.[23] Fifty percent had attempted or seriously considered suicide. A study of runaway and nonrunaway children by the Division of Adolescent Medicine at the Children's Hospital of Los Angeles found that 85 percent of the runaways were clinically depressed and 21 percent had severe mental health problems.[24]

The runaways were four times as likely to have emotional problems as the nonrunaways.

A recent study of runaway children produced the following disturbing findings:

- Half the runaways were physically or sexually abused at home.
- Sixty percent had parents who were alcoholics, drug abusers, or law violators.
- One in 4 were born to mothers under the age of 17.
- Seventy percent of the runaways used drugs.
- One in 4 female runaways had been raped.
- Thirty-six percent had been pregnant.
- Only 23 percent of the females used birth control.
- Half the male runaways under age 14 were sexually active.
- Eighty percent of the runaways had serious emotional or behavioral problems.
- Only 13 percent were functionally literate.
- Only 1 out of 3 ever seeks help from a shelter.[25]

AIDS AND THE RUNAWAY

The greatest danger now faced by runaway and homeless youth is AIDS (Acquired Immune Deficiency Syndrome). The high-risk factors are there at every turn. "They have sex with strangers. They use intravenous drugs or love somebody who does. The boys commit homosexual acts, and the girls may have lovers who earn a living that way. Some try to practice safe sex, 'if the john doesn't object'."[26]

Many believe that adolescents will figure prominently in the third wave of the AIDS epidemic. If this is true, it appears that runaway youths may well be at the center of the epidemic as the following quotation illustrates:

> If geography is destiny, runaway and homeless kids gravitate to the very locations around the country where their risk is greatest. Not only are these kids at higher risk with every sexual contact than their suburban counterparts, but they also have higher levels of drug use and sexually transmitted diseases. Often their immune systems are already compromised by repeated exposure to infections. All of these conditions may increase the risk for developing AIDS.[27]

It is estimated that at least 200,000 runaways each year are involved in high-risk activities for contracting AIDS such as prostitution and drug use.[28] A nurse at Covenant House, New York City's largest shelter for runaways, estimated that 40 percent of the children living on the streets may carry the AIDS virus.[29] Some suggest the percentage is even higher. Jim Kennedy, a physician at Covenant House, recently tested a small sample of children there for AIDS. Twenty-seven percent tested positive for HIV (Human Immunodeficiency Virus). He estimated that 15 percent of the 11,000 children who pass through Covenant House each year would be HIV-positive, if tested. However, for those engaged in prostitution regularly, Kennedy estimated a rate of infection surpassing 50 percent.[30]

RUNAWAY AND HOMELESS YOUTH ACT

The crisis of runaway and homeless children in this country and the association with prostitution, pornography, drug abuse, and delinquency led to the passage of the Runaway and Homeless Youth Act of 1978 (RHYA). The act made grants available to states, localities, and nonprofit organizations for runaway shelters.[31] Amended in 1980, the RHYA recognized that many "runaways" are in fact "throwaways," clarified the requirements of runaway houses with respect to runaway and missing children as well as their families, and called for the development of model programs designed to help chronic runaway youths.[32] (See also Chapter 18.)

4. Missing and Abducted Children

Children face an additional danger to running away or being thrown out of their homes. Each year thousands of children are reported missing from home—either through kidnapping by a parent or by a total stranger. In many instances, the child is never heard from again. In some cases, the results prove to be tragic. A recent example is the discovery of the body of a 12-year-old girl who had been abducted from a slumber party two months earlier allegedly by a man with two kidnapping convictions and a history of mental problems. Missing children represent one of the most serious forms of child victimization and exploitation today, but it is often one of the least to be investigated and resolved by police departments and other agencies.

PARENTAL KIDNAPPING

Many children are abducted by a parent—often the result of a divorce, separation, or bitter custody battle. Parental kidnapping, also known as "child snatching," accounts for in excess of 100,000 abductions per year.[1] The American Bar Association (ABA) estimates that 7 out of 10 children kidnapped by a noncustodial parent will never see the custodial parent again.[2]

Fathers are most often the abductors, as they seek to circumvent a legal system that in 92 percent of the cases grants custody of the child or children to the mother.[3] Thousands of dollars may be spent futilely in an effort to locate the missing child, an innocent victim and pawn in the parental conflict. In many instances, the child is returned only after the conflict is resolved satisfactorily for the parent kidnapper. Because of the domestic nature of such abductions, they are not often at the top of the list for police departments with shrinking budgets. Even when the attention is there, locating a bitter parental kidnapper can often be like searching for a needle in a haystack the size of the United States. In some cases, the noncustodial parent takes the child overseas, further lessening the chance of ever reuniting child and custodial parent.

The laws vary from state to state with respect to parental kidnapping and prosecution, much less conviction—which further complicates the task of finding the child, returning them home safely, and making the child snatcher fully accountable for his/her actions.

Although in most cases of parental kidnapping the child is not harmed physically, the emotional harm of the abduction and inaccessibility to both parents can be considerable.

ABDUCTED CHILDREN

Child snatching by a stranger is usually even more ominous for the child and his/her parents. Such a kidnapper is rarely motivated by anything that could possibly be in the child's best interest. It is unknown just how many children are abducted each year. However, a conservative estimate is that 150,000 children under 9 years of age are reported missing annually who are presumed to have been kidnapped.[4]

Not all missing and/or abducted children are reported to authorities. Some are runaways, others are throwaways who have been further victimized through kidnapping by pedophiles, pimps, and others who exploit and abuse them. Estimates of unsolved or undiscovered cases of missing children range from hundreds of thousands to millions every year.[5] More than 4,000 bodies of missing children are discovered annually, with many more feared dead, drugged, or kept prisoner by a kidnapper.[6]

LOCATING MISSING CHILDREN

Recent years have seen important strides on the federal and state levels, as well as through national organizations, to help locate missing and abducted children. In 1980, Congress passed the Parental Kidnapping Prevention Act.[7] This empowered the Federal Parental Locator Service to assist in the search for children abducted by parents. The purpose of the act was to determine child custody rights, enforce them, and to investigate or prosecute in parental kidnapping cases.

The intent was to deter child snatching and make child custody decrees uniform across the United States by requiring states to honor a custody decree of any other state. The act does not make parental child kidnapping a federal crime, but it does enable the FBI to assist in the search for abducted children once a state arrest warrant has been issued for the parent kidnapper.

In many states, parental abduction of children is not considered a felony, hampering the effectiveness of the federal Parental Kidnapping Prevention Act. Furthermore, in as many as half the cases of abduction that occur before divorce proceedings have begun, neither federal nor state statutes apply. This means that in such cases, spousal consent may not be necessary for a parent to legally remove a child from the home.

The Missing Children Act, enacted in 1982, was in direct response to the growing numbers of missing and abducted children in this country.[8] The act enables the descriptions of missing and runaway children to be entered into the FBI's National Crime Information Center computer to which local law enforcement have access. This helps the police to better identify and locate missing children and gives parents a means for having their missing children registered across the country, increasing the chances for locating them. The act also allows for FBI intervention once a kidnapping has been established.

There are two major drawbacks regarding the effectiveness of the Missing Children Act. One is that most police departments will not act on a missing child report until after 24 hours—often the most critical time to locate an abducted child. Secondly, not all police agencies are on-line with the national computer due to outdated equipment, budget constraints, or inadequately trained staff. Further hampering the usefulness of the computer tracking in the recovery of missing children can be inaccurate information provided by parents on the child.

The National Center for Missing and Exploited Children was established in 1984 to serve as a clearinghouse for disseminating information on missing children, reporting or sighting missing children, reporting cases of child pornography, and identifying missing and exploited children.[9] On May 25, 1984, the nation began observing National Missing Children's Day.

Other national organizations providing information and support regarding missing, abducted, and exploited children include the American Humane Association, the National Center on Child Abuse and Neglect, National Clearinghouse on Runaway and Homeless Youth, National Resource Center on Child Sexual Abuse, National Criminal Justice Reference Service (NCJRS), and the National Network of Runaway and Youth Services. Refer to Chapter 18 for additional responses to the victimization and exploitation of children.

PART II

The Sexploitation of Children

5. The Sexual Abuse and Exploitation of Children

The victimization of children is perhaps greatest and most widespread in the area of sexual abuse and exploitation. Children can be sexually exploited in many ways including incest, molestation, sodomy, pedophilia, exhibitionism, forcible and statutory rape, child prostitution, and child pornography. The perpetrators can be parents, guardians, caretakers, family friends, acquaintances, or complete strangers. Although female children tend to be most often associated with child sexual abuse and exploitation, recent studies have shown that male children are victimized just as often.[1]

Child sex victims range from totally accidental victimization involving little victimogenesis to seductive sexual partner with extensive victimogenesis. In many instances, the child may consent to the sexual victimization unintentionally or unwittingly, or offer only passive resistance; in other cases of sex exploitation, the victim and offender are in a symbiotic relationship or form a cooperative dyad.[2] At its worst, the sexually abused child is completely powerless, vulnerable, and exploited by the powerful, nonvulnerable exploiter.

The type of therapy for child sexual abuse victims "seems to be related to where they are situated along the victim continuum in conjunction with such factors as the degree of physical force or violence used by the offender and the intensity of the victim-offender relationship prior to the sex offense."[3]

THE SEXUAL EXPLOITATION
OF CHILDREN HISTORICALLY

Children have been misused for sexual purposes throughout history, providing a disturbing precedent for virtually every form of child sexual exploitation in the modern age. In Victorian England, for example, defloration of young girls was a routine practice. "Enthusiasts [have] always claimed that there is a special pleasure in deflowering a virgin, because of the emotional thrill, a blend of aggression, possessiveness, and mild sadism."[4]

Sexual exploitation of children has historically been a reflection of customs, culture, religion, superstition, and economics. In Babylonia, children were forced to be temple prostitutes, and in Rome during Caesar's reign, child prostitution was widely supported; at one point even infants were used in brothels.[5] Pederasty—sexual relations between men and boys—and homosexuality involving children have always been around but only became a commercial enterprise during the surge in child prostitution in the nineteenth century, particularly in Great Britain and the United States. A study done in England in 1869 estimated that of 9,000 prostitutes working on a seaport, 1,500 were younger than 15 years of age, and of these, one-third were under the age of 13.[6]

Sexual assaults against children throughout history are well represented in the literature. In nineteenth century London, for example, the rape of young virgins was said to be "a highly organized and efficient business."[7] Child rape has been shown to be especially prevalent during times of war.[8] A study to determine how various groups in our society differ in the degree of seriousness they give to forms of child maltreatment found that there is a greater consensus about the seriousness of child sexual abuse than any other type of child victimization.[9]

DEFINING CHILD SEXUAL ABUSE

The Child Abuse Prevention and Treatment Act (Public Law 100-294) defines child sexual abuse as

> (a) the employment, use, persuasion, inducement, enticement, or coercion of any child to engage in, or assist any other person to engage in, any sexually explicit conduct or simulation of such conduct

for the purpose of producing any visual depiction of such conduct, or (b) the rape, molestation, prostitution, or other such form of sexual exploitation of children, or incest with children.[10]

A report sponsored by the American Bar Association (ABA), the Legal Resource Center for Child Advocacy and Protection, the American Public Welfare Association, and the American Enterprise Institute suggested definitional guidelines for Child Protective Service (CPS) agencies with respect to child sexual abuse and exploitation. The report defined sexual abuse as "vaginal, anal, or oral intercourse; vaginal or anal penetrations; or other forms of contact for sexual purposes." Sexual exploitation was defined as "using a child in prostitution, pornography, or other sexually exploitative activities."[11]

The sexual abuse and exploitation of children come in many forms and degrees. Below are typical examples:

- *Familial Sexual Abuse.* Perpetrated by a member of the nuclear family such as a father or father substitute, mother or mother substitute, or a sibling.
- *Extended Familial Sexual Abuse.* Perpetrated by nonnuclear family members such as grandparents, uncles, aunts, or cousins.
- *Caretaker Sexual Abuse.* Perpetrated by someone responsible for the child's care and well being that is nonfamily, such as babysitters and day care workers.
- *Nonstranger Sexual Abuse.* Perpetrated by someone known to the child but not a caretaker, such as an adult friend, scout leader, or postman.
- *Peer Sexual Abuse.* Perpetrated by another child that is a nonfamily member.
- *Stranger Sexual Abuse.* Perpetrated by someone unfamiliar to the child or family.
- *Ritualistic or Satanic Sexual Abuse.* Perpetrated by persons in groups that practice rituals or satanism.

THE PREVALENCE OF CHILD SEXUAL ABUSE

Due to the broad range of ways in which children are sexually abused, accurately assessing its scope is virtually impossible. There is no central, national or uniform recording system for tracking the sexual abuse of children. Estimates of child sexual abuse in large urban areas have been put at 4,000 cases annually,[12] with 5,000 cases of father-daughter incest each year nationally,[13] and between 200,000 and 500,000 cases of sexual abuse annually perpetrated on female children aged 4 to 14.[14] In one large city with advanced victim services, 24 percent of all sexual assaults were on children under the age of 14.[15]

According to the National Committee for Prevention of Child Abuse's (NCPCA) annual fifty state survey, about 17 percent of all child abuse and neglect cases involve sexual abuse.[16] In David Finkelhor's article "How Widespread Is Child Sexual Abuse?", the author found that as many as 52 percent of the women and 9 percent of the men studied had been sexually abused during their childhood.[17] In its 1991 Summary Data Component, the National Child Abuse and Neglect Data System (NCANDS) estimated that 129,697 reports of child sexual abuse were substantiated or indicated after investigation.[18]

When including unreported child sexual victimization and sexual assault falling under criminal statutes, the incidence of child sexual abuse in this country is undoubtedly much higher.

THE RISK FACTORS OF CHILD SEXUAL ABUSE

Although all children are potentially at risk to become the victims of sexual abuse, research has shown that certain factors may make some children more susceptible to victimization than others. These include:

- Being a female.
- Absence of parents/guardians.
- A family cycle of sexual or physical abuse.
- Being part of a stepfamily.
- Being the oldest child.
- The absence of a supportive family relationship.
- Substance abuse in family.
- Unstable family situation (such as frequent moves).
- Poor or nonexistent family bonding.
- Mental manipulation or exploitation.

According to the American Humane Association, the average age of sexually abused children is 9.3 years. The AHA found that over 78 percent of the sexually maltreated children studied were females and that the sexual abuse of girls seemed to increase proportionately with

with age.[19] The National Incidence Study (NIS) reported that the incidence rate for sexual abuse was highest among female children aged 12 to 17.[20]

The Child Victimization Study found that reported sexual molestation cases involved primarily male perpetrators against female victims and were more likely to involve middle class families than physical abuse or neglect cases.[21]

THE CHARACTERISTICS OF CHILD SEXUAL ABUSE

Because of the complexities of child sexual abuse, few conclusive characteristics or causes of the problem can be stated. In general, there are symptoms and correlates that appear to operate in conjunction with the sexual abuse of children. These include other family dysfunctional behaviors such as child physical abuse, wife abuse, emotional abuse, intergenerational abuse, and alcohol or drug abuse. There is also evidence of some sex abusers being driven in part by recurring sexual fantasies.[22]

Studies indicate that victims of intrafamilial sexual victimization are at greater risk for repeated sexual abuse than those abused by non-family perpetrators.[23] Some data suggest that sexually abused daughters often may unconsciously "seek abusive environments in which they are subsequently victimized (through rape or spousal abuse) and are frequently unable to protect their children from being abused."[24]

Transgenerational sexual abuse is believed by some to be also a learned behavior, which may result in "an escalating geometric progression of abuse in subsequent generations as some abused children in turn abuse their own children."[25] Many other sexual abuse victims neither "learn" nor continue the cycle of abuse in adulthood.

ADULT PERPETRATORS OF CHILD SEXUAL ABUSE

Most sexual abuse of children is committed by adults—often family members or family acquaintances, but adult strangers are also well represented among abusers and exploiters. As a result of this range of adult victimizers, no single profile of a child sexual abuser has been established.

Some researchers have attempted to isolate characteristics and behavioral patterns of child sex abusers. P.H. Gebhard and associates conducted one of the most comprehensive studies ever of sex offenders in a study of 1,500 inmates. They defined the offenders' sexual abuse of children as uncommon behavior motivated by abnormal and/or pathological desires.[26] Other researchers have found that by comparison to the population at large, child sex offenders are more likely to be of subnormal intelligence than superior intelligence.[27] Subnormal intelligence has been found to be present more frequently in sex offenders convicted of incestuous relations, statutory rape, and bestiality than offenders convicted of exhibitory acts, forcible rape, and disseminating obscene materials.[28]

Most child sex offenders tend to be young, unmarried, and familiar to some degree with their victims. There does not appear to be any consistent offender profile with respect to education and socio-economic backgrounds, although some studies show sex offenders to be disproportionately represented among poorly educated, socially and economically disadvantaged groups.[29]

CHILD PERPETRATORS OF CHILD SEXUAL ABUSE

There is growing evidence that many child sex victims are being victimized by other children. Notes David Finkelhor:

> It is increasingly recognized that there are many adolescents who abuse younger children both inside and outside their families. Because such cases are less likely to come to agency attention and because more information is greatly needed, it is important for research to include such abuse within their purview.[30]

A study of sexually aggressive children by the Department of Social and Health Services in the state of Washington found the following:

- Sixty-four percent had been sexually abused.
- Fifty percent of the perpetrators and victims lived in the same home.
- Half had had 2 to 5 victims.
- Twenty-six percent of the perpetrators of child sexual abuse were preadolescent children.
- Forty-eight percent of the aggressors were aged 13 to 14.[31]

The National Adolescent Perpetrator Network issued a report that further underscored the problem of child-to-child sexual abuse. The report noted that 50 percent of the sexual molestation of boys and 15 to 20 percent of the sexual abuse of girls was perpetrated by other children.[32] At present, this remains a vastly underreported but highly disturbing dimension of child sexual victimization.

THE EFFECTS OF
CHILD SEXUAL ABUSE

Most experts concur that the short- and long-term effects of child sexual abuse can be significant to the child victim. Their normal, healthy development having been interfered with, sexually abused children are often "unable to cope emotionally, intellectually, and/or physically with sexual stimulation and responsiveness, regardless of whether the child finds the experience emotionally satisfying, erotically pleasurable, or negative in some fashion."[33]

One study reported that the psychological scarring and emotional stress of child sexual victimization and exploitation often leads to substance abuse "to deaden memories and desensitize present experiences."[34] Other findings show similarities in the social maturation and psychological effects of victims of incest and child pornography. Most child sexual abuse victims experience feelings of guilt, betrayal, rage, worthlessness, and withdrawal—all of which have been shown to manifest themselves in both inwardly self-destructive behavior and outwardly socially aberrant behavior.[35]

The physical effects of child sexual abuse have been well documented and include lacerations to the genitals, sexually transmitted diseases, pregnancy, internal injuries, broken bones, and even death. There is also a strong correlation between child sexual abuse, child physical abuse, and victim-turned-sex offender.[36]

More in-depth discussion on specific dimensions of child sexual abuse including incest, rape, other sex offenses, child prostitution, and child pornography can be found in subsequent chapters of Part II.

6. *Incest and Child Molestation*

The sexual violation of children is most painful and tragic when it occurs at home with the perpetrator being a family member. Incestuous acts of molestation affect millions of families each year, including child victims, adult survivors, secondary victims, and perpetrators of incest—many of whom were themselves incest victims. Yet this form of sexual abuse is amongst the most secretive, making detection and treatment that much harder to come by. This chapter will explore the dynamics of incest and familial child molestation.

A HISTORICAL CONDEMNATION OF INCEST

Perhaps no other form of sexual abuse and exploitation has been more condemned throughout history than incest. The word *incest* derives from the Latin term *incestum*, which means unchaste and low. Incest is commonly defined as "sexual intercourse between relatives within the prohibited degrees of relationship defined by the law."[1] Anthropologists have found that there is a near universal incest taboo.[2] Prohibitions against incestuous relations have been severe and precise as evidenced in Leviticus, the Book of Laws (18:6–18; 20:11–21). The description of consanguinity defined the nature of punishment to be inflicted upon those guilty of incest, including burning, flogging, exile, and death. Incest, along with murder and idolatry, was forbidden even if for medical reasons or to save one's life.

Despite the strong taboos against incest, particularly in Western societies, this type of behavior has a long and storied history. Moses was the offspring of an aunt-nephew marriage (Numbers 26:59; Exodus 6:20), Abraham married his paternal sister Sarah (Genesis 29:12), and Jacob was wed to his two sisters (Genesis 29:15–30). In some nonliterate societies, incest was condoned by the privileged classes only. In ancient Peru the Incas married their sisters, while in Africa the kings of Golzales and Gaboon wed their maturing daughters and the queens their eldest sons.[3] Among sectarian groups, the Mormons sanctioned virtually all types of incest before outlawing such practices in 1892.[4]

In most modern societies, incest is considered a criminal offense, though definitions of incest can vary widely from country to country and even state to state. Meanwhile, the practice of incest and child molestation continues to make its presence felt to thousands, perhaps millions, of victims.

DEFINING INCEST TODAY

The problem of defining incest in the 1990s is as complex as the problem itself. In some states, incest is recognized as sexual intercourse between blood relatives; other states define it as *any* sexual act between various combinations of "legal" relatives (such as a stepfather and stepdaughter). The dictionary definition of incest is "sexual intercourse between people regarded as too closely related to marry each other."

Increasingly professionals have broadened the meaning of incest to include not only sexual intercourse but also sodomy, oral sex, fondling, masturbation, exhibitionism, voyeurism, pedophilia, and other sexual acts (see Chapter 7). The perpetrators can be anyone in the immediate, natural family; extended family members such as an uncle or grandfather; or nonnatural family or household members such as an adopted father or stepmother. Given this range of potential perpetrators and victims of incest, one can only imagine the difficulty in adequately addressing the problem, identifying the participants, and dealing with the complex issues surrounding incest.

THE EXTENT OF INCEST

How widespread is incest? Reliable figures are hard to come by, given the loyalty of secrecy and silence present in so many incestuous families.

David Finkelhor estimated that 75 to 90 percent of the incest cases go unreported.[5] Noted one researcher: "The family as a whole supports actively or passively their own incestuous equilibrium."[6]

Estimates of incest in the United States have ranged from tens of thousands of cases per year to well over a million cases annually.[7] Psychiatrist G. Pirooz Sholevar estimated the number to be between 11 and 33 million.[8] A report from the Family Violence Research Program at the University of New Hampshire estimated that 5 to 15 percent of all females under the age of 17 in the United States are victims of familial sexual abuse.[9] Social worker Mary Donaldson estimated that as many as 28 percent of all females in this country are victims of incest or other types of sexual abuse.[10] It is believed that as many as 1 in 10 females in the United States may be affected by incest.[11]

THE NATURE OF INCEST

Incest knows no boundaries with respect to race, ethnicity, religion, class, or income. "We know that incest cuts across every social, economic, and educational barrier," noted clinical social worker Susan Forward.[12] Consequently, victims come from all walks of life and share a common bond of betrayal and exploitation by those often closest to them. Although incest victims can be any age, studies show that incestuous relationships generally start when the victim is between 6 and 11 years old, and last for at least two years.[13]

Typically, the active aggressor of incest is a male, while the passive victim is most often a female. It is estimated that in 90 to 97 percent of all incest cases the perpetrator is male, while more than 85 percent of the reported victims are female.[14] H. Stoenner found the ratio of female-to-male victims of reported incest to be 10 to 1.[15]

Approximately 78 percent of all incest reported today involves father-daughter, 18 percent sibling-sibling, 1 percent mother-son, and the remainder multiple incestuous relationships.[16] According to Rita Justice and Blair Justice in *The Broken Taboo: Sex in the Family*, "The typical [incestuous] father is white and middle class, has a high school education and often some college, and holds a white-collar job or skilled trade. He's most often in his late thirties, married more than ten years. His wife is slightly younger than he is."[17] Other characteristics that typify the incestuous father include being in a state of reassessment of his life, and suffering from depression, spousal rejection, loneliness, and diminished potency.

The typical daughter incest victim pattern is as follows:

- She is often the eldest daughter.
- She is usually entering adolescence.
- Her median age is 8½, with most victims between the ages of 5 and 16.

A typology of other types of incestuous relations can be seen below:

Type of Incest	Motivations *(Individual Psychopathology)*
Father-Son	Homosexual conflict.
Sibling (Older)-Sibling	Expression of unconscious conflict.
Mother-Daughter	Psychosis/infantilism.
Mother-Son	Substitute gratification for absent father.
Grandfather-Granddaughter	Assertion of manhood.[18]

FATHER-DAUGHTER INCEST

Men who molest their own daughters represent by far the greatest number of reported cases of incest, with some estimates placing the actual incidence of father-daughter incest at three-quarters of all incestuous relationships. The sexual abuse of daughters can begin in infancy and continue well into their adult lives. Incestuous fathers tend to be mostly middle-aged men (30 to 50 years of age) with the average age being mid-thirties.

The majority of incestuous fathers have introverted personalities, an intrafamily background, and are socially isolated. Many are gradually heading towards incestuous contact with their daughters. In some cases, the wife may unwittingly aid and abet in the incestuous behavior by arranging situations that isolate the father and daughter from others.

One of the most comprehensive studies to date on men who sexually molest their daughters was conducted recently by sociologists David Finkelhor and Linda Williams, whose sample consisted of 118 incestuous fathers.[19] They established five categories of incestuous fathers:

- *Sexually Preoccupied*—Men who have a conscious or obsessive sexual interest in their daughters.
- *Adolescent Regressives*—Men who become sexually attracted to their daughters as they reach puberty.
- *Instrumental Self-Gratifiers*—Fathers who see their daughters in nonerotic terms and feel guilty about the incestuous acts.
- *Emotionally Dependent*—Fathers who are emotionally needy, depressed, and/or lonely.
- *Angry Retaliators*—Men who molest their daughters out of anger towards them or their mother who may be neglectful or have deserted them.

The men in the last category accounted for about 10 percent of the incestuous fathers and were the most likely to have criminal records involving rape or assault. The largest percentage of incestuous fathers were adolescent regressives who comprised approximately one-third of the sample, followed by sexually preoccupied men who comprised just over one-fourth of the incestuous fathers.

The researchers also found that alcohol or drugs played a role in the incest for 43 percent of the men, while marital discord was blamed in part for the incestuous relations in 43 percent of the cases. Seventy percent of the incestuous fathers reported being sexually abused as children.

A high proportion of father-daughter incest involves stepfathers and stepdaughters.[20] A typical situation is a man who has married a woman with a daughter by a previous marriage. His sexual attraction to the daughter as a sex object may continue for years, though he may also view her as a child dependent.

INCESTUOUS WOMEN

Women are generally less likely to be incestuous than men. Psychologist Ruth Mathews studied more than 100 female sex offenders and divided them into four major categories:

- *Teacher-Lover*—Older women who have sexual relations with a young adult.
- *Experimenter-Exploiter*—Females from rigid families where sex education is proscribed.

- *Predisposed Women*—Those with a predisposition to molest children because of their own history of being physically or sexually abused.
- *Male-Coerced Women*—Women who sexually abuse children because men force them to do so.[21]

According to Mathews, more than one-third of the survivors of incest she interviewed said they had been molested by women. Nevertheless, *true* female pedophiles accounted for only about 5 percent of her sample. Most of the molesters themselves had been abused beginning at age two and up.

Many believe that incestuous mothers may be far more prevalent than the statistics would suggest. Kathy Evert, a therapist, surveyed 93 women and 9 men who were molested by their mothers.[22] About 80 percent reported that the molestation by their mother was the most closely guarded secret in their lives. Psychologist A. Nicholas Groth contended that sexually abusive women may not be identified as such because of the relative ease in which they can molest children under the guise of normal child care.[23]

MOTHER-SON INCEST

Studies show that in mother-son incest, the mother is often severely disturbed as well.[24] In this incestuous relationship, the father is usually absent and the mother seeks sexual gratification from the son. It has been suggested that mothers' engaging in sexual activity with their adolescent sons, referring to them as their "lovers," is socially more acceptable than father-daughter incestuous relations. Apparently only the most blatant examples incur societal condemnation and intervention.

MOTHER-DAUGHTER INCEST

Mother-daughter incest is even rarer than mother-son incest, and relatively little is known about the contributing factors. The molester here is usually also extremely disturbed and exhibits infantile and/or psychotic behavior. By turning to her daughter for emotional nurturance, she may effect a complete role reversal in their relationship.

R. Medlicott pointed to a case of mother-daughter incest where the mother slept with the daughter to avoid the father, whereby she then initiated sexual contact with the daughter.[25] R. Lidz and T. Lidz studied the adverse factors of a mother's homosexual attraction towards her daughter.[26] In three cases, the incestuous relationship involved intimacy while the daughters were asleep; touching and anal contact, combined with aloofness, increasing the victims' insecurities. All three daughters became schizophrenic in adulthood.

FATHER-SON INCEST

As with mother-daughter incest, the incidence of father-son incest is very rare. When it does occur, it is generally believed to be a reflection of interactional family disturbances and intrapsychic conflicts of the incestuous father. Studies have shown that father-son incest often involves a combination of individual and familial pathologies.[27] A recent case of parricide in which two boys were on trial for killing their wealthy parents was sensationalized after the boys alleged years of incestuous relations with their father led to the murders.

SIBLING-SIBLING INCEST

Though the incestuous relationship of father and daughter is far more likely to be reported and condemned, evidence suggests that incest between siblings is far more prevalent. A number of studies have found that brother-sister incestuous relations may be five times as common as incest involving father-daughter.[28]

Yet because of definitional issues, misdiagnosis, and silence within the family, sibling-sibling incest is largely hidden or disregarded for its seriousness. "Sibling abuse has been ignored in part," notes Vernon Wiehe, author of *Sibling Abuse: Hidden Physical, Emotional, and Sexual Trauma*, "because the abusive behavior of one sibling toward another is often excused as normal behavior. Sibling rivalry must be distinguished from sibling abuse."[29]

In brother-sister incest, the sister has often had previous sexual experiences (in many cases with an incestuous father). The youngest sister in a family is especially at risk. The brother may have coerced the sister into sexual relations after having assumed a father role in the family (usually after the biological father has abandoned the family). The idolizing sister may succumb to her brother's request while experiencing little guilt at the time.

GRANDFATHER-GRANDDAUGHTER INCEST

The dynamics of grandfather-granddaughter incest are similar to those of father-daughter incest, particularly when the grandfather is young. However, when the grandfather is older, the incestuous relationship is more often perpetrated to bolster the molester's ego and help him reassert his manhood and self-esteem which have decreased due to his natural physical deterioration.[30]

There is also evidence to indicate that much incest is trigenerational—that is, the grandfather may have sexually molested his daughter first, followed by the granddaughter. The grandfather may himself have been sexually molested during childhood.[31] One study found that grandfather-granddaughter incest accounted for 9 to 11 percent of all incest cases.[32]

MULTIPLE INCEST

Incest involving multiple intrafamilial combinations can occur as well. K. C. Meiselman reported that nearly 30 percent of her sample had either been actively incestuous with more than one family member or knew of other incestuous relationships within the family.[33] This indicates that once the incest taboo is broken in a family, it may become more acceptable amongst family members, thereby increasing the chances of it spreading beyond the initial incestuous relationship.

INCEST AND VICTIM-PROVOCATION

The role of the victim of incest has long been debated with respect to precipitation, provocation, and culpability in one's own victimization. Researchers such as L. Bender and A. Blau[34] have accused children as young as four years old of "unusual attractiveness, seduction, and outright instigation of incest in the home."[35] According to Marshall Schechter and Leo Roberge, the physiological and social changes experienced by female incest victims during their adolescent years result in an increased sexual drive which in turn "produces an acceptance of the incestuous relationship if not at times seductive partner whose tenuous oedipal resolution make her especially vulnerable."[36]

Most behavioral scientists who study victim-provocation in incestuous relationships believe that only a small minority of incest victims actively solicit or encourage incestuous contact with adults.[37] Moreover, many reject altogether the notion of victim culpability in incest victimization, placing the entire burden of guilt and blame on the adult perpetrator. Insists one social worker and writer: "It's always the responsibility of the adult to control any destructive interaction, no matter what the child's behavior is."[38]

THE EFFECTS OF INCEST ON THE VICTIM

Few, if any, victims of incest emerge unscathed. For some the short- or long-term effects may be minimal. For others the results may be dramatic and traumatic for a lifetime. In young children, incest can lead to a range of physical and emotional problems including internal bleeding; injuries to the vagina, anus, and stomach; bed wetting; nightmares; suicide; running away; and precociousness.[39] Teenage victims of incest have been associated with sexual promiscuity, child prostitution and pornography, substance abuse, sexually transmitted diseases, and psychological dysfunctions.[40]

Adult survivors of incest are also often unable to escape its devastating effects. Many suffer from flashbacks, sexual problems, sexual identity, adult prostitution, weight gain, psychological and social disorders, and other mental and physical issues. There is also the strong correlation between incest victimization and a cycle of incestuous behavior, as well as other forms of child abuse, domestic violence, and criminal behavior.[41]

What all victims of incest seem to have in common are feelings of shame, denial, self-blame, anger, guilt, and, most of all, distrust. An attorney recounts the typical example of a young woman who was sexually molested by her father beginning at age 12:

> Lisa doesn't want to think she's been damaged by what happened to her, but ... she's had a real problem with trust. She was vulnerable at twelve, and look what happened to her. For the next two years ... she had sexual problems. She had a problem being touched. She had an overreaction to anything sexual or exploitative of women. She couldn't stand to see nudity in movies. She was really fearful about having children of her own, especially girls.... But Lisa minimized

what happened to her and put all her efforts and energies into ap-
pearing normal. That was her coping mechanism.[42]

At age 19, the aforementioned victim filed a civil suit against her father,
charging him with incestuous assault and battery. The case was even-
tually settled out of court.

THE VICTIMIZATION OF SECRECY

Aside from the incest victims' victimization itself, what may be most
torturing is the secrecy surrounding the incestuous relations, often
permeating the entire family. Wrote researcher Sandy Rovner:

> Incest has always been something nobody wants to talk about. The
> taboo is so deep-seated, and the act so steeped in humiliation, rage,
> shame, and guilt that perpetrator and victim may be caught in a this-
> is-happening-but-it's-not-happening twilight zone. For the rest of
> the family, all of the human mind's boundless capacity to not "see,"
> to deny, rationalize or reject reality comes into play.[43]

Maintaining the silence and secrecy of incest victimization is often
more a reflection of fear than anything else. The fear of the molester,
being believed, self-doubts, shame, confusion, uncertainty, the future... Consequently, many incest victims never speak out or admit to
themselves that they were victims—thereby continuing the violation,
torture, guilt, and denial.

Those who do break the conspiracy of silence can then begin the
process of recovery. But, as writer Heidi Vanderbilt notes, recovery can
be as difficult as the victimization of incest:

> Recovery—which for many may include gaining the ability to feel—
> requires an almost heartbreaking commitment to truths nobody wants
> to hear, to things nobody wants to say, to memories nobody wants to
> have. Victims of incest have lost their innocence, memories, parents,
> families, trust, the opportunity to grow up and develop in the ways
> and in the time allowed to children who were not abused.
> ... Confronted by memories and their implications, the victim can
> swing wildly between denial that the abuse ever happened and accep-
> tance of the fact that it did. With acceptance comes grief. Then rage.
> And, finally, self-forgiveness followed by resolution.[44]

INCEST AND THE LAW

Currently incest is a felony violation of the law in every state. However, the particular statutes covering incest as well as its definition and penalties vary from state to state, jurisdiction to jurisdiction. As a result, treatment for the victim and offender is nonuniform and even nonexistent in some cases.

Other cases of alleged child molestation never make it to police or social workers, much less the courts. Kee MacFarlane, a program analyst with the National Center on Child Abuse and Neglect, admitted that "the process of trying the father and dragging the child through court can be more harmful than the incest itself."[45] Consequently, many families refuse to press charges or testify.

Furthermore, such groups as Victims of Child Abuse Laws (VOCAL), a national organization devoted to fighting child abuse laws, further complicate bringing child molesters to justice and charges of incest to light, perpetuating the cloak of secrecy and cycle of incest.

7. Statutory Rape
and Other Sex Crimes

Many experts believe that children are victims of sex crimes more than any other kind of offense. One reason for this is the wide range of sex offenses perpetrated upon children and the difficulty in identifying victims and sex offenders. Many of these sex crimes remain largely hidden from everyone but the victim and perpetrator, often allowing the victimization to continue for years unnoticed or uninterrupted. In recent years, society has begun to focus more closely on the sexual exploitation of children beyond forcible rape, incest, and child molestation. Such child sex offenses as day care sexual abuse and ritualistic abuse of children have been brought to light through high profile police and media investigations. This chapter will explore these and other sex crimes victimizing children every day in this country.

STATUTORY RAPE

Rape victimization of children is generally viewed in terms of forcible rape. The number of children who are forced into nonconsensual sexual relations annually is indeed staggering. A Bureau of Justice Statistics report estimated that between 1973 and 1987 an average of 54,400 females aged 12 to 19 were rape victims.[1] Since only a fraction of rapes or attempted rapes are believed to be reported, the actual number of victims is likely much higher.

But what about nonforcible child rape or statutory rape? This sex

71

offense consists of intercourse between an adult and a consenting minor—generally a person under the age of 18, depending on the state. Because of its consensual nature, relatively little attention or seriousness to statutory rape is applied by the public, media, or law enforcement. Indeed, the occurrence of consensual sexual relations involving children is so widespread today, it has made statutory rape laws virtually unenforceable.

The following findings on teenage sexual activity provide dramatic indications of its prevalence and implications:

- In the United States, 11.5 million teenagers have had sexual relations, including 6.5 million males and 5 million females.
- Seven out of every 10 females have had sexual intercourse by age 20.
- Eight out of every 10 males have had sexual intercourse by age 20.
- Four out of every 10 teenage females become pregnant before they reach age 20.
- More than 1 in every 10 teenage females gets pregnant each year.
- Twenty-seven percent of the unmarried, sexually active females aged 15 to 19 had never used any type of birth control.
- The 10 to 24-year-old age group accounted for 62.5 percent of gonorrhea cases and 40 percent of the cases of syphilis in 1985.
- Almost half of the estimated 20 million persons infected with sexually transmitted diseases are under the age of 25.[2]

When considering statutory rape, little data exists on its relationship to adolescent sexuality and promiscuity. In a study of child sex offenses, female victims were described as having a "collaborative" role in the sexual offense in 7–8 percent of 330 court cases,[3] as "nonobjecting" in 40 percent of 1,194 court cases,[4] as "encouraging" the sex offender in 66–95 percent of all sex offenses,[5] as "fully participatory" in 60 percent of 73 court cases,[6] and as "seducers" in 185 court cases.[7]

Statutory rape is often absent of physical force or violence, making it that much more difficult to detect or respond to. One study found that force was used on the child sex victim in only 4 percent of 333 court cases.[8] This is related to the fact that most victim-perpetrators had a relationship prior to the sexual offense, often making physical force unnecessary for the success of the offense. H. Gagnon found that 1.9 percent of child victims studied sustained forced, vaginal or oral, penetration and 2.7 percent were physically assaulted.[9]

The most frequent forms of sexual contact occurring between child victim and sex offender are exhibition of sexual organs; genital and non-genital petting or fondling; consensual oral, vaginal, or anal contacts; and attempted penetration of the vagina without force.[10] In a study of sex offenders, P.H. Gebhard and colleagues found that the median age of men convicted of heterosexual offenses with female minors was 25.[11] In most of the cases, the victim did not discourage or report the rape.

PEDOPHILIA

Pedophilia, also referred to as child molestation, is a term used to describe occasions in which a child is the favored sexual object of an adult. This form of child sexual abuse is the most common and normally consists of nonviolent sexual contact with a child including genital viewing or fondling, orogenital contact, penetration, and any other immoral or indecent behavior involving sexual activity between an adult and child. (See also Chapter 6 on incestuous child molestation.)

It is estimated that anywhere from one to more than two million children are the victims of child molesters annually.[12] An eighteen month study of child molestation cases reported to child protection agencies in Brooklyn and the Bronx, New York, revealed that:

- Child molestation is statistically more prevalent than child physical abuse.
- The median age of sexually molested children was 11.
- Younger children, including infants, are also vulnerable to molestation.
- Female victims of child molestation outnumbered male victims 10 to 1.
- The molesters were male in 97 percent of the cases.
- In 75 percent of the cases the molester was known to the victim or victim's family.
- The median age of the molester was 31.
- In over 40 percent of the cases, the molestation had occurred over a length of time varying from a few weeks to 7 years.
- Sixty percent of the victims were molested through force or threat of force.
- Two-thirds of the children suffered some form of identifiable emotional trauma; 14 percent had become severely disturbed.[13]

Studies have found the pedophile or pedophiliac to be frequently passive, immature, and insecure regarding his inability to engage in normal adult heterosexual relations. J. M. Reinhardt postulated that some young or middle-aged pedophiles turn to children only after failure to achieve sexual satisfaction with adults.[14] Older pedophiles, usually those over fifty, have been shown to molest children due to diminishing physical and mental abilities brought about by the aging process.

Albert Cohen identified three classes of pedophiles: (1) the *immature* child molester who only desires to fondle, touch, or caress the child, (2) the *regressed* child molester, characterized by feelings of self-doubt and sexual inadequacy, and (3) the *aggressive* child molester who is often sadistic and violent in his desire for sexual excitement and stimulation.[15] Johan Mohr, R. E. Turner, and M. B. Jerry established five types of pedophilia:

- *Heterosexual Hebephilia*—sexual relations of any nature where the female partner is pubescent.
- *Heterosexual Pedophilia*—sexual relations of any nature when the female partner has not shown any pubertal changes.
- *Homosexual Hebephilia*—sexual relations of any nature when the male partner is pubescent.
- *Homosexual Pedophilia*—sexual relations of any nature where the male partner of the same sex has not shown any pubertal changes.
- *Undifferentiated Pedophilia*—sexual relations of any nature when the partner's gender is not differentiated.[16]

The role of the victim in pedophilia was examined in a study of 73 female victims of child molestation. The female victims were divided into two categories: (1) *Participant Victims*—those who played a role in initiating and maintaining the relationship, and (2) *Accidental Victims*—those who did not have an active role in their molestation.[17] A significant factor in participatory victimization appears to be the victim's seductive behavior towards adults. Evidence shows that when participant victims of child molestation are deprived of the care, affection, and approval they need at home, they are more likely than accidental victims to seek such nurturance elsewhere.[18]

There are presently a number of organizations that support sexual activity between children and adults and seek to abolish statutory rape and the age of consent laws. In Wales, England, the Paedophiliac Information Exchange (PIE) is organized for the express purpose of advocating consensual adult-child sexual practices. The Rene Guyon Society, based in California, professes to having 2,500 members who admit to having intercourse with a young child. The Society's slogan is "Sex by year eight or else it's too late." Other politically active pedophile groups include the Childhood Sexuality Circle which boasts more than 10,000 members, and the North American Man-Boy Love Association (NAMBLA).[19]

EXHIBITIONISM

Exhibitionism as a sexual deviation refers to the intentional, inappropriate exposure of genitalia to either a woman or child. Though most exhibitionists are male, some women are known to be exhibitionists. This sexual perversion ranks alongside pedophilia as one of the most common sex offenses against children.

Exhibitionism is a compulsive behavior characterized by a person who feels compelled to exhibit oneself to relieve "unbearable anxiety." J. L. Mathis reported that the exhibitionist is driven by a force within that is uncontrollable.[20] P. H. Gebhard and associates characterized the exhibitionist as such:

- He is fairly normal behind his exhibitionism.
- He has little rationale for his behavior.
- He attaches particular importance to his audience's reaction.
- He has an irresistible compulsion to be an exhibitionist and a sort of stupefaction during the exposure.
- His childhood was often extremely difficult in some manner.[21]

J. C. Coleman found exhibitionism to correlate with personal immaturity (such as shyness, self-doubts about masculinity, and feelings of inferiority in approaching members of the opposite sex), and interpersonal stress and acting out (such as an inability to cope with an intense conflict). Regarding the latter correlation, Coleman observed:

> Often the married exhibitionist appears to be reacting to some conflict or stress situation in his marriage, and his behavior is in the nature of a regression to adolescent masturbatory activity. In some instances, an exhibitionist may state that exhibiting himself during masturbation is more exciting and tension reducing than utilizing pictures of nude women.[22]

Exhibitionism has also been associated with other mental disorders including schizophrenia and brain deterioration.

The most frequent places for exposure are public—such as parks, theaters, or streets. However, when a child is the exhibitionist's target, the exposure occurs most often in or near schools and playgrounds and in cars. Estimates place the number of child victims of exhibitionists to be between 20 and 50 percent.[23]

The act of exhibitionism tends to vary with the circumstances and the offender—ranging from exposure of the flaccid penis in which sexual stimulation is not present, to exposure of the erect penis in which masturbation often occurs along with intense sexual gratification. Mathis noted that "the exhibitionist does not expose himself as a prelude to sex or as an invitation to intercourse; rather, the exhibitionist seems more intent on evoking fear or shock."[24] The typical exhibitionist favors strangers for his exposure; when his target is a child, he prefers a group of children.

Although exhibitionism is one of the most frequent sex offenses known to law enforcement, it is also one of the most underreported.[25] The majority of complaints come from parents whose children have been victimized by exhibitionists. In general, exhibitionism is looked upon as more a nuisance crime than a sex offense. It is not yet fully known what the short- and long-term effects are for a child victim of an exhibitionist.

TRIOLISM

Triolism is a variation of exhibitionism and voyeurism in which the adult (triolist) receives sexual gratification by viewing others, as well as himself, in group sexual activity. It is when triolism involves children that it is of most concern to law enforcement, particularly since it has been linked to child pornography as well.

Children are easily lured into participating in triolism. Triolists offer them money for a minimal amount of work. The offender is usually addicted to triolism involving children, especially its relatively low cost compared to other sexual activity such as prostitution. The typical pattern of triolism victimizing children is as follows:

> To earn his extra money, the child gets others from among his friends to go to the offender's house or the back of his store and engage in acts, which are in themselves fun, while the pervert watches.[26]

BESTIALITY/ZOOERASTIA

Although the terms bestiality and zooerastia are often used separately, they both refer to the same sexual perversion—sexual intercourse between a human and an animal. Bestiality is a legal term, zooerastia a medical one. Despite laws that prohibit this and its rarity, bestiality does occur in our society. Men who engage in this practice have also been known to lure children into participating. This is especially true in rural areas where animals are often in abundance.

One case told of a boy coerced into entering a man's shanty after which the man had the boy "playing" with the man's dog. Shortly thereafter, the dog performed oral copulation on the boy. Gebhard and colleagues found in their study that 17 percent of farm boys were reported to have experienced orgasm resulting from contact with animals.[27] The majority of the contacts took place during preadolescence and lasted over a two or three year period.

The incidence of bestiality involving children in this country is unknown, given the hidden and hard to detect nature of the sexual abuse and exploitation. As with other sex offenses against children, the number of child victims is likely much higher than most conservative estimates.

COPROLAGNIA/UROLAGNIA

Coprolagnia/urolagnia is another extreme sexual perversion associated with child molestation. It involves sexual gratification by smelling, eating, throwing, or handling excrement, urine, or other filth. Richard von Krafft-Ebing described the coprolagnia/urolagnia pathological person as one "driven by an irresistible urge to touch or swallow feces, sputum, nasal mucus, earwax, or menstrual blood."[28] Surprisingly, this has been shown to be one of the most commonly encountered activities for law enforcement.

The strong relationship between being addicted to coprolagnia/urolagnia and child molestation has been documented in several cases.[29] In one example, an officer who was aware that in many instances child molesters handle filth (in one form or another), arrested a local person for a minor offense. During the booking, the officer found the offender in possession of pictures and written material that referred to urine and excrement. The man later admitted to molesting local children. He was ultimately confined to a mental institution.

Robert Morneau and Robert Rockwell made an interesting observation with respect to the correlation between coprolagnia/urolagnia and child molestation:

> An officer who is booking a suspect for any crime and discovers excrement on his person (many times carried in dried form) should realize, at the very minimum, he may have a child molester on his hands...
>
> Just as a child molester might be recognized from his interest in filth, anyone who is arrested as the result of a complaint that he is a child molester should be interviewed about unrelated cases where coprolagnia or urolagnia were part of the offense.[30]

NECROPHILIA

Necrophilia refers to the desire to have sexual intercourse with the dead. This sexual perversion often involves deceased children as victims and men as offenders. Researchers have distinguished four primary types of necrophiliac offenders: (1) the *true necrophiliac,* (2) the *sadonecrophiliac,* (3) the *sadomasochistic necrophiliac,* and (4) the *necrofetishist.*[31] Because these types can overlap, it is often difficult for police to identify the necrophiliac offender or his particular motivation.

Necrophiliacs are often morticians or others who work or have worked in a mortuary. A macabre example of necrophilia can be seen in a criminal investigation report in which a man with a history of sexual perversion is being questioned in connection with the sexual assault and murder of a young girl:

> He admitted he had worked years before as a mortician's assistant ... fascinated by the bodies, especially those of young girls.... The mortician's vehicle was pressed into service as an ambulance. This man described how he became sexually aroused when driving back into town because of the screams and crying of the injured and dying children he was transporting.
>
> That night, working late and alone in the mortuary, he was seized with a compulsion to have intercourse with the corpses. He spoke ... of having intercourse with one young girl who was mutilated and since additional wounds would not likely be noticed, he cut her stomach open at some point so he could see his penis down inside her.[32]

A key factor in necrophilia is the complete passivity of the female victim, allowing the perpetrator to do as he pleases without resistance or fear of detection or reprisal.[33] A further element of this sexual perversion often has to do with religious fanaticism and the necrophiliac offender's belief that he is following God's orders. Many male child sex offenders who murder their victims use this delusional, irrational reasoning in perpetrating "some perverted act with the child just before death or even after. Their justification is found in the commands of the Lord, which reached them in clear language ordering the brutal violation."[34]

The act of necrophilia is usually accompanied by disfigurement of the body. The necrophiliac receives gratification in two ways: (1) from mutilating the dead and (2) the realization that others (especially family members) will be repulsed by the deed. Defenselessness, helplessness, and decomposition of the victim are crucial in carrying out necrophilia.

RITUALISTIC SEXUAL ABUSE

A form of child sexual abuse that seems to be increasing in prevalence is that involving ritualism or satanism. Ritualistic or satanic sexual abuse of children is usually related to religious, supernatural, or magic practices. It is estimated that 1 to 5 percent of all child sexual abuse cases may involve some form of ritualistic or satanistic practice.

Three types of ritualistic child sexual abuse have been identified:

- *Cult-based*, where the sexual abuse is secondary to a larger goal.
- *Pseudo-ritualistic*, where sexual abuse is the primary goal.
- *Psychopathological*, where there is a single perpetrator.[35]

Ritualistic abuse perpetrators include:

- Organized groups, including families and communes.
- National and international organizations with local and regional affiliates.
- Persons who dabble in ritualism for fun, curiosity, or sexual experimentation, while often using drugs or alcohol.
- Mentally unbalanced individuals.

Many groups that practice ritualism or satanism are highly structured and may involve the child's own parents and siblings, as well as their "cult parents" in their indoctrination. "Children may be taken from natural parents and placed in the care of other group members as a means of ensuring continued group involvement by natural parents."[36]

Ritualistic sexual abuse of children often includes other forms of sexual abuse discussed in this chapter such as bestiality and necrophilia. Drug abuse is highly associated with ritualistic abuse, which may also involve the murder of the child victim as part of the ritual.

Currently there are no formal national networks of professionals addressing ritualistic abuse. The Resource and Education Network on Ritualistic Abuse (RENRA) exists in Los Angeles with a focus on information gathering and sharing.

8. The Prostitution of Children

Child prostitution reflects perhaps the quintessential exploitation and violation of children in our society. Each year, thousands of children sell their bodies for money, drugs or shelter. In spite of laws meant to protect children from prostitution and sexual exploitation, the reality is this is a booming business that shows no signs of diminishing.

Indeed, the prostitution of children is rooted in a long, sad, and storied history of child sexploitation. "Many societies considered it proper and actually encouraged treating children as marketable commodities and selling them into slavery or prostitution."[1] In ancient Egypt, the "most beautiful and highest born Egyptian maidens were forced into prostitution . . . and they continued as prostitutes until their first menstruation."[2] In India and China, children were regularly sold into prostitution by their parents and for centuries Persia was renowned for its boy brothels.[3] Child brothels "flourished in Europe during the Nineteenth Century, and freelance child prostitution was rampant in both Europe and America during the early 1800s, as men demanded more esoteric forms of sexual titillation."[4]

Today, child prostitution continues to be rampant in the United States with the stakes for child victims greater than ever.

THE DYNAMICS OF CHILD PROSTITUTION

Sexual misuse and exploitation of children as young as age 3 has become a multimillion dollar industry in America, with child prostitution accounting for a large chunk of illicit revenue. Child prostitution is commonly defined as the use of or participation of children—age 17 and under—in sexual acts with adults or other minors where no force is present, including intercourse, oral sex, anal sex, and sadomasochistic activities where payment is involved. As opposed to other forms of child sexual abuse such as statutory rape and incest, it is the selling of sexual favors that differentiates child prostitution. Payment often comes in money but also drugs, food, clothing, shelter, or other material items. Occasionally parents involved in the sex-for-sale industry sell their own children into prostitution, often when they are too young to fully understand what is happening to them.

How large is the problem of child prostitution? Estimates vary from tens of thousands to more than one million children active in the profession.[5] Some experts estimate that the figures for child prostitutes nationwide could be much greater, and this is just for children under the age of 16; the numbers perhaps doubling when 16- and 17-year-olds are included.[6] It is generally believed among authorities that there are as many girls as boys, and vice versa, working the streets as prostitutes.

There is evidence that the number of child prostitutes is increasing. In a recent 50 state survey, it was found that child prostitution had risen in 37 percent of the affected cities.[7] This was attributed in large measure to more children running away or being thrown out of troubled homes (See also Chapter 3). The two-year study also found that:

- Most child prostitutes are runaways with drug or alcohol problems.
- The majority are between 13 and 17 years of age, though many were found to be much younger.
- Most child prostitutes are found in central business districts, arcade game rooms, and bus and train depots.

Child prostitutes are often recruited from midwestern cities and rural areas. More than one million children run away from home each year, and many of them turn to prostitution for survival. "The children who run look for companionship, friendship, and approval from those they meet. Many such youths are easy marks for gangs, drug pushers, and pimps. Runaways often sell drugs or their bodies, and steal to support themselves."[8]

What children find in the world of prostitution is often far worse than what they may have imagined or were led to believe. Substance abuse, physical abuse, virtual slavery, sexually transmitted diseases, and sometimes death are typical circumstances they encounter as child prostitutes.

Their customers are almost exclusively men. "Many are married, including the ones primarily interested in boys, and of high stature and power. Nearly all feel inadequate and unable to relate meaningfully to peer sexual partners."[9]

Contrary to popular belief, child prostitutes are not primarily children from lower socioeconomic circumstances. In a study of prostitutes, Mimi Silbert found that 70 percent of her sample group were from families of average or higher incomes.[10] A Minnesota study of juvenile prostitutes found that nearly 1 in 4 had parents with some college education and many had fathers who were in skilled or professional occupations.[11] Jennifer James indicated a "phenomenal" increase in the number of "affluent and overindulged" child prostitutes.[12]

GIRL PROSTITUTES

By some estimates, girl prostitutes account for as many as two-thirds of all child prostitutes.[13] Girl streetwalkers may face greater risks than their boy counterparts with respect to crime, violence, abuse, and other hazards of the profession.[14] They also appear to be victims of a double standard when it comes to being arrested for prostitution. In 1992, slightly more females under the age of 18 were arrested for prostitution and commercialized vice than males under the age of 18. Many prostitutes are arrested as runaways. There were 82,922 girls arrested as runaways compared to 63,178 boys in 1992.[15]

Most girl prostitutes are between the ages of 15 and 17. James's study placed the median age at 16.9 years.[16] Arrest data show that 1 in every 2 females under the age of 18 arrested for prostitution or commercialized vice is 17.[17] Researchers have found that the vast majority of girl prostitutes are under age 16 when they enter the business, with the average age for entry into prostitution 14.[18]

Girl prostitutes come from all racial and ethnic groups, yet evidence indicates that white females comprise the majority of girls prostituting themselves. Studies in San Francisco[19] and Minneapolis[20] found that 80 percent of the girls in the sample were white, while 6 in 10 from James's study were white girls.[21] Black girls account for the second highest percentage of female juvenile prostitutes, with estimates ranging from 10 to 50 percent of those sampled.[22] Studies have found that Hispanic girls make up between 2 and 11 percent of the girl prostitutes in this country.[23]

Most girls entering prostitution come from broken homes and/or were victims of sexual or physical abuse. In Maura Crowley's study of female runaway prostitutes, 85 percent of the girl prostitutes reported the absence of one or both parents during their childhood.[24] The Huckleberry House study found that 70 percent of its sample group of girl prostitutes came from homes where one or both parents were missing.[25]

Even more common among girl prostitutes is sexual abuse including incest, molestation, and rape. The Huckleberry House found that 90 percent of the female prostitutes had been sexually abused before entering the profession.[26] Nearly two-thirds of the girl prostitutes in Mimi Silbert's sample were victims of incest.[27]

Physical child abuse is also strongly related to the background of girl prostitutes. Studies have shown that two-thirds of the girl prostitutes were physically abused at home.[28]

The Role of the Pimp

Entry into prostitution for many girls involves a pimp, usually a man whom they work for, live for, and sometimes die for. "It is generally accepted that most female prostitutes are physically, psychologically, and emotionally coerced by a pimp into becoming a prostitute."[29] In both James's and Dorothy Bracey's studies of juvenile prostitution, the authors speak of the "pimp's charm, flattery, and emotional manipulation as prominent in a girl's decision to enter the prostitution business."[30]

Although some studies have found that physical intimidation by pimps is rarely used to force girls into prostitution, once a young girl is part of a pimp's stable, "she is generally subject to his rules, regulations, and manipulation which includes falling in love, working for him, believing him, giving him much of her earnings, and violence."[31]

A typical example of the girl prostitute–pimp relationship can be seen in a recent article on child prostitution:

In New York City, a girl's pimp kept her on the street six nights a week. She hated being a prostitute, but the pimp was the only person who had shown her any kindness. When she could stand it no longer and told him she had to quit, he broke her jaw. At the hospital where the jaw was wired shut, she was given pain pills and told to rest. But her pimp put her on the street the next night.

Later, she tried to commit suicide using the pills, but she vomited, breaking the wires in her jaw. Her pimp would not allow her to return to the hospital and sent her back on the street.... She turned herself in to the police.

When asked her age, she replied, "I'll be 15 tomorrow."[32]

Motivating Factors For Entry Into Prostitution

Experts have linked female prostitution with psychological factors such as depression, emotional deprivation, and schizophrenia; as well as situational correlates such as child abuse and neglect, early sexual experiences, and rape.[33] Many studies have found economic deprivation or need to be a significant motivational factor in a girl's decision to enter into prostitution. James noted: "The apparent reason for prostitution among adolescents is for economic survival and to meet other needs."[34] Most child prostitutes interviewed acknowledge this to be true, supported by the reality of child prostitution in which prostitution is "one of the few ways for unskilled, undereducated, underaged persons to make money for food or shelter."[35]

BOY PROSTITUTES

The prostitution of boys has received greater attention in recent years with the AIDS virus. However, the selling of boys' bodies has long been a major problem. In a study of boy prostitutes, Robin Lloyd estimated that in the United States there were 300,000 males under the age of 18 who sold sex for money or other items.[36] Others believe the numbers of boy prostitutes to be even higher.

Boy prostitutes are referred to on the streets as "chickens," while the men who cruise the streets in search of boy prostitutes are known as "Chicken-Hawks" or "Chicken-Queens." Much of the boy prostitution takes place in large cities with a significant gay population. Boys can also be found selling sex in the suburbs and rural communities. The areas most frequented by boy prostitutes include adult bookstores, public parks, alleys, and doorways of businesses.

The first national study of boy prostitutes was conducted by the Urban and Rural Systems Associates of San Francisco.[37] Their findings on the typical juvenile male prostitute can be seen below:

- Boy prostitutes sell their bodies to survive financially, explore their sexuality, or make contact with gay men.
- The average age of the boy prostitute is 16.
- Two-thirds of the teenage male prostitutes are white, one-fourth black.
- The majority of boy prostitutes are runaways or throwaways.
- Most juvenile male prostitutes come from broken homes.
- A large percentage of boy prostitutes have been sexually, physically, or emotionally abused.
- Many teen prostitutes have failed in or dropped out of school.
- Delinquency and criminal activities are prominent among boy prostitutes.
- Pimps are virtually nonexistent in the adolescent male prostitution subculture.
- Money is the primary motivating factor for most boy prostitutes.
- Gay-identified boy prostitutes find the lifestyle initially exciting.

It is estimated that as many as half of all boy prostitutes are "thrown out of their houses because of sexual identity issues."[38] The vast majority of boy prostitutes are streetwalkers. In the book *Children of the Night*, O. Kelly Weisberg found that 94 percent of the boys sampled practiced their trade on the streets.[39]

A typical example of the way a boy prostitute operates is described by a Baltimore police detective with the sex offenses unit:

> The boy will usually find a set of marble steps, sit, and observe passing cars. Eye contact is the key. The "Chicken-Hawk" will stare at the boy he feels could be a "hustler." If a period of eye-contact is made between both, the "Chicken-Hawk" will still circle the block several times, making eye-contact at each passing. Finally the "Chicken-Hawk" will nod and, if the boy returns the nod, a deal is in the making. At times, the "chickens" would work as teams, usually two together. If the customer wanted two boys, he would use hand signals, indicating how many boys he wanted and how much he was paying.[40]

The Men Who Sexually Exploit Boys

Most men who solicit boys as prostitutes are pedophiles. Many "Chicken-Hawks" seek out any male hustlers, including adult male prostitutes. Some favor boys from a specific age group "and will not pick up any other boys who might be older or younger than he desires."[41] A profile of the typical "Chicken-Hawk" can be seen below:

* He is often middle-aged.
* Relates to children well, usually better than to adults.
* Is generally non-violent.
* He sees the boy victim as the sexual aggressor.
* Is usually single, but can be married.
* He associates with other pedophiles and "Chicken-Hawks."
* Often sexually molested as a child.
* Pretends to be the boy's friend.
* Is often a white-collar worker or professional.

Boy Prostitutes and Law Enforcement

Many boy prostitutes never come into contact with the criminal justice system despite evidence that many tend to be involved in more serious criminal activity than girl prostitutes, including assaults and robberies. D. Sweeney estimated that 70 percent of the teenage male prostitutes are never arrested or detained, compared to data which indicates that approximately 75 percent of the girl prostitutes have had some contact with the police, courts, or juvenile detention.[42]

This disparity is generally attributed to the greater difficulty in identifying boy prostitutes whose hustling is not as well exposed as girl prostitutes'. Laws also tend to be stricter as to what undercover police officers can do or say when targeting boy prostitutes compared to girls.

Kelly Weisberg's research did suggest a high incidence of boy prostitutes coming into contact with the criminal justice system. About two-thirds of the teenagers sampled had been arrested at least once, with prostitution-related charges accounting for one-third of the arrests.[43]

CHILD PROSTITUTION AND
SUBSTANCE ABUSE

A strong correlation exists between child prostitution and drug or alcohol use/abuse. It is estimated that between one-fifth and one-half of all child prostitutes use drugs regularly.[44] Marijuana is the drug used most often by teenage prostitutes; however, narcotics and psychedelic drugs as well as alcohol abuse have also been frequently associated with child prostitutes.[45] The Huckleberry House study found that 83 percent of the boy prostitutes sampled had tried marijuana, and 77 percent continued to smoke marijuana.[46] Another study found that 29 percent of the teenage male prostitutes used hard drugs, while 42 percent were heavy drinkers or alcoholics.[47]

Many young prostitutes were experienced in drug and alcohol use well before entering the world of prostitution. Often the victims of sexual or physical abuse, they had begun using drugs or alcohol to "Deaden memories and desensitize present experiences."[48]

AIDS AND CHILD PROSTITUTION

Sexually transmitted diseases among child prostitutes are epidemic and are one of the unfortunate realities of the victimization of child prostitution. Notes the writer of an article about teenage runaways and prostitutes: "They know they're flirting with disease. There's an epidemic of old venereal infections, crabs and chlamydia, secondary syphilis and super-gonorrhea, resistant to penicillin."[49] But now child prostitutes and runaways face the deadly threat of the AIDS virus (Acquired Immune Deficiency Syndrome), increasing their risks for pain, suffering, and death tenfold. Although AIDS can be contracted through various means including dirty needles and tainted blood, "sex more than anything puts runaway kids at risk for AIDS.... Their bodies become the currency of exchange...."[50] Many experts believe that "any kid on the street for a month will have to turn to prostitution. They don't have alternatives."[51]

One article speaks of the severity of the situation for teenagers who sell their bodies:

> AIDS has a potentially disastrous effect on what is going on in the streets, particularly in the inner cities where sex, drugs and poverty cross paths that often lead out to the suburbs and all across the coun-

try. Many of these runaway and homeless adolescents, between 20,000 and 40,000 in New York City, up to 1.2 million nationwide, are caught at the juncture of risks.[52]

The numbers indicate that for many child prostitutes the risk of contracting AIDS has already been realized. Recently 27 percent of the adolescents sampled at Covenant House, New York City's largest shelter for runaways, tested positive for HIV (Human Immunodeficiency Virus).[53] It was estimated that for those child prostitutes hustling every night, the rate of exposure would exceed 50 percent. The Centers for Disease Control recently found the rate of AIDS among prostitutes to be much higher than that for the public-at-large.[54]

The implications for child prostitutes, runaways, and throwaways goes well beyond contracting the AIDS virus itself. As AIDS moves into the population of victimized children, the questions outweigh the answers, as evidenced by the following thoughts from the director of a New York outreach program:

> Who will visit them in the hospital, bring them cards and candy, answer the questions about death and God their desperate eyes will ask? Where will they sleep between hospital visits?... Who will attend the funerals and weep beside their graves? Who will bury our children?[55]

9. *Child Pornography*

Child pornography was described by one writer as "the most inhuman of crimes. For pleasure and profit, pornographers have murdered the childhood of a million girls and boys, victims who must live with the dreadful memories of their experience."[1] Often referred to as "kiddie porn" and "chicken porn," child pornography is defined as photographs, videos, books, magazines, and motion pictures that depict children in sexually explicit acts with other children, adults, animals, and/or foreign objects. Many young child porn victims are subjected to every form of abuse, sadism, perversion, and bestiality. A particular magazine vividly depicts adults in various sexual acts with toddlers. Some audio tapes, accompanied by explicit narrative description, record the screams of a young girl being raped.

It is unknown just how long children have been the preferred victims of pornographers. However, it is generally believed that the modern era of child pornography began in China during the mid–1400s with the sex manual, *The Admirable Discourses of the Plain Girl*, in which intercourse and other sexual acts involving children were graphically described.[2]

Although there are laws against child pornography in the United States, most criminologists and sociologists agree that they are inadequate in halting the spread and availability of child pornography.

HOW WIDESPREAD IS CHILD PORNOGRAPHY?

The evidence suggests the problem of child pornography is alive and well in the United States, despite tough laws, increased crackdowns on child pornographers by law enforcement agencies, and efforts at community awareness. It is estimated that the child porn business takes in as much as $6 billion annually.[3] In Los Angeles alone, it is estimated that 30,000 children are sexually exploited by child pornographers each year.[4] One recent study found that at least 264 different magazines depicting sexual acts involving children were produced and distributed in this country each month.[5] A magazine of obscene pictures of children can be produced for as little as 50 cents and sold for twenty times as much.[6] Child pornography accounts for approximately 7 percent of the pornography in America.[7]

Recent examples illustrate the severity of the problem:

- A woman was alleged to have made $500,000 yearly by supplying 80 percent of the child pornography market.
- Houston police raided a warehouse full of child pornographic materials including 15,000 color slides of boys engaged in homosexual acts, more than 1,000 magazines and paperbacks, and over 1,000 reels of film.
- Forty thousand pictures depicting sexual relations between boys and with men were seized from the home of a suspected Hollywood pornographer.

Child pornographers have little difficulty recruiting willing participants with a potentially large pool of susceptible children, including their own, runaways, throwaways, child prostitutes, and neighborhood children looking for excitement or adventure. These children are often induced through gifts, money, or a place to hang out; many others are forced to cooperate with pornographers through fear, intimidation, abduction, torture, and blackmail.

WHO ARE THE CHILD PORNOGRAPHERS AND EXPLOITERS?

They are usually men from all walks of life and backgrounds. "The men who support this industry do so to rationalize and seek justification for their perverted and deviant mentality, whereas the pornographers who bring children into this seedy world are primarily interested in capitalizing monetarily from the sickness of disturbed, immature pedophiles who receive their only sexual satisfaction with children."[8]

The FBI's pedophile profile describes the typical child exploiter or pornographer as "intelligent enough to recognize they have a problem," but somehow justifying that "what they're doing is right."[9] One FBI agent notes the mindset of the pedophile: "Pedophilia is a way of life. They believe there's nothing wrong with it, so naturally they're looking for other individuals who support their thinking."[10]

Their most powerful allies are groups such as the Rene Guyon Society and the North American Man-Boy Love Association which openly support child pornography and consensual sexual relations between minors and adults (see Chapter 7). Despite the existence of such groups and affiliate chapters throughout the country, law enforcement is often powerless to stop or prevent their activities or membership "without an allegation or a reason to conduct" an investigation.[11]

THE LEGAL BATTLE
AGAINST CHILD PORNOGRAPHY

Before 1978, there was little federal or state legislation that specifically addressed the use of children in sexually explicit acts or material. Public outcry against child pornography led to a series of Congressional hearings in the late 1970s. As a result, Congress enacted the Protection of Children Against Sexual Exploitation Act of 1978.[12] The act was meant to stop the production and dissemination of child pornography by prohibiting the transportation across state lines of children for purposes of sexual exploitation.

The federal legislation provided punishment and penalties against persons who use, employ, or persuade minors (defined as persons under 16 years of age) to participate in sexually explicit visual or printed materials or productions. Penalties include a fine up to $10,000 for a first offense and up to 10 years imprisonment.

In 1982, the U.S. Supreme Court upheld a New York statute that prohibited the production and sale of materials portraying children in sexually explicit photographs, films, or performances.[13] This decision thereby added child pornography to the category of "speech" not protected by the First Amendment.

Since 1978, 48 states have designed legislation to combat child pornography. In 1993, President Clinton directed the Attorney General to draft new, tougher laws against child pornography in response to the Justice Department changing its interpretation of hard-core pornography in a Supreme Court case that involved videos of young girls posing seductively.

THE EFFECTS
OF CHILD PORNOGRAPHY

Child victims of pornographers face a lifetime of victimization. The physical and emotional scars of child pornography include children being molested, abused, exploited, often drugged, psychologically manipulated, imprisoned, and humiliated. There are also the ramifications of pictures or videos resurfacing after the child has participated, causing anxiety, helplessness, hopelessness, and withdrawal for the victim, as illustrated by the following example:

> Margie, a shy nine-year-old, was lured into a porn-photo session by a Little League coach who used provocative photographs of Brooke Shields as a child to entice her. Although the coach has been convicted, not all the photos of Margie were found. Presently, she refused to go to her school's open house because she dreamed that her teacher had the missing photographs displayed for everyone to see.[14]

Child pornography has also been linked to other forms of child abuse, violence, and sexual assault against children and women, and to sadistic pornography.[15] In *Children and Criminality*, the author notes that

> while it is difficult to distinguish between child molesters and the providers of children and child pornography as to which may be the most harmful to the child, it seems that our efforts must first be directed toward eliminating the mass marketing of child pornographic material, for it is this practice that promotes child sexual abuse and provides the sex offender with easy access to children and/or the sick fantasy of being with children.[16]

PART III

Violence and Victimized Children

10. *Violent Crimes Against Children*

In the past decade, the rate of violent crimes perpetrated against persons under the age of 20 has risen steadily. This is particularly true for teenage victims. Why is this? There are any number of possible reasons including the plethora of guns in our society, increased and more sophisticated gang activity, drugs and alcohol, a surge in domestic violence and family dysfunction, cutbacks in law enforcement across the country, and a seemingly general decline in moral values and self-restraint. The violence against children is merely a reflection of the larger problem of an increasingly violent society where few of us feel safe even in our own homes, much less on the streets. This chapter will be limited to examining official and victimization data with respect to violent crime victimization of children. For discussion on the cause and effect of violent criminality against children refer to Chapters 1, 2, and 11.

THE RATE OF VIOLENT CRIME
AIMED AT YOUTH

The *National Crime Victimization Survey* (NCVS) estimated that in 1991 there were 2,054,320 violent crimes perpetrated against persons aged 12 to 19 in the United States. These crimes included rape, robbery, and assault, but excluded murder.[1] Victimization rates for child victims of violent crimes can be seen in Table 10-1. The highest rate of

TABLE 10-1

Victimization Rates for Persons Aged 12 to 19, by Type of Crime and Age of Victims

Type of Crime	Rate per 1,000 Persons in Each Age Group	
	12–15	16–19
All personal crimes[a]	**163.9**	**185.1**
Crimes of violence	62.7	91.1
Completed	23.6	32.4
Attempted	39.1	58.7
Rape	1.1[b]	3.5
Robbery	10.0	8.3
Completed	5.9	4.9
With injury	1.5[b]	2.6
From serious assault	0.3[b]	1.0[b]
From minor assault	1.2[b]	1.6[b]
Without injury	4.4	2.4
Attempted	4.1	3.4
With injury	1.3[b]	0.9[b]
From serious assault	0.4[b]	0.3[b]
From minor assault	0.9[b]	0.6[b]
Without injury	2.8	2.5
Assault	51.6	79.2
Aggravated	12.9	25.5
Completed with injury	5.5	7.8
Attempted with weapon	7.5	17.6
Simple	38.7	53.8
Completed with injury	12.0	17.7
Attempted without weapon	26.7	36.0
Population in each age group	13,783,200	13,364,290

[a] Includes crimes of theft.
[b] Estimate is based on about 10 or fewer sample cases.

Source: U.S. Department of Justice, *Criminal Victimization in the United States, 1991: A National Crime Victimization Survey Report* (Washington, D.C.: Government Printing Office, 1992), p. 23.

victimization for crimes of violence was in the 16 to 19 age bracket. Only among completed or attempted robberies was the victimization rate greater for persons aged 12 to 15.

Table 10-2 reflects violent crime victimization of persons aged 12 to 19, by sex and race in 1991. Male juveniles had a significantly higher rate of victimization than their female counterparts. In the 12 to 15 age group, males were more than 2.6 times as likely as females to be the victim of a violent crime, and twice as likely among 16 to 19 year olds.

Blacks had a higher rate of violent crime victimization than whites in both age categories. When considering race, sex, and age, black males had a considerably higher victimization rate than white males, or females of either race. Black males aged 16 to 19 had a rate of 147.5 victimizations per 1,000 black persons in that age group and were more than five times as likely to be a victim of violence than black females aged 12 to 15.

MURDERED CHILDREN
IN THE UNITED STATES

There were 3,990 persons under the age of 20 as victims of murder or nonnegligent manslaughter in the United States in 1992, according to the FBI's *Uniform Crime Reports* (UCR). While this sum comprises just 17.7 percent of the total 22,540 murder victims in 1992, the number of juvenile homicide victims grew 5.7 percent from 1991 and 71.4 percent from 1983 when 2,328 persons under the age of 20 were murdered in this country.[2]

Table 10-3 breaks down child murder victims in 1992 by age, sex, race, and weapons used. Most of the children murdered were between the ages of 15 and 19, male, black, and the victims of firearms. Nearly 11 percent of the murders in this country in 1992 were of people under age 18. Juveniles aged 15 to 19 accounted for 71.5 percent of all homicides of persons under age 20. Younger children (infants to age 4) were murdered in greater numbers than middle aged children (age 5 to 14). Male juveniles were 3.5 times more likely to be murdered in 1992 as female juveniles. For those aged 15 to 19, 6 males were murdered for every female.

Black youths accounted for 51 percent of all murder victims under age 18 and 58.4 percent of those aged 15 to 19. These percentages are especially unsettling considering that blacks under the age of 20 constitute only about 13 percent of the nation's juvenile population.

TABLE 10-2

Violent Crime Victimization Rates
for Persons Aged 12 to 19,
by Sex, Age, and Race, 1991

	TOTAL POPULATION	CRIMES OF VIOLENCE[a]
SEX AND AGE		
Male		
12–15	7,066,340	90.3
16–19	6,766,590	121.3
Female		
12–15	6,716,860	33.7
16–19	6,597,690	60.1
RACE, AGE, AND SEX		
White		
12–15	11,003,290	60.3
16–19	10,686,350	89.7
Male		
12–15	5,610,640	84.3
16–19	5,394,180	118.7
Female		
12–15	5,392,640	35.2
16–19	5,292,160	60.1
Black		
12–15	2,219,640	82.4
16–19	2,114,640	106.5
Male		
12–15	1,137,690	133.9
16–19	1,060,590	147.5
Female		
12–15	1,081,950	28.4
16–19	1,054,050	65.1

[a] Rate per 1,000 persons in each age group.

Source: Compiled from U.S. Department of Justice, *Criminal Victimization in the United States, 1991: A National Crime Victimization Survey Report* (Washington, D.C.: Government Printing Office, 1992), pp. 24, 28–29.

The availability of firearms in this country is strongly related to the murder victimization of children. Of the total homicides of persons under age 18 in 1992, 60.4 percent were attributed to use of firearms — primarily handguns. More than 85 percent of the murdered youths aged 15 to 19 were victims of firearms.

Most murders of children tend to occur from juvenile gang violence, domestic violence, and in relation to brawls or incidents influenced by alcohol or narcotics.[3]

TEENAGE RAPE VICTIMS

According to victimization and official data, more than 100,000 rapes are reported each year. Of these, approximately one-third of the victims are under the age of 20.[4] A National Crime Survey of female rape victims from 1973 to 1987 found that on average 54,400 victims were between the ages of 12 and 19 annually. Most teenage victims — 37,600 per year — were aged 16 to 19.[5]

The victimization rate for preteen and teenage rape victims in 1991 was 4.6 per 1,000 persons aged 12 to 19, as reported by the NCVS.[6] For victims aged 16 to 19, the rate was 3.5 per 1,000, which represented the highest victimization rate of seven age groups from 12 to 15 to 65 and over. Rape victims aged 12 to 15 were victimized at a rate of 1.1 per 1,000, the third highest rate by age group.

When considering the victimization rate for female preteens and teens only, the rate of rape victimization is even higher. Compare the following two year rates for rape victimization:

Age	Females 1990	Females 1991	All Persons 1990	All Persons 1991
12–15	3.4	2.0	1.8	1.1
16–19	2.5	7.1	1.4	3.5

Females aged 16 to 19 had a rape victimization rate more than twice that of all persons 16 to 19 victimized in 1991 and significantly higher than all other age brackets of female rape victims. This indicates both the predominantly female nature of rape victimization and the highest risk group for victimization.

Black teenagers have a higher rate of rape victimization than white teenagers, as do teens of other minority groups. However, more white teens are victims of rape each year than the total of nonwhite victims.[7]

TABLE 10-3

Murdered Children in U.S.,
by Age, Sex, Race, and Weapons Used, 1992

AGE	Total	SEX		RACE			WEAPONS USED			
		Male	Female	White	Black	Other	Firearms	Knives or cutting instruments	Blunt objects (Clubs, hammers, etc.)	Other[b]
Total Murder Victims in U.S.	22,540	17,576	4,936	10,647	11,175	548	15,377	3,265	1,029	2,869
Percent Distribution[a]	100.0	78.0	21.9	47.2	49.6	2.4	68.2	14.5	4.6	12.8
Total Murder Victims Under 18	2,428	1,748	679	1,103	1,240	72	1,468	172	97	691
Infants (under 1)	254	137	116	147	99	3	11	4	15	224
1 to 4	408	237	171	204	192	12	61	19	41	287
5 to 9	126	64	62	60	56	10	47	8	8	63
10 to 14	351	230	121	163	171	14	252	35	12	52
15 to 19	2,851	2,444	407	1,114	1,664	60	2,433	230	40	148

[a] Due to rounding and unknown ages or circumstances, percentages may not add up.
[b] Includes use of hands, fists, drownings, explosives, poison, etc.

Source: U.S. Federal Bureau of Investigation, *Crime in the United States: Uniform Crime Reports 1992* (Washington, D.C.: Government Printing Office, 1993), pp. 16, 18.

TABLE 10-4

Assault and Robbery Victimization of Persons Under Age 20, 1988–1990[a]

		TYPE OF CRIME		
		ASSAULTS		ROBBERIES
Year	Total	Aggravated	Simple	Total
1988	1,501,990	516,950	985,030	258,760
1989	1,569,360	517,570	1,051,770	273,660
1990	1,589,980	547,530	1,042,430	314,150

[a] Totals are for persons aged 12 to 19.

Source: Derived from data in U.S. Department of Justice, *Criminal Victimization in the United States: 1973–90 Trends* (Washington, D.C.: Government Printing Office, 1992), pp. 27, 42–43.

Hispanic and non–Hispanic teenagers have similar rates of victimization, but below that of black teens.[8]

Most rapes of persons under 20 occur at the victim's home, at night, and without the use of weapons.[9]

ASSAULTIVE CRIMES AGAINST CHILDREN

Recent years have seen an increase in assaultive crimes such as robberies and assaults in which children and young adults are victims. Much of this can be attributed to the increased availability of handguns and the more violent turn society seems to have taken in the late '80s, early '90s. Table 10-4 illustrates this trend for robberies and assaults of persons aged 12 to 19 between 1988 and 1990. Assaults of persons under age 20 rose nearly 6 percent during the period, while robberies grew more than 21 percent.

Victimization rates in 1991 for robberies and assaults were highest among all age groups for persons aged 16 to 19, according to the NCVS. A person in this age category was more than 4 times as likely

TABLE 10-5

Violent Crimes Victimization Rates for Persons Age 19 and Under, by Age, Sex, Race, and Type of Crime, 1991[a]

	Crimes of Violence[b]	ASSAULT			ROBBERY		
		Total	Aggravated	Simple	Total	With Injury	Without Injury
AGE							
12–15	62.7	51.6	12.9	38.7	10.0	1.5	4.4
16–19	91.1	79.2	25.5	53.8	8.3	2.6	2.4
SEX AND AGE							
Male							
12–15	90.3	74.8	21.1	53.7	15.1	4.3	10.9
16–19	121.3	108.2	39.3	68.9	13.1	4.4	8.7
Female							
12–15	33.7	27.2	4.3	22.9	4.5	1.3[c]	3.3[c]
16–19	60.1	49.5	11.2	38.3	3.4[c]	2.6[c]	0.8[c]
RACE AND AGE							
White							
12–15	60.3	51.1	12.8	38.3	7.8	2.9	4.8
16–19	89.7	76.7	24.6	52.1	9.2	3.5	5.7
Black							
12–15	82.4	62.9	16.1	46.8	19.5	2.1[c]	17.4
16–19	106.5	97.8	29.5	68.3	5.2[c]	3.6[c]	1.6[c]

[a] Rate is based on per 1,000 persons in each age group.
[b] Includes rape victimization.
[c] Estimate is based on 10 or less sample cases.

Source: U.S. Department of Justice, *Criminal Victimization in the United States, 1991: A National Crime Victimization Survey Report* (Washington, D.C.: Government Printing Office, 1992), pp. 24, 28.

to be a robbery victim and 28 times a victim of an aggravated assault as a person age 65 or older. Children aged 12 to 15 had a higher rate of robbery victimization than did persons aged 16 to 19 in 1991, but older teens were almost twice as likely to be the victims of an assault.

Table 10-5 shows victimization rates for persons aged 12 to 19 by age, race, sex, and type of violent crime in 1991. Males and blacks aged 16 to 19 had the highest victimization rates among youths, while older female teens were nearly twice as likely to be victims of violent crimes as younger female teens. Male youths had significantly higher victimization rates than their female counterparts. For example, males aged 16 to 19 were 9 times more likely to be victims of aggravated assault than females aged 12 to 15.

Black teens were disproportionately represented as victims of assaultive crimes in 1991. There were 97.8 assaults of blacks aged 16 to 19 for every 1,000 blacks in that age group. Younger black teens had a significantly higher rate of robbery victimization and robbery without injury than did older black teens, with ratios of 3.75 and 10.8 respectively. Victimization data for other minority groups and Hispanics indicate that their rate of assaultive crimes victimization is higher relative to their population figures.[10]

The percentage of juvenile victims sustaining physical injury and taking self-protective measures during a robbery or assault in 1991 can be seen in Table 10-6. About one-third of the persons aged 12 to 19 were physically injured during an assault or robbery. Over 40 percent of those aged 16 to 19 sustained injury during a robbery.

Most victims of violent crimes aged 12 to 19 took some form of self-protective measures. Three out of every 4 persons aged 16 to 19 sought to protect themselves, including 8 out of 10 victims of an aggravated assault. Victims were least likely to take self-protective measures when the crime was a robbery where no injury was sustained.

A study of the places where violent criminal victimization of teenagers occurs is shown in Table 10-7. Most victimizations tend to occur at school or on the streets. Robberies of teenagers are perpetrated about one-third of the time on the streets, while about one-quarter of the aggravated assaults take place on the street.

OFFENDER CHARACTERISTICS

Most perpetrators of violent crimes against persons under the age of 18 tend to be characteristic of the victims themselves—that is, of

TABLE 10-6

Violent Victimizations Against Teenagers, by Type of Crime, Age of Victim, and Place of Occurrence, 1985–88

| | CRIMES OF VIOLENCE | | | | | | | |
| | Total | | Robbery | | Aggravated Assault | | Simple Assault | |
Place of Occurrence	12–15 years	16–19 years	12–15 years	16–19 years	12–15 years	16–19 years	12–15 years	16–19 years
Total[a]	100%	100%	100%	100%	100%	100%	100%	100%
At school	37	17	32	9	23	9	43	24
In building	20	9	19	4	9	4	24	13
On property	17	8	13	5	14	5	19	11
Street	25	26	35	38	28	27	21	22
Near victim's home	11	7	9	6	13	9	11	7
At victim's home	4	8	4	10	5	7	4	7
Home of friend, relative, or neighbor	8	11	4	12	11	7	11	
Park, field, or playground[b]	5	5	5	5	6	8	5	4
Public transportation, parking lot	5	13	5	15	7	15	4	12
Restaurant, commercial building	2	8	4	5	1	9	3	9
Other place	3	5	2	4	5	5	2	5

[a] Percents may not sum to 100 because of rounding.

[b] Excludes school playgrounds, which are classified as school property.

Source: U.S. Department of Justice, Bureau of Justice Statistics, *Teenage Victims* (Washington, D.C.: Government Printing Office, 1991), p. 8.

TABLE 10-7

Percent of Violent Crime Victimizations Involving Victim Injury and Self-Protective Measures for Persons Aged 12 to 19, 1991

PERCENT OF VICTIMS SUSTAINING PHYSICAL INJURY

Age of Victim	Robbery and Assault	Assault	Robbery
12–15	32.9	33.8	28.3
16–19	33.3	32.3	42.1

PERCENT OF VICTIMS TAKING SELF-PROTECTIVE MEASURES

Age of Victim	Crimes of Violence	ASSAULT			ROBBERY		
		Total	Aggravated	Simple	Total	With Injury	Without Injury
12–15	69.7	70.4	72.1	69.6	64.6	70.2	61.7
16–18	74.4	77.6	81.5	75.6	59.6	68.0	55.5

Source: U.S. Department of Justice, *Criminal Victimization in the United States, 1991: A National Crime Victimization Survey Report* (Washington, D.C.: Government Printing Office, 1992), pp. 84, 88.

---

similar age range, gender, race, and ethnicity. Of the 1,306 murders of persons under the age of 18 in the United States in 1992 in which there was a single offender, 26 percent were committed by persons under age 18.[11] More than 9 out of every 10 black homicide victims and 8 of every 10 whites slain in this country were the victims of same race offenders. While 87 percent of the males murdered in single victim-offender circumstances were killed by males, 9 of every 10 females slain were the victims of males.

In a study of female rape victims between 1979 and 1987, 36 percent of the victims aged 16 to 19 and 27 percent of those aged 12 to 15

TABLE 10-8

Percent Distribution of Single- and Multiple-Offender Victimizations of Persons Aged 12 to 19, by Type of Crime and Perceived Age of Offender(s), 1991

Percent of Single-Offender Victimizations

Type of Crime	Number of Single-Offender Victimizations	Total[a]	Under 12	Perceived Age of Offender					
				Total	12–20			21–29	30 & over
					12–14	15–17	18–20		
Crimes of violence[b]	1,312,780	100%	1.8[c]	68.5	22.2	23.8	22.5	15.7	10.8
Robbery	123,800	100%	3.5[c]	52.6	27.5	11.0[c]	14.0[c]	22.3	9.8[c]
Assault	1,131,830	100%	1.7[c]	72.6	22.5	26.4	23.7	14.3	9.0

Percent of Multiple-Offender Victimizations

Type of Crime	Number of Multiple-Offender Victimizations	Total[a]	Perceived Age of Offender				
			All Under 12	All 12–20	All 21–29	All 30 & over	Mixed Ages
Crimes of violence[b]	741,540	100%	0.5[c]	64.2	1.7[c]	1.1[c]	24.2
Robbery	123,310	100%	0.0[c]	64.8	3.7[c]	0.0[c]	14.7[c]
Assault	613,290	100%	0.6[c]	64.6	1.3[c]	1.3[c]	25.8

[a] Includes data for offenders in which perceived age is unknown or unavailable.
[b] Includes data on rape.
[c] Estimate is based on 10 or less sample cases.

Source: U.S. Department of Justice, *Criminal Victimization in the United States, 1991: A National Crime Victimization Survey Report* (Washington, D.C.: Government Printing Office, 1992), pp. 60, 65.

reported the rapist to be age 20 or younger.[12] More than 6 out of every 10 rape victims under age 20 were victimized by offenders under age 21.

Single and multiple-offender violent crime victimizations of persons under age 20 by type of crime and perceived age of offenders in 1991 can be seen in Table 10-8. Nearly 7 out of every 10 single-offender crimes of violence victimization of persons younger than 20 were believed to be perpetrated by offenders between the ages of 12 and 20. Victims aged 12 to 19 were assaulted 73 percent of the time and robbed over half the time by offenders aged 12 to 20. In 64.2 percent of the multiple-offender violent crime victimizations, the offenders were perceived to be between the ages of 12 and 20.

In the NCS report, *Teenage Victims*, other findings of victim-offender characteristics in violent crime victimizations of teenagers include:

- Young teenage victims (age 12 to 15) are the most likely to have known their offenders casually or by sight.
- Robbery victims are proportionately less likely to know their perpetrators than victims of assault.
- Male teenagers are the victims of male offenders in better than 9 out of every 10 crimes of violence.
- Female teens are victimized by all male offenders in 6 violent crimes out of 10.
- Female teenagers are twice as likely as female adults to be the victims of violent crimes committed by other females.
- The vast majority of teenage victimizations are intraracial.
- Teenage victimizations are more likely to be intraracial than adult victimizations.
- More than 8 out of 10 black teens are victimized in crimes of violence by other blacks.
- White teenage robbery victims are victimized by white offenders in about half the cases, with 4 out of 10 perpetrators being black.[13]

REPORTING CRIMES OF VIOLENCE
TO THE POLICE

Violent crimes against persons under the age of 20 are less likely to be reported to the police than victimizations of persons over 20. In 1991, 35.6 percent of the crimes of violence perpetrated against persons 12 to 19 were reported to the police—compared to more than 50 percent in the four older age groups, as reported by the NCVS.[14] The highest percentage of reporting for teenage victims of violent crimes was for the crime of rape, where better than 4 out of every 10 victimizations was reported to the police in 1991. About one-third of those victimizations involving strangers and nonstrangers were reported.

In *Teenage Victims* it was found that:

- Robberies and simple assaults were most often reported when older teens were victimized than younger ones.
- Rapes were more likely to be reported when the victim was a younger teen rather than an older teen.
- The proportion of teenage victimizations reported to the police increased as did the seriousness of the crime.
- In one-third of the reported crimes of violence against teenagers, the most important reason for reporting was to prevent the crime from happening again.
- For younger teens, the reason most often given for not reporting a violent crime was that it was not considered important enough.
- For older teens, the reasons most often used for not reporting a violent crime were that it was a personal, private matter or unimportant.[15]

11. School Violence and Victimization

An increasing problem in our society is the level of crime and violence in and around schools. This is due in large part to the easy access of guns, alcohol, and drugs by teenagers, and the proliferation of juvenile gangs onto campuses across America. The victimization of children at school by other children has led to tighter security at schools, stricter rules and regulations for students, and greater involvement of parents and police in school safety. School violence continues to be one of the major forms of child victimization and school grounds one of the most dangerous places for adolescents in the nineties.

THE SCOPE OF SCHOOL VIOLENCE

School violence has become an "epidemic of violence" in our nation's school system, according to recent studies. In 1994, the National School Boards Association (NSBA) released the findings of a 5-year survey of 729 school districts on school violence. Eighty-two percent of the districts reported that school violence had increased over the five-year period; 78 percent reported student assaults against other students; 60 percent that there were student attacks against teachers; and 61 percent reported school violence in which weapons were involved. In 15 percent of the school districts—39 percent of which were urban—students were scanned with metal detectors. Nearly 8 in 10 districts attributed the increase in school violence primarily to "changing family situations."[1]

111

TABLE 11-1

Percent Distribution of School Violence, by Type of Crime and Place of Occurrence, 1991

Type of Crime	Number of victimizations[a]	Percent of Victimizations		
		Total	Inside school building	On school property
Crimes of Violence	641,977	100%	49.1%	50.9%
Completed	205,445	100%	43.5	56.5
Attempted	439,573	100%	51.6	48.4
Rape	5,314	100%	67.7[b]	32.3[b]
Robbery	39,395	100%	40.6[b]	50.4[b]
Completed	32,179	100%	41.3[b]	58.7[b]
Attempted	8,034	100%	40.9[b]	59.1[b]
Assault	602,597	100%	49.6	50.4
Aggravated	94,641	100%	36.2	63.8
Simple	503,625	100%	51.9	48.1
Personal larceny with contact	26,205	100%	61.8[b]	38.2[b]
Motor vehicle theft	44,358	100%	.....	100%

[a] Totals may not add up due to rounding.
[b] Estimate is based on 10 or fewer sample cases.

Source: Derived from U.S. Department of Justice, *Crime in the United States, 1991: A National Crime Victimization Survey Report* (Washington, D.C.: Government Printing Office, 1992), p. 75.

The *National Crime Victimization Survey Report* (NCVS) estimated that there were 641,977 crimes of violence inside school buildings or on school property in 1991 (see Table 11-1). Most victimizations were assaults and simple assaults. Violent crimes were more likely to occur on school property than in school buildings and be attempted than completed at schools.

In *Teenage Victims*, it was reported that between 1985 and 1988, a high percentage of violence against teenagers occurred at school. As

TABLE 11-2

School Violence by Type of Crime, Place of Occurrence, and Age of Victim, 1985–1988

| | **PERCENT OF VIOLENT CRIMES** | | | | | | | |
| | Total | | Aggravated Assault | | Simple Assault | | Robbery | |
Place of Occurrence	Age 12–15	Age 16–19	Age 12–15	Age 16–19	Age 12–15	Age 16–19	Age 12–15	Age 16–19
Total[a]	100%	100%	100%	100%	100%	100%	100%	100%
At school	37	17	23	9	43	24	32	9
Inside school	20	9	9	4	24	13	19	4
On school property	17	8	14	5	19	11	13	5

[a] For all crimes against persons in these age groups.

Source: U.S. Department of Justice, *Teenage Victims: A National Crime Survey Report* (Washington, D.C.: Government Printing Office, 1991), p. 8.

shown in Table 11-2, 37 percent of the violent crimes against those 12 to 15 years of age from 1985 to 1988 were committed in school buildings or on school property. For teenagers 16 to 19 years of age, 17 percent of the violent victimizations happened at school. Younger teens experienced the highest percentage of their victimizations for simple assaults (43 percent) and robberies (32 percent) on school grounds, whereas one-fourth of older teenagers' simple assaults occurred at school.

Perhaps the most definitive study of school violence was conducted over a six-month period in 1989 by the Justice Department as a School Crime Supplement (SCS) to the NCVS (see Table 11-3). In surveying more than 10,000 students 12 to 19 years of age, the SCS found that 9 percent had been crime victims in or around school within the six month period. Two percent of the students reported being victims of one or more violent crimes.

The degree and type of victimization varied in relation to age, race, ethnicity, family income, place of residence, type of school, and

TABLE 11-3

Students Reporting Victimization at School, by Personal and Family Characteristics, 1989

STUDENT CHARACTERISTICS	Total # of Students	Percent of students reporting victimization at school		
		Total	Violent[a]	Property[b]
Sex				
Male	11,166,316	9%	2%	7%
Female	10,387,776	9	2	8
Race				
White	17,306,626	9	2	7
Black	3,449,488	8	2	7
Other	797,978	10	2	8
Hispanic origin				
Yes	2,026,968	7	3	5
No	19,452,697	9	2	8
Not ascertained	74,428	3[c]	(d)	3[c]
Age				
12 years	3,220,891	9	2	7
13 years	3,313,714	10	2	8
14 years	3,264,574	11	2	9
15 years	3,214,109	9	3	7
16 years	3,275,002	9	2	7
17 years	3,273,628	8	1	7
18 years	1,755,825	5	1[c]	4
19 years	231,348	2[c]	(d)	2[c]
# of times family moved in last 5 yrs.				
None	18,905,538	8	2	7
Once	845,345	9	2[c]	7
Twice	610,312	13	3[c]	11
3 or more	1,141,555	15	6	9
Not ascertained	51,343	5[c]	5[c](d)	
Family income				
Less than $7,500	2,041,418	8	2	6

STUDENT CHARACTERISTICS	Total # of Students	Percent of students reporting victimization at school		
		Total	Violent[a]	Property[b]
Family Income				
$7,500 to $9,999	791,086	4	1[c]	3
$10,000 to $14,999	1,823,150	9	3	7
$15,000 to $24,999	3,772,445	8	1	8
$25,000 to $29,999	1,845,313	8	2	7
$30,000 to $49,999	5,798,448	10	2	8
$50,000 and over	3,498,382	11	2	9
Not ascertained	1,983,849	7	3	5
Place of residence				
Central city	5,816,321	10	2	8
Suburbs	10,089,207	9	2	7
Nonmetropolitan area	5,648,564	8	1	7
SCHOOL CHARACTERISTICS				
Type of school				
Public	19,264,643	9	2	8
Private	1,873,077	7	1[c]	6
Not ascertained	416,372	6	3[c]	4[c]
Grade in school				
6th	1,817,511	10	3	8
7th	3,170,126	9	2	8
8th	3,258,506	9	2	8
9th	3,390,701	11	3	9
10th	3,082,441	9	2	7
11th	3,223,624	8	2	7
12th	3,171,819	6	1	5
Other	439,364	5	3[c]	3[c]

[a] Includes the crimes of rape, robbery, simple, and aggravated assault.
[b] Includes personal larceny, with and without contact, and motor vehicle theft.
[c] Estimate is based on 10 or fewer sample cases.
[d] Less than 0.5 percent.

Source: U.S. Department of Justice, Bureau of Justice Statistics, *School Crime* (Washington, D.C.: Government Printing Office, 1991), pp. 1–2.

grade level. Male and female students were equally likely to experience criminal victimization or violent criminality (9 percent); students of different races were victimized about the same in crimes of violence (2 percent); students over age 17 generally experienced less violent crime victimization than younger students; and 15-year-olds experienced the highest percentage of crimes of violence among all students (3 percent).

School violence and family income had no consistent relationship. However, students who had moved 3 or more times in the previous 5 years were 3 times as likely to be victims of violent crimes as students who had not moved at all during the preceding 5 years. Students living in central cities or suburbs were twice as likely to experience violent victimizations as students residing in nonmetropolitan areas.

Public school students were more likely than private school students to be victimized and experience crimes of violence. High school seniors were the least likely to be violent crime victims, while sixth and ninth graders were the most likely victims of violence.

Other findings of note from the SCS include:

- Approximately 21.6 million students, ages 12 to 19, were enrolled in public and private schools during the time of the survey.
- Sixteen percent of the respondents reported that a student had assaulted or threatened a teacher during the previous 6 months.
- Hispanic students were more likely to experience crimes of violence than non-Hispanic students.
- Nine out of 10 students were non–Hispanic.
- Fifty-two percent of the students were male, 48 percent female.
- Eight out of 10 students were white, 16 percent black.
- Nearly half the students lived in suburbs, about one-quarter resided in central cities, and one-quarter lived in nonmetropolitan areas.

The scope and characteristics of school crime and violence can be further assessed in relation to overall crime statistics. Table 11-4 reflects the percentage of school-related violent crimes by selected characteristics in the United States in 1991. Nearly one-fifth of all assaults by unarmed offenders occurred inside schools and on school property, while twice as many assaults by armed offenders took place on school property as inside school buildings. School-related robberies accounted for just over 4 percent of all robberies and were perpetrated most often by unarmed offenders.

TABLE 11-4

Percentage of School-Related Violent Crime Victimizations, by Selected Characteristics of Total Crime, 1991

Type of Crime and Offender	Percent of Total Victimizations		
	Inside School Building	On School Property	Total School Incidents
Assault			
By armed offenders	2.1	4.3	6.4
By unarmed offenders	9.3	7.9	17.2
Robbery			
By armed offenders	0.0[a]	1.7[a]	1.7[a]
By unarmed offenders	4.2[a]	4.2[a]	8.4[a]
Relationship and Type of Crime			
Involving Strangers			
Crimes of Violence	3.1	3.7	6.8
Rape	2.0[a]	2.0[a]	4.0[a]
Robbery	1.2[a]	1.9[a]	3.1[a]
Assault	3.8	4.4	8.2
Involving Nonstrangers			
Crimes of Violence	8.7	8.3	17.0
Rape	2.2[a]	0.0[a]	2.2[a]
Robbery	3.1[a]	3.8[a]	6.9[a]
Assault	9.5	9.0	18.5

Type of Crime	On the Way to or from School
Crimes of Violence	3.9
Rape	4.6
Robbery	2.8
Aggravated assault	3.2
Simple assault	4.6

[a] Estimate is based on about 10 or fewer sample cases.

Source: Derived from U.S. Department of Justice, *Crime in the United States, 1991: A National Crime Victimization Survey Report* (Washington, D.C.: Government Printing Office, 1992), pp. 76–77, 79.

Nearly 7 percent of violent crime involving strangers in 1991 occurred in or outside schools, with school assaults accounting for 8.2 percent of stranger assaultive crimes. Seventeen percent of crimes of violence involving nonstrangers were committed at schools, including almost one-fifth of all assaults committed by nonstrangers.

Violent victimizations on the way to or from school were responsible for nearly 4 percent of all violent crimes, with rape and simple assaults representing the highest percentage of school-related crimes of violence.

DRUG AND ALCOHOL USAGE AT SCHOOL

Students are using and abusing drugs and alcohol across the country. Consider the following findings on teenagers, alcohol and drugs:

- The United States has the highest rate of teenage drug use in the industrialized world.
- Between 1975 and 1980, 93.2 percent of students in a nationwide survey admitted drinking alcohol during their lifetime.
- In another survey from 1975 to 1982, 70 percent of the teens said they had drunk alcohol within the past month.
- Three million teenagers aged 14 to 17 are estimated to abuse alcohol.
- A 1991 survey found that 20.1 percent of the respondents aged 12 to 17 had used illicit drugs at some point, 14.8 percent within the past year, and 6.8 percent in the past 30 days.
- One in every three 12- to 17-year-olds has tried marijuana.
- Nearly one in every 5 high school seniors has tried cocaine or crack.
- Teenage use of amphetamines such as "speed" is increasing.
- Drug use among juveniles is 10 times more prevalent than parents realize.[2]

According to the SCS, 3 in 10 students felt that marijuana and alcohol were easy to obtain at school with only half as many students believing they were impossible to obtain (see Table 11-5). Twenty percent of the students believed uppers and downers were easy to get, while 14 percent felt that other types of drugs were easy to obtain.

Two-thirds of the male and female, black and white, and Hispanic and non–Hispanic students reported the availability of drugs at school.[3]

TABLE 11-5

Availability of Drugs or Alcohol at School, by Type of Drug

Drugs or Alcohol at School	Percent of students reporting that obtaining a drug or alcohol at school was					
	Total[a]	Easy	Hard	Impossible	Not known	Drug not known
Alcohol	100%	31%	31%	16%	22%	1%
Marijuana	100%	30	27	16	25	1
Cocaine	100%	11	33	25	31	1
Crack	100%	9	29	28	32	2
Uppers/downers	100%	20	26	17	31	5
Other drugs	100%	14	27	19	37	3

[a] Detail may not total 100% because of rounding. The total number of students represented was 21,554,092.

Source: U.S. Department of Justice, *School Crime: A National Crime Victimization Survey Report* (Washington, D.C.: Government Printing Office, 1991), p. 3.

The confidence in availability of drugs increased with age. Over three-fourths of the students aged 17 to 19 believed drugs were accessible, compared to just over half the students age 12.

The relationship between availability of drugs or alcohol and victimization of students can be seen in Table 11-6. Students who reported that drugs or alcohol were easy to obtain were more likely to have been victims of crime and violent crime than students who believed that alcohol or drugs were hard or impossible to get. Twice as many students who felt that marijuana, cocaine, crack, and uppers and downers were easy to get were victims of violent crimes as students who felt these drugs were hard to come by.

GANGS AND SCHOOL VIOLENCE

Many believe that the rise in school violence is related to the presence and activity of gangs in and around schools in the United States. There

TABLE 11-6

Victimization of Students, by Availability of Alcohol or Drugs at School

Alcohol or drug and availability	Total number of students	Percent of students victimized		
		Total	Violent	Property
Alcohol				
Easy	6,637,706	11%	2%	9%
Hard	6,712,646	9	2	7
Impossible	3,407,854	8	2	7
Not Known	4,673,642	8	2	6
Marijuana				
Easy	6,568,766	11%	3%	9%
Hard	5,918,567	8	1	7
Impossible	3,494,543	8	2	7
Not Known	5,396,256	8	2	6
Cocaine				
Easy	2,297,249	11%	4%	9%
Hard	7,034,616	10	2	8
Impossible	5,354,381	9	2	7
Not Known	6,655,588	8	2	6
Crack				
Easy	1,862,226	12%	4%	9%
Hard	6,338,322	9	2	7
Impossible	6,018,289	10	2	8
Not Known	6,988,776	8	2	6
Uppers/Downers				
Easy	4,399,177	12%	3%	10%
Hard	5,555,802	8	1	7
Impossible	3,723,187	8	2	6
Not Known	6,760,441	8	2	6
Other Drugs				
Easy	2,992,401	13%	4%	10%
Hard	5,895,744	8	1	7
Impossible	4,019,868	8	1	7
Not Known	8,029,741	8	2	7

Source: U.S. Department of Justice, *School Crime: A National Crime Victimization Survey Report* (Washington, D.C.: Government Printing Office, 1991), p. 5.

are estimated to be 2,200 juvenile gangs in the country, consisting of approximately 96,000 members.[4] In Los Angeles alone there are believed to be some 600 youth gangs, totalling about 70,000 members of virtually every ethnic and racial group.[5] Experts have found gang members to be responsible for as much as one-third of all violent crimes "and maintaining a state of siege in many inner city schools."[6]

In the SCS survey, 79 percent of the students said no gangs existed at their schools, 15 percent reported that there were gangs at school, and 5 percent were uncertain (see Table 11-7). Of the students who reported that gangs existed at school, 37 percent said gang members never fought at school, while 19 percent believed that gang members fought once or twice a year, and 16 percent reported that gang members fought once or twice a month.

Sixteen percent of the students said that a gang member had attacked or threatened a teacher during the 6 months prior to the interview, 73 percent reported no such attacks or threats, and 11 percent were unsure.

Students who reported gangs were at their schools were more likely to have been victims of a crime or violent crime than students who said there were no gangs at school. Other findings of the SCS related to gangs and school are as follows:

- Twenty percent of black students reported the presence of gangs at school, 14 percent white students, and 25 percent students from other racial groups.
- Male and female students were relatively equal in their percentage reporting gangs.
- Thirty-two percent Hispanic students reported gangs at school compared to 14 percent non–Hispanic students.
- Gangs were most likely to exist in schools with students aged 14 to 17.
- Students in households with an income under $30,000 a year were more likely to attend schools with gangs than students in households with higher annual incomes.
- Central city students were more than 3 times as likely to report gangs in school as nonmetropolitan area students.
- Seventy-eight percent of students at schools where gangs were present reported that drugs could be obtained at school, compared to 66 percent of students at schools where there were no gangs.

TABLE 11-7

Students Reporting Gangs at School and Attacks on Teachers

	Total number of students	Percent of students reporting[a]
Street gangs at school		
Present	3,300,826	15%
Not present	17,041,519	79
Not known or not ascertained	1,211,747	5
Frequency of fights between gang members[b]		
Never	1,678,041	37%
Once or twice a year	843,607	19
Once or twice a month	743,649	16
Once or twice a week	337,868	7
Almost every day	219,516	5
Not ascertained	689,894	15
Attacks or threats on teachers		
Yes	3,468,631	16%
No	15,639,976	73
Not known or not ascertained	2,445,485	11

[a] Percentage distribution may not total 100% because of rounding.
[b] Excludes cases in which the student indicated that there were no gangs at school.

Source: U.S. Department of Justice, *School Crime: A National Crime Victimization Survey Report* (Washington, D.C.: Government Printing Office, 1991), p. 8.

FEAR OF SCHOOL CRIME AND VIOLENCE

The greatest victimization most students likely experience at school is the fear of crime and violence. The SCS found that victims of violent crimes were about 3 times as likely as nonvictims to report the fear of

FIGURE 11-1

Percent of Students Fearing Victimization by Gang Presence at School and Areas to Fear or Avoid

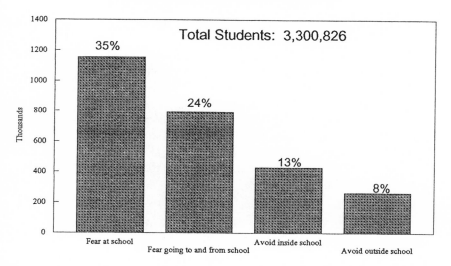

Source: U.S. Department of Justice, *School Crime: A National Crime Victimization Survey Report* (Washington, D.C.: Government Printing Office, 1991), p. 3.

being assaulted at school.[7] Student victims of an assault or robbery in the past 6 months were more than twice as likely to avoid certain places at school for fear of being attacked as student victims of theft, and 5 times more likely than students who had not experienced a violent victimization at school.

Six percent of all students reported avoiding places inside or outside school for fear of victimization. School restrooms (2.7 percent) and school hallways (2.1 percent) were the most often mentioned places to avoid.

Students at schools with gangs were twice as likely to fear being attacked as students at schools with no gangs. Figure 11-1 gives the percentages of places that students fear or avoid when gangs are present at school. Thirty-five percent of the students feared an attack at school, 24 percent going to or from school; while 13 percent avoided areas inside school and 8 percent avoided being in certain areas outside of school.

Additional findings from the SCS with respect to students' fear of victimization include:

- Male and female students are equally likely to fear an attack at school as are students of different racial groups.
- Female students are more afraid of being attacked going to and from school than male students.
- Black students are more likely to fear being attacked going to and from school than students of other racial groups.
- Hispanic students are more likely than non–Hispanic students to fear violent crime at school or going to or from school.
- Younger students both fear more school crime and avoid more places at school as a result than older students.
- Public school students fear victimization at school and avoid certain areas at school as a result, more than students attending private schools.

SELF-PROTECTION AND SCHOOL SECURITY

The relationship between self-protection, school security, and violent victimization at school was examined in the SCS survey. Two percent of the student respondents took self-protective devices to school during the 6 months prior to the interview including guns, knives, razor blades, and brass knuckles.[8] Male students were more likely than female students to have in-school objects for protection. Central city students were more likely than suburban students to report bringing objects to school that could be used as weapons.

School security measures such as hall monitors seemed to have little effect on violent crime in school. Students reported that violent crime occurred as frequently in schools employing security measures as in schools that did not. Black and Hispanic students were more likely to attend schools with security measures than students of other racial groups and non–Hispanic students. Students from nonmetropolitan areas were the most likely to attend schools with teacher monitors, and students at suburban schools the least likely.

Students attending schools employing hall monitors as security were more likely to fear victimization than students at schools without hall monitors or security patrols.

PART IV

The Violent Victimization of Women

12. Violent Crimes Against Women

Women of the nineties are the victims of an increasing number of acts of violence including domestic violence, sexual violence, campus violence, drug-related violence, and work-related violence. Consequently, more women are at risk than ever before to become a victim of violence despite new laws aimed at curbing the victimization of women and putting offenders behind bars and keeping them there longer. To protect themselves, more and more women have enrolled in self-defense classes and purchased handguns.

This chapter will look at official and victimization statistics on violent crimes against women, while subsequent chapters will examine in greater depth specific crimes in which women are being made victims of violence.

THE PREVALENCE OF FEMALE VIOLENT VICTIMIZATION

The Bureau of Justice Statistics reports that approximately 2.6 million females are the victims of a violent crime in the United States each year, including such crimes as rape, aggravated assault, and robbery.[1] The rate of victimization in 1992 for crimes of violence against females aged 12 and over can be seen in Table 12-1. The highest victimization rate among individual crimes was for assaults at 21.1 per 1,000 females, followed by robberies at 3.9 per 1,000.

TABLE 12-1

Victimization Rates for Females
Age 12 and Over, by Type of Crime, 1992

Type of Crime	RATE PER 1,000 PERSONS AGE 12 OR OLDER
	Female
All personal crimes[a]	**81.8**
Crimes of violence	25.9
Completed	9.6
Attempted	16.2
Rape	0.8
Completed	0.2[b]
Attempted	0.5
Robbery	3.9
Completed	2.7
With injury	1.5
From serious assault	0.7
From minor assault	0.8
Without injury	1.2
Attempted	1.2
With injury	0.3[b]
From serious assault	0.1[b]
From minor assault	0.2[b]
Without injury	0.9
Assault	21.1
Aggravated	6.1
Completed with injury	2.0
Attempted with weapon	4.1
Simple	15.0
Completed with injury	4.7
Attempted without weapon	10.4
Population age 12 and over	107,150,610

[a] Includes crimes of theft.
[b] Estimate is based on about 10 or fewer sample cases.

Source: U.S. Department of Justice, *Criminal Victimization in the United States, 1992: A National Crime Victimization Survey Report* (Washington, D.C.: Government Printing Office, 1994), p. 22.

TABLE 12-2

Violent Crime Victimization Rates for Women, by Age and Race and Age, 1992

AGE	Total Population	Rate per 1,000 persons in each age group Crimes of Violence
16–19	6,641,980	58.7
20–24	9,224,530	53.4
25–34	21,079,350	34.7
35–49	28,065,230	18.8
50–64	17,216,270	8.0
65 and over	18,015,410	3.3
RACE AND AGE		
White		
16–19	5,362,500	51.9
20–24	7,508,090	51.0
25–34	17,414,450	32.6
35–49	23,673,130	20.0
50–64	14,916,270	7.6
65 and over	16,161,410	2.7
Black		
16–19	1,052,120	94.8
20–24	1,314,120	77.7
25–34	2,872,230	48.1
35–49	3,370,440	12.9
50–64	1,821,880	12.1[a]
65 and over	1,541,840	9.6[a]

[a] Estimate is based on 10 or fewer sample cases.

Source: U.S. Department of Justice, *Criminal Victimization in the United States, 1992: A National Crime Victimization Survey Report* (Washington, D.C.: Government Printing Office, 1994), pp. 24, 29.

Table 12-2 breaks down victimization rates for women by age, and race and age in 1992. As we see the highest rate of victimization for crimes of violence was for women aged 16 to 19, followed by those aged 20 to 24. Women in the 16 to 19 age group were more than three times

TABLE 12-3

Murdered Females in U.S., by Age, 1992

Total	4,936
Percent of all murders	21.9
Under 18	679
Over 18	4,193
15 to 19	407
20 to 24	630
25 to 29	706
30 to 34	662
35 to 39	525
40 to 44	388
45 to 49	253
50 to 54	175
55 to 59	93
60 to 64	105
65 to 69	110
70 to 74	103
75 and over	245
Unknown	64

Source: U.S. Federal Bureau of Investigation, *Crime in the United States: Uniform Crime Reports 1992* (Washington, D.C.: Government Printing Office, 1993), p. 16.

as likely to be victims of violence as those aged 35 to 49, while those aged 16 to 24 were seven times more likely to be victimized as those aged 50 and over.

Black women aged 16 to 19 had the highest violent crime rate of victimization for all women when age and race were considered. Among black women only those aged 16 to 24 had a rate of victimization more than six times greater than those aged 35 and over. White women aged 16 to 24 had the highest victimization rate among white women of all ages. Studies show that Hispanic women are disproportionately victimized by violent crimes compared to non–Hispanic women.[2]

MURDERED WOMEN IN AMERICA

In 1992, there were 4,193 females 18 years of age and over murdered in the United States.[3] Table 12-3 breaks down female murder victims by age. More than 90 percent of all female victims were slain by males, 29 percent by husbands or boyfriends. The circumstances for which women were murdered can be seen in Table 12-4. Most felony murders of women came as the result of robberies and rapes. Arguments were responsible for the vast majority of nonfelony type murders.

FORCIBLE RAPE

No crime epitomizes the victimization of women more than the crime of rape. Each year, well over 100,000 rapes are reported in the United States, while many more go unreported. In 1992, 141,000 forcible rapes were reported to the NCVS.[4] In about half the cases, the victim was violated by someone she was acquainted with. Though the percentage is relatively small, some rape victims also lose their lives in the process. There were 127 murders of women in this country attributed to rapists in 1992.[5]

Between 1987 and 1991, an estimated 132,172 women were raped each year, representing one rape victim for every 600 women in this country.[6]

Table 12-5 shows when, where, and what time single-offender rapes occur and the nature of the victim-offender relationship. More than 40 percent of all rapes take place at or near the victim's home, including over half the nonstranger rapes. About two-thirds of all rapes occur at night, while most tend to happen between 6 P.M. and 6 A.M., whether the rapist is a stranger or nonstranger.

In *Female Victims of Violent Crime*, the following percent distribution of known and unknown rapists to the victim was reported:

Percent of Rapist or Attempted Rapist

Rape	Total	Intimate	Other Known	Stranger
Total	100%	14%	28%	54%
Completed	100%	20%	29%	46%
Attempted	100%	10%	27%	58%

TABLE 12-4

Circumstances in Which Females Were Murdered, 1992

Total[a]	4,936
Felony Type Total	927
Rape	127
Robbery	322
Burglary	78
Larceny-theft	4
Motor vehicle theft	13
Arson	55
Prostitution and commercialized vice	21
Other sex offenses	19
Narcotic drug laws	120
Gambling	1
Suspected Felony Type	63
Other Than Felony Type Total	2,643
Romantic triangle	83
Child killed by babysitter	14
Brawl due to influence of alcohol	36
Brawl due to influence of narcotics	31
Argument over money or property	75
Other arguments	1,416
Gangland killings	14
Juvenile gang killings	42
Institutional killings	2
Sniper attack	5

[a] Includes other types of killings not specified.

Source: U.S. Federal Bureau of Investigation, *Crime in the United States: Uniform Crime Reports 1992* (Washington, D.C.: Government Printing Office, 1993), p. 21.

In 42 out of every 100 completed or attempted rapes, the rapist was known to the victim, whereas in 54 of 100 rapes the rapist was a stranger to the victim. Intimates accounted for one-fifth of the completed rapes. In one-third of completed or attempted rapes, the victim was acquainted with her rapist.[7]

TABLE 12-5

Place and Time of Single-Offender Rape Incidents, by Victim-Offender Relationship, 1987–91

| | Percent of Rape Victimizations | | |
| | Victim-Offender Relationship | | |
Place and Time of Rape	Total	Non-stranger	Stranger
Percent of Rape Cases	100%	55%	44%
Place of Occurrence			
Total	100%	100%	100%
At or near own home	43	52	25
At or near friend's home	16	21	25
Commercial establishment or school	6	9	4
Public parking area or garage	5	4	8
Open area or public area	18	5	43
Not ascertained	12	9	12
Whether Incident Took Place in Daylight or Dark			
Total	100%	100%	100%
Incident occurred-			
During daylight	32	31	33
While dark	62	64	59
At dawn or dusk	6	4	8
Time of Day			
Total	100%	100%	100%
6 AM-Noon	16	15	18
Noon-6 PM	16	18	14
6 PM-Midnight	37	38	32
Midnight-6 AM	31	25	34

Source: U.S. Department of Justice, *Violence Against Women: A National Crime Victimization Survey Report* (Washington, D.C.: Government Printing Office, 1994), p. 11.

As shown in Table 12-6, between 1987 and 1991, black women had the highest rape victimization rate, nearly twice that of white women. Other racial minorities such as Native Americans and Asians collectively had a higher rate of rape victimization than white women; however, a greater number of white women are raped each year than the combined total of minority women.

Women aged 20 to 24 had the highest rape rate and were twice as likely to be raped as women aged 25 to 34. When marital status is considered, women separated, divorced, or never married were 9 times more likely to be the victim of rape as those married or widowed.

A disproportionate number of reported rape victims—tend to reflect women from lower income families. This may not accurately reflect the socioeconomic background of rape victims since many middle and upper class rapes may go unreported. See Chapter 13 for more detailed discussion on rape and sexual assault.

ASSAULTIVE CRIMES
AGAINST WOMEN

Approximately 2 million women are the victims of assaults and robberies in the United States each year. Many of these victimizations involve other crimes such as murder and rape. In 1992, the rate of assaults against women was 21.1 victimizations per 1,000 females while the rate of robbery victimizations was 3.9 per 1,000 persons.[8]

Figure 12-1 compares assault victimization of women by the age group of the victim from 1988 to 1990. Most victimizations occurred in the 25 to 34 age group, followed by women 35 to 49 years of age. Young women, aged 16 to 19, were slightly more likely to be victims of an assault than women aged 20 to 24, while the lowest risk groups were women aged 50 and over.

The vast majority of assaultive victimizations of women are simple assaults. As shown in Figure 12-2, simple assaults accounted for 60.2 percent of the assaultive crimes against women in 1990, followed by aggravated assaults at 21.3 percent. Robberies, which include those involving serious or minor assaults, comprised nearly one-fifth of all assault victimizations of women.

TABLE 12-6

Average Annual Rate of Rape, by Selected Characteristics of Female Victims, 1987–1991

Victim Characteristics	Average Annual Rate[a] Rape[a]
Total	1.3
Race	
White	1.1
Black	2.0
Other[b]	1.3
Ethnicity	
Hispanic	1.1
Non-Hispanic	1.2
Age	
12–19	1.8
20–24	3.1
25–34	1.5
35–49	0.7
50–64	0.2
65 or older	0.1[c]
Family Income	
Less than $9,999	2.4
$10,000–19,999	1.4
$20,000–29,999	1.0
$30,000–49,999	1.0
$50,000 or more	0.5
Marital Status	
Never married	2.9
Married	0.3
Widowed	0.3
Divorced/separated	2.8

[a] Rate is per 1,000 females age 12 or over.
[b] Includes American Indians, Asians, Aleuts, and Eskimos.
[c] Estimate is based on 10 or fewer sample cases.

Source: U.S. Dept. of Justice, *Violence Against Women: A National Crime Victimization Survey Report* (Wash. D.C.: Government Printing Office, 1994), p. 3.

FIGURE 12-1

Comparison of Assaults on Women, by Age of Victim, 1988–1990

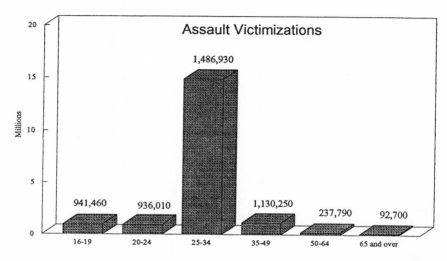

Source: U.S. Department of Justice, *Crime Victimization in the United States: 1973–90 Trends* (Washington, D.C.: Government Printing Office, 1992), pp. 57–62.

VIOLENCE BY INTIMATES

Much of the violence against women is inflicted by intimates, such as a spouse or boyfriend. In 1991, 54 percent of the violent victimization of females was committed by nonstrangers.[9] A study of violence against women from 1987 to 1991 found that women were victimized by intimates at a rate nearly eleven times that of men.[10] Women were 14 times as likely to be the victims of violence perpetrated by a spouse, ex-spouse, or boyfriend. Intimates were responsible for 2.9 million violent victimizations of women during the five-year span, averaging 572,032 victimizations per year (see Table 12-7). Most single-offender violent victimizations by intimates were perpetrated by boyfriends and spouses, followed by ex-spouses. White and black women had similar rates of victimization by intimates or relatives, while women with incomes of under $10,000 were five times more likely to experience

FIGURE 12-2

Distribution of Assaultive Crimes Against Women, 1990

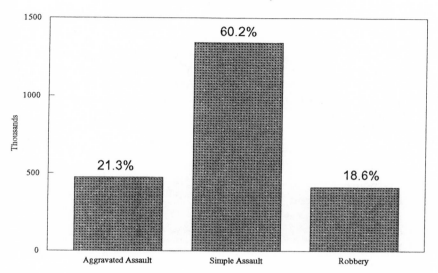

Source: U.S. Department of Justice, *Crime Victimization in the United States: 1973–90 Trends* (Washington, D.C.: Government Printing Office, 1992), pp. 26, 41.

violence by intimates than women with family incomes of over $30,000.

The highest annual rate for female victimization by intimates was for simple and aggravated assaults. Women were twice as likely to be injured if the offender was an intimate rather than a stranger.

Nonintimates but persons known to the victims were the offenders in more than one-third of all violent crimes against women.

VIOLENCE BY STRANGERS

Strangers are responsible for nearly half of all violent crime victimizations of women. Between 1987 and 1991, 2.8 million victimizations involved strangers, an average of 571,114 million victimizations annually.[11] One-third of the victimizations in which a weapon was used involved strangers, who were more likely than other offenders to be armed with guns.

TABLE 12-7

Violence Against Women,
by Single-Offender Intimates, 1987–1991

Victim-Offender Relationship	Percent of Single-Offender Violent Victimizations
	Average Annual Number of Victimizations
Intimate/Relative	572,032
Total	33.0%
Spouse	9.6%
Ex-spouse	4.0%
Boyfriend/girlfriend	14.0%
Parent	0.8%
Child	1.3%
Brother/sister	1.6%
Other relative	2.0%
Acquaintances	35.0%
Unknown Relationship	1.0%
Total[a]	100.0%

[a] Includes stranger victimization.

Source: U.S. Department of Justice, *Violence Against Women: A National Crime Victimization Survey Report* (Washington, D.C.: Government Printing Office, 1994), p. 6.

Figure 12-3 displays percentages of violent crimes against women committed by strangers by type of crime in 1991. Strangers accounted for 46.1 percent of the violent crimes against women. In nearly 3 out of every 4 robberies and 7 out of 10 robberies involving injuries to the victim, the victimization was attributed to a stranger. Half the rapes in 1991 were stranger perpetrated.

FIGURE 12-3

Percent of Violent Victimizations of Women Involving Strangers, 1991

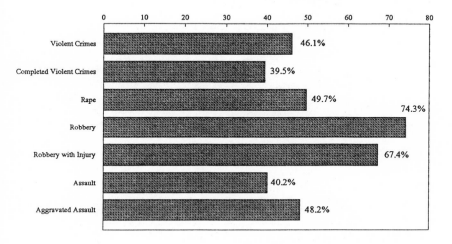

Source: U.S. Department of Justice, *Crime Victimization in the United States: 1973–90 Trends* (Washington, D.C.: Government Printing Office, 1992), p. 56.

SELF-PROTECTION OF FEMALE VIOLENT CRIME VICTIMS

The majority of female victims of violent crimes take some self-protective measures during their victimization (Figure 12-4). In more than 7 out of 10 violent victimizations in 1991, the victim took protective measures. The percentage of self-defense was highest for rape victimization at nearly 84 percent, followed by aggravated assaults, where 77 percent of the victims employed self-protection methods.

Of the women who used self-protection measures during a violent victimization, one-fifth involved resistance of the victimization or capturing the offender. Nearly another one-fifth either ran away or hid from their attacker. Just over one percent of the victims used or threatened to use a weapon to protect themselves from victimization.[12]

FIGURE 12-4

Percent of Female Violent Victimizations in Which Victims Employed Self-Protective Measures, by Type of Crime, 1991

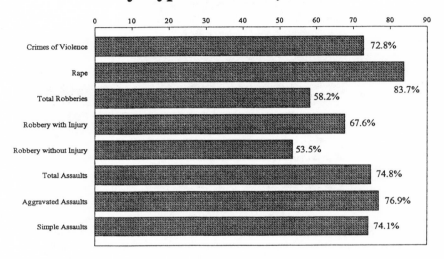

Source: U.S. Department of Justice, *Crime Victimization in the United States: 1973–90 Trends* (Washington, D.C.: Government Printing Office, 1992), p. 84.

REPORTING VIOLENT CRIMES TO THE POLICE

More than half the female victims of violent crimes report the victimization to the police. The NCVS found that 55 percent of the violent victimizations of women were reported to the police in 1991. The percentage distribution of reported violent crimes involving strangers and nonstrangers is shown in Table 12-8. Women reported an equal percentage of stranger and nonstranger violent victimization to the police in 1991. The highest percentage of reported stranger victimization was for robbery with injury and serious assault at 86.3 percent and 100 percent respectively. However, the latter percentage was based on only 10 or less sample cases. Reporting victimization involving non-

TABLE 12-8

Percent of Violent Victimizations of Women Reported to the Police, by Type of Crime, and Victim-Offender Relationship, 1991

Type of Crime	Percent of Victimizations Reported to the Police		
	All Victimizations	Involving Strangers	Involving Nonstrangers
Crimes of violence	**55.1%**	**55.1%**	**55.2%**
Completed	63.2	65.5	61.7
Attempted	49.6	49.5	49.7
Rape	60.2	60.4	60.0
Robbery	61.2	62.5	57.3
Completed	70.4	73.0	62.3
With injury	78.3	86.3	66.0[a]
From serious assault	93.0[a]	100.0[a]	83.9[a]
From minor assault	72.7	81.5	58.1[a]
Without injury	66.6	68.4	58.5[a]
Attempted	38.3	35.2	46.1[a]
With injury	31.0[a]	32.0[a]	26.6[a]
From serious assault	67.2[a]	61.3[a]	100.0[a]
From minor assault	13.8[a]	17.2[a]	0.0[a]
Without injury	42.6	37.6	52.5[a]
Assault	53.5	51.9	54.7
Aggravated	65.0	62.3	67.5
Completed with injury	64.4	59.5	66.2
Attempted with weapon	65.3	63.0	68.7
Simple	49.8	47.4	51.1
Completed with injury	60.0	57.0	60.8
Attempted without weapon	44.4	44.8	44.0

[a] Estimate is based on about 10 or fewer cases.

Source: U.S. Department of Justice, *Criminal Victimization in the United States, 1991: A National Crime Victimization Survey Report* (Washington, D.C.: Government Printing Office, 1992), p. 103.

strangers had the highest percentage for attempted robbery with injury from serious assault and completed robbery with injury from serious assault at 100 percent and 83.9 percent respectively. Each figure was based on 10 or fewer sample cases. Six in 10 rapes, over half the assaults, and 65 percent of the aggravated assaults involving strangers or nonstrangers were reported to the police.

The reasons most often given for reporting violent victimization to the police were to prevent further victimization, to stop or prevent the incident, and because it was a criminal offense.[13]

Not reporting violent crime victimization to the police was most often due to an object recovered or the offender unsuccessful in the victimization, a private or personal matter, or it was reported to another source.[14]

WOMEN'S FEAR OF VIOLENT CRIME

Recent studies suggest that many women are fearful of becoming a victim of crimes of violence and are more likely to feel the need to take self-protective measures to ensure their own safety. In a study of perceived danger from gun violence in their neighborhoods or place of work, nearly 4 in 10 women felt threatened.[15] When asked in a Gallup Poll if there was more crime in their neighborhood than a year ago, 6 in 10 women felt that there was more crime.[16] The same poll asked women if they were afraid to walk alone at night in their own neighborhood. Fifty-nine percent of the respondents said yes.[17]

These attitudes and perceptions on the part of women emphasize the problem of violent crime in our society and the vulnerability women are experiencing. In a national survey, one-fifth of the females felt it was necessary to take the law into their own hands for their personal safety from crime.[18] This fear of crime has led to an increased use by women of handguns for personal protection. In a 1993 survey regarding the presence of firearms in the home, 43 percent of the women respondents reported having a gun in their home.[19] Forty-five percent of the women polled did not believe there should be a law banning handguns.[20]

13. Rape and Sexual Assault of Women

A forcible rape occurs every six minutes in the United States. It is estimated that as many as 150,000 rapes were committed in this country in 1993.[1] The vast majority of the victims were women. As they were in the 1980s, sexual assaults continue to be a major problem in the 1990s. High profile rape cases and charges of sexual harassment have helped bring about an increased awareness of the broad nature of rape and range of rapists in this final decade of the twentieth century. No longer is rape viewed as largely a stranger perpetrated act of violence. Instead, we are now paying greater attention to nonstranger rape assaults such as marital rape, acquaintance rape, and date rape. This has resulted in improved laws against rape and more harsh punitive actions against rapists, yet the battle is far from being won by victims and potential victims.

THE HISTORICAL RAPE OF WOMEN

The rape victimization of women has a history as old as human existence. Forcible rape was once the means by which a man could "seize or steal" a woman to be his wife. She represented little more than a trophy—with no legal, social, or human rights.

Over time, the tolerance of rape declined and, in many instances, the culpability shifted to the victim. Herodotus, often referred to as "the father of history," documented this way of thinking in 500 B.C. when he observed:

> Abducting young women is not, indeed, a lawful act; but it is stupid
> after the event to make a fuss about it. The only sensible thing is to
> take no notice; for it is obvious that no young woman allows herself
> to be abducted if she does not want to be.[2]

In other words, Herodotus was placing the blame for the rape squarely
on the victim. Sadly, many people today continue to blame the victim
for somehow or some way being responsible for her rape.

Many feel that the institution of marriage and family is historically
a reflection of the violation of women. In a historical review of rape,
Susan Brownmiller, author of *Against Our Will: Men, Women and
Rape*, described rapists as "shock troops" whose existence more or less
forced women into marriage as a means of protecting themselves from
rapists.[3] Brownmiller further contended that the predatory nature of
men and their desire for property are the fundamental causes of rape
and sexual inequality.

WHAT CONSTITUTES RAPE?

The word *"rape"* is derived from the Latin word *"rapere,"* which means
"to steal, seize, or carry away." In today's times, rape is often classified
in state statutes as "criminal sexual assault" and "sexual battery," and
includes such sexual offenses as sodomy, oral, and anal copulation involving female and male victims. For purposes of discussion in this
chapter, we shall adopt a definition of rape consistent with that in many
state statutes, victimization and official measurements of rape: carnal
knowledge of a female through the use of force or the threat thereof,
and this includes attempted rape.

THE EXTENT OF RAPE

By most accounts, the number of rapes being perpetrated throughout
this country annually is staggering. Estimates of rape vary from source
to source. The *Uniform Crime Reports* (UCR) estimates that 109,062
forcible rapes were reported to law enforcement agencies in the United
States in 1992, an increase of 2.3 percent over 1991.[4] The *National
Crime Victimization Survey's* (NCVS) estimate of reported rapes in
1992 was 141,000 rapes.[5] The NCVS rate of 70 female rape victims per
100,000 females was 61 percent higher than the UCR rate of 42.8 rape
victimizations per 100,000 persons. The NCVS estimated that 132,172
women were raped each year between 1987 and 1991.[6]

A San Francisco survey on the incidence of rape suggests the annual total may be much higher. Based on interviews with females 18 years of age or older, the survey found a rape rate of 3,548 per 100,000 women.[7] Extrapolating the incidence rate over the entire country, the indication is that more than 1.5 million rapes and attempted rapes occurred the year of the survey.

Even the above estimates may be underestimating the scope of rape in the United States. It is widely believed that the vast majority of rapes are never reported to the police or victimization interviewers. Rape experts estimate that anywhere from 40 to 90 percent of rape victimizations go unreported.[8] The reasons for this include fear of reprisal, a private concern, lack of proof, embarrassment, shame, and the belief that the police or courts will be ineffective and/or insensitive. Thus the problem of rape is compounded for the silent victim and mitigated for the rapist offender.

THE CHARACTERISTICS
OF RAPE VICTIMIZATION

The circumstances surrounding rape victimization can vary considerably from incident to incident. Studies show that general characteristics of a rape assault can be seen as follows:

- Two-thirds of all rapes occur at night.
- Four in 10 rapes occur in the victim's home.
- In 7 of 10 rapes, the victim and offender are acquainted.
- Rape is largely an intraracial crime.
- Most rapes occur without the use of a weapon by the perpetrator.
- Injuries occur to rape victims in more than half the assaults.
- Women aged 16 to 24 are three times as likely to be raped as other women.
- The vast majority of rape victims are white.
- Black women have the highest rate of rape victimization.
- Hispanic and non–Hispanic women are equally likely to be rape victims.
- Women who live in the city are at greater risk as rape victims than those who live in suburbs or rural areas.
- Women who live alone are more likely to be rape victims than women who live with someone.

- Women who live in dormitories, boarding houses, and apartment complexes are more likely to be raped than other women.
- Unemployed women and students face a greater risk of rape than women in general.
- Half of all rape victims are on the lowest end of the economic scale.[9]

An important characteristic of rape victimization worth noting is that despite its seriousness, rape and attempted rape actually account for about 3 percent of the violent crime in the United States. Nevertheless, hundreds of thousands of women are at risk daily to be the victim of a sexual assault.

DISPELLING THE MYTHS ABOUT RAPE

Over the years, any number of myths and misconceptions have helped shape attitudes and beliefs about rape, the rape victim, and offender. Many of these myths continue not only to influence opinions, but legislation and the criminal justice system response to rape and other sexual assaults.

Myth: Women Cry Rape Falsely

Police often cite unfounded rapes as proof that women falsify rape allegations as a means to exact revenge or punishment on boyfriends and lovers or to protect themselves from gossip or censure. The truth is that false claims of rape are relatively rare, accounting for only about 2 percent of the charges of rape.[10]

Even when charges of rape are dismissed by the police or district attorney, it is rarely due to conclusive proof that the complainant was untruthful but rather is usually because of a lack of evidence. This underscores the difficulty rape victims face in being believed, much less having the allegations result in a conviction.

Myth: Rape Is a Victim-Precipitated Crime

This theory assumes that victims of rape "got what they deserved" or were "asking for it" by their mode of dress or behavior. There have been studies that have described rape as victim-precipitated or provoked merely because the victim responded politely to a rapist's verbal overtones. A recent study by the National Commission on the Causes and Prevention of Violence reported that only 4 percent of the rapes that were investigated involved a woman's precipitative behavior.[11] In *Patterns in Forcible Rape*, Menachem Amir found that the victim's behavior is not as significant in the assault as the "offender's interpretation of her actions."[12]

Myth: All Women Secretly Desire to Be Raped

The seduction theme is not uncommon in women's sexual fantasies, according to psychologists. However, such fantasies are controlled completely by the woman including time, place, and partner. Fantasies to be seduced or made love to by a known or unknown man tend to be representative of the woman's desire to feel guiltless in sexual encounters—not a wish to be raped.

Myth: Only Young and Attractive Women Are Raped

Rape can and does happen to women of all ages, shapes, sizes, and physical appearances. There is no truth to the contention that younger, more attractive women are at higher risk than other women. On the contrary, reported cases of rape have included infant victims and women in their nineties. Vulnerability by the victim and opportunity for the rapist are primary factors in rape. Often the rapist does not even remember or care what the victim looked like.

Myth: Rape Is Motivated by the Desire for Sexual Gratification

Most studies indicate that rape is motivated predominantly by aggression, dominance, and hatred rather than pleasure. Many convicted rapists were married when the rape occurred; others who were unmarried indicate they had access to ready and willing sexual partners. Wives of rapists often describe sex with their husband as good or satisfactory.

Myth: Rape Cannot Occur If the Woman Resists

One of the more irresponsible and potentially dangerous myths is that if a woman resists or does not want sexual relations to take place, then a rape is not possible. Many professionals such as doctors and lawyers still retain this misconception. The fallacy of such a belief is that it assumes that rape and consensual sex are one and the same. They are not. Rape is the forced sexual aggression of the offender, regardless of the victim's wishes; normal sexual relations are by mutual consent. Nonresistance to rape does not reflect compliance by consent but rather fear, intimidation, the shock of the attack, being overpowered, and a desire to survive the rape. To date, no foolproof method has been developed for resisting a potential rapist that would prevent the rape, injury, or even death for the victim.

Myth: Most Rapists Are Strangers

The raw statistics fail to support this notion. For example, in 1991, 51 percent of the rapists were reported to be nonstrangers.[13] When factors such as hidden rape are considered (including acquaintance and marital rape), the evidence suggests that rape victims are even more likely to know their offenders than the data indicate. The NCVS study of completed rapes between 1979 and 1987 found that in only 3 of 10 cases, or 30 percent, was the rapist reported to be a stranger.[14] More than half of the rapists were intimates (i.e., spouse, boyfriend).

Myth: It Can't Happen to Me

Rape can happen to any woman at any time. Currently there is a 1 in 10 chance that a female will be sexually assaulted during her lifetime.

THE DIVERSITY OF RAPE

As indicated at the opening of this chapter, with the nineties has come greater recognition of the range of rape assaults occurring across this country. While much of our attention in the past has been on stranger rape — victimization that seemed to better fit our concept of immorality and sexual deviancy—today we are expanding our scope of the many ways in which women are being subjected to the forced sexual assault of men. These include variations on rape victimization such as date rape, marital rape, and gang rape. What we now know is that sexual assaults of women have been vastly underestimated and rapist types cannot be narrowly defined.

Stranger Rape

Rape perpetrated by a stranger continues to be the standard by which we measure rape and rapists. Tradition tells us that the majority of rapes are committed by men the victims are not familiar with. Many statistics continue to support this. The National Crime Survey reports that 54 of 100 attempted or completed rapes are committed by strangers.[15] In rapes reported to the police over a recent 15-year period, 57 percent involved strangers. In 1991, of the females who reported rape to the police, 60.4 percent of the rapists were identified as strangers.[16] The typical characteristics of stranger rape are as follows:

- More attempted stranger rapes occur than completed stranger rapes.
- While the rapist may be a stranger, the victim is often known by the offender.
- Unlocked doors and windows help make stranger rape a distinct possibility and easier for the offender.
- Stranger rapists are more likely to use a weapon in the assault than nonstrangers.
- Victims are less likely to offer resistance to a stranger rapist than an acquaintance rapist.
- Stranger rapes are reported to the police more often than non-stranger rapes.

Acquaintance Rape

Acquaintance rape assaults involving nonromantic social acquaintances, relatives, friends, co-workers, and/or neighbors account for nearly one-third of all reported rapes. According to law enforcement agencies and rape counselors, as many as 60 percent of all rapes involve acquaintances of the victims.[17] The secrecy of acquaintance perpetrated rape indicates that unreported assaults may make this the most frequent form of rape.

Acquaintance rape has become a key target of anti-rape activists in the nineties as the reality of nonstranger rape is brought to light, and with good reason. In 1990 alone, there were 76,030 reported rapes involving nonstrangers. This amounted to more than half the total number of reported rapes. Important trends concerning acquaintance rape include:

- In 4 of 10 rape attempts, the victim knows the offender other than intimately.
- In more than half the acquaintance rapes, the perpetrator is well known to the victim.
- Casual acquaintances account for about 40 percent of the acquaintance rapes.
- Nearly all acquaintance rapes tend to be with one offender.
- More than half of the multiple offender acquaintance rapes are perpetrated by casual acquaintances.
- Most nonstranger rapes occur in the evening and at night.
- Victims are less likely to take self-protective measures against an acquaintance than a stranger.

Date Rape

One myth that has become outdated in recent years is the notion that it cannot be rape if the woman was dating the alleged rapist or was otherwise romantically involved with him. We now recognize the epidemic of date rape in this country, although there is still much resistance to the notion, in many cases from the victims themselves. Self-blame and stereotypes of rapists have contributed to keeping this form of rape underreported and understudied.

The difficulty in recognizing date rape for what it is—a sexual assault—can be illustrated in a recent study at the University of California in which more than half the female students felt that under some circumstances it was permissible for a man to use physical aggression to obtain sexual favors from his date.[18] Another study conducted by *MS.* magazine found that nearly three-quarters of the victims of rape, as legally defined, did not identify the assault as such.[19]

As more attention and education are focused on date rape, more and more victims are coming forward and breaking the silence. In the process, the following facts have emerged about date rape:

- Most victims are single women between the ages of 15 and 25.
- One in 8 women are the victims of date rape.
- Two in 10 female college students are the victims of rape or attempted rape.
- Half of the female victims of rape are victimized by first dates, casual dates, or romantic acquaintances.

Marital Rape

Marital rape, also known as spousal and conjugal rape, is being addressed now more than ever as women are made more aware that rape is an act of violence and a crime, even when perpetrated by a spouse. Changing criminal statutes and court decisions have supported the woman's right against marital rape. This is in direct contradiction to tradition and sexist views which embrace the man's right to "seize a woman" as his wife and "rape her" at his discretion. To many, intercourse continues to be presumed implicit in marriage and, therefore, not subject to rape laws.

As the strong association between battered women and forced sexual relations has been established, support for the notion and prevention of marital rape has grown. The FBI estimates that 25 million women in the United States are sexually assaulted by their spouses annually.[20] Other experts suggest the numbers may be much higher since victims of marital rape are less likely to report their assault than other victims of nonstranger rapes.

Currently more than half the states consider marital rape to be a crime. By the turn of the century, the entire country should have criminal statutes in effect against marital rape.

The followings facts are now known regarding marriage and rape victimization:

- Intimates are responsible for half of all completed rapes.
- Battered women are likely to be victims of marital rape.
- Spousal sexual assaults are more common than stranger sexual assaults.
- Battered women are more likely to be raped by their spouse than unbattered women.
- A marriage license is not a license to rape.

THE MEN WHO RAPE WOMEN

Who are these men that sexually assault women? What do they look like? What motivates them to rape? Realistically, what can be done to prevent this crime of violence? Of course, there are no simple answers to these questions. Characterizing rapists may be the first important step. Even this can only be generalized, since no two rapists are identical in appearance, style, targets, circumstances, or motivation.

The typical rapist can be characterized as follows:

- Age 21 to 29.
- Likely to occupy the lower end of the economic scale.
- The same race or ethnicity as his victim.
- Alcohol or drugs are a factor in half his rapes.
- Nonstranger to the victim.
- Single rather than multiple offender.
- Predominantly white.
- Blacks have the highest rate of rape among racial groups.
- Most rapists are unarmed.
- Lives in the same neighborhood as the victim.
- Assaults the victim in or near her own home.
- Most multiple offenders are young, under the influence of drugs or alcohol, and peer pressure.[21]

More than 50 types of rapists have been identified by criminologists and sex researchers. In almost all typologies, the act of rape is seen not as an "aggressive expression of sexuality but rather as a sexual expression of aggression."[22] The following categories of rapists have emerged:

- *The Sociopath Rapist.* The most common type of rapist. He is impulsive; motivated primarily by sex. The rape itself is a manifestation of deviant behavior.
- *The Situational Stress Rapist.* He is rarely violent or dangerous. The rape is often due to situational stress (i.e., unemployment). He usually has no history of sexual deviations or violent behavior.
- *The Masculinity Conflict Rapist.* A broad spectrum of rapists whose commonness is a real or perceived deficiency in their masculinity. The rape is often planned, dangerous, and violent.
- *The Substance Abuse Rapist.* He is usually under the influence of

drugs or alcohol, or both. This plays a primary role in the rape, though often in combination with other factors.

- *The Double-Standard Rapist.* He divides women into good ones to be treated with respect, and bad ones who do not deserve respect and consideration.
- *The Acquaintance Rapist.* He knows and possibly dates his victim, gaining her trust. He usually plans the rape, enjoys overpowering his prey, and has extreme self-confidence.
- *The Sadistic Rapist.* A small percentage of rapists, but amongst the most frightening. He usually plans the rape, has a history of perversion and hostility toward women, and derives pleasure in ritualistic degradation of women.
- *The Unpredictable Rapist.* Often psychotic, he gives no indication based upon his past of his potential to rape.[23]

Within these typologies, the rapist's own interpretations of the assault may differ considerably depending on the individual. In almost all cases, the rapist who admits to sexual contact with a victim either defines his actions as rape or goes into a classic denial that a rape occurred, such as the date rapist.

A number of theories have been established to explain why men rape. *Interactionist theories* hypothesize that "social interaction is mediated by signs and symbols, by eye contact, gestures and words."[24] This school of thought assumes that rapists respond to their interpretations of the woman's actions and inactions. One such interactionist theory is the victim-precipitation theory which posits that the rape victim is culpable to some degree due to the real or perceived communication between her and the rapist for consensual sexual relations.

Psychoanalytic theories regard rapists as emotionally disturbed and often with an intense hatred of women developed during childhood, triggering latent homosexual tendencies.[25] The rape is seen as a reflection of this hatred and an overpowering need of the rapist to assure himself of his own masculinity.

Opportunity structure theory contends that rapists view women as possessors of saleable sexual properties. "When bargaining for sex, men reportedly use various forms of coercion. They may make promises they cannot or will not really fulfill. They may harass women or threaten them with physical harm."[26] This theory explains rape as a consequence of some men lacking the necessary social and economic means to attract women they desire, meaning they must resort to sexual violence to achieve their desires.

A biological predisposition to rape has been advanced by feminist writers, such as the following excerpt from *Against Our Will*:

> In terms of human anatomy, the possibility of forcible intercourse incontrovertibly exists. This single factor may have been sufficient to have caused the creation of a male ideology of rape. When men discovered that they could rape, they proceeded to do it.[27]

In general, such theories tend to be flawed, primarily because they cannot account for all rapists and rapes or be validated scientifically. In many instances, the rapist fails to fall into any category or typology other than their willingness to rape and violate.

THE EFFECTS OF RAPE ON THE VICTIM

The tragedy of rape victimization goes well beyond the act of forcible rape. For victims, there is often a sense of hopelessness, helplessness, frustration, guilt, and uncertainty about the future. Recovery can sometimes be as painful and difficult as the assault. Legal and medical costs to rape victims are on the rise and may take years to complete. Loss of work time or employment, change in residence, and school withdrawal are often inevitable consequences of being raped. Suicide is another consequence, where the rate of attempts to end a victim's life is 8 times greater than that of nonrape victims.

Further responses to rape that seem to manifest themselves among most rape victims are:

- Disruption of normal adaptive patterns.
- Appetite and sleep disturbance.
- Lowered attention span.
- Regression to a more dependent state.
- Diminished functioning level.
- Increased emotional susceptibility.

The long-term effects of rape may well depend on the level of assistance the victim receives. Personal and professional help is essential if the recovery is to be successful and the time of recovery mitigated. For most victims, the violation of self can never be completely overcome even in a high tech society that seems to have all the answers for dealing with any problem.

THE CRIMINAL JUSTICE SYSTEM RESPONSE

Criminal justice for rape victims is more promising now than in past years. Officials within the system have become more sensitive to the criticism of neglecting rape victims in favor of their assailants. This has resulted in improved forensic techniques, specialized training for trial attorneys and staffers, better victim services, and greater involvement of female criminal justice professionals in the investigative and prosecution stages of charges of forcible rape.

Despite these advances, the reality is that it continues to be difficult to obtain justice for rape victims. Only a fraction of rapists are ever arrested and, of those, relative few are tried and convicted. Nonstranger rapists are even more likely to walk away from the system. Evidentiary requirements, varying departmental policies, discretionary practices, victim cooperation and credibility, and inconsistent rape statutes and cooperation between various branches of the criminal justice and social services systems all play major roles in limiting the effectiveness of justice for victims of rape.

RAPE CRISIS CENTERS

Since the first rape crisis centers opened in the United States in the early 1970s, their philosophy has remained essentially the same: to offer support and comfort to rape victims that otherwise might be unavailable to them. The centers are staffed by trained volunteers, many of whom were victims of sexual assaults.

Many rape crisis centers are facing funding problems and staff shortages. Their role in assisting rape victims through counseling, referrals, education, hotlines, and sympathy is invaluable and should assure the survival of rape crisis centers for years to come.

14. Battered Women

Perhaps the classic symbolization of the victimization of women is the battered woman. Not only have women been the victims of abusive husbands or boyfriends throughout history, but this form of victimization and domestic violence continues to be amongst the most hidden and painfully prevalent issues of our time. A recent study of domestic violence found women to be victims of intimates at a rate three times as often as men.[1] In this chapter, we will examine the problem of battered women and its implications for women and our society.

A DARK HISTORY OF WIFE ABUSE

Wife battering has been in existence since ancient times, often thought of as an acceptable and even expected practice. Historical literature is replete with examples of the cruelties inflicted upon women by their spouses. One article recounts the "scalding death of Fausta ordered by her husband, the Emperor Constantine, which was to serve as a precedent for the next fourteen centuries."[2]

Friedrich Engels postulated that wife abuse began "with the emergence of the first monogamous pairing relationship which replaced group marriage and the extended family of early promiscuous societies."[3] Another theory advanced that the historical condoning of violence against women is rooted in the "subjugation and oppression of women through the male partner exercising his authority as head of the family."[4]

In western society, wife battering has flourished since the Middle Ages. The rampant violence towards wives in Europe came to America

156

with the colonists. "During one period, a husband was permitted by law to beat his wife so long as his weaponry was not bigger than his thumb."[5] Such laws remained on the books until the end of the nineteenth century.

DEFINING THE BATTERED WOMAN TODAY

For many, a battered woman continues to reflect physical abuse of some nature. One study defined battered women as

> adult women who were intentionally physically abused in ways that caused pain or injury, or who were forced into involuntary action or restrained by force from voluntary action by adult men with whom they have or had established relationships, usually involving sexual intimacy.[6]

With advances in understanding relationships and the effects of behavior, the definition of the battered woman has broadened in recent years. The term now reflects not only physical abuse of women such as beatings with fists or other objects, choking, whipping, but also psychological or emotional abuse, including threats, insults, intimidation and degradation. The perpetrators of battering include not only husbands, ex-husbands, or lovers, but children and grandchildren as well.[7]

Referring to battered women has also taken on many now common phrases such as "the battered wife or woman syndrome," "wife abuse," "woman battering," and "conjugal violence." Most important is the recognition that women can be victimized by their mates in many ways, each of which can be devastating to the woman's physical and emotional well being.

HOW WIDESPREAD IS THE PROBLEM?

While most experts agree that the battering of women has reached epidemic proportions, researchers have found that women actually reporting this occurrence is far less frequent. A recent study estimated that only 1 out of every 270 incidents of wife abuse is ever reported to law enforcement.[8] In a study of women victims of battering, Denver psychologist Lenore Walker, who has done extensive research on the subject and authored several books on family violence, indicated that less than 10 percent ever reported serious violence to the police. The severe underreporting of domestically violated women can generally be attributed to the following reasons:

- Victim denial.
- Protection of the batterer.
- Disavowal techniques to keep it in the family.
- Silent desire to be abused.
- Fear of alternatives (i.e., continued abuse, loss of support).
- Shame.

Despite the cloak of silence that greatly hampers efforts at discovering and assisting battered women, researchers have found the problem to be staggering. Over a five-year period (1987–1991), the *National Crime Victimization Survey* found that 2.9 million women were the victims of violence by intimates, for an average of 572,032 victimizations per year.[9] Diana Russell, a professor of sociology and author of *Rape in Marriage*, recently completed a survey of sexual assault of San Francisco women. Twenty-one percent of the respondents who had ever been married reported being physically abused by a husband at some stage in their lives.[10] According to a National Family Violence Survey conducted by sociologists Murray Straus and Richard Gelles, in 1985 1.7 million women were seriously physically abused by husbands or partners.[11]

Estimates of battered women have soared as high as 1 woman out of every 2. Social scientists contend that every year as many as 2 million women in the United States are beaten by their spouses.[12] According to FBI statistics, woman battering is one of the most frequently occurring crimes in the nation, with a beating taking place every 18 seconds.[13] In 1992, 29 percent of the women murdered in the United States were killed by husbands or boyfriends.[14]

WHO IS THE BATTERED WOMAN?

The popular myth is that battered women are of the lower class, undereducated, and minority segments of our population. However, these groups are overrepresented in the statistics because of their greater dependency (and therefore visibility) on society's institutions for their basic survival needs.

Recent studies indicate that as many as 80 percent of the cases of battering have gone undiagnosed because of the more privileged environment in which they occur.[15] Women of every age, race, ethnicity, and social class are being battered by their husbands and lovers. What these women have in common is a low self-esteem that is usually related to repeated victimization. For some victims, this characteristic is limited only to their relationship with men; for others, low self-esteem pervades their entire existence.

Battered women typically view themselves and all women as inferior to men, have a tendency to cope with anger through denial or turning it inward, and suffer from depression, psychosomatic illnesses, and feelings of guilt. According to Terry Davidson, author of *Conjugal Crime: Understanding and Changing the Wife Beating Pattern*, victims of spousal abuse "may exemplify society's old image of ideal womanhood—submissive, religious, nonassertive, accepting of whatever the husband's life brings.... The husband comes first for these women, who perceive themselves as having little control over many areas of their own lives."[16]

WHO ARE THE BATTERERS OF WOMEN?

Just as the victim of battering can be any woman, the perpetrator can also be any man. Certain patterns have emerged in the character of an abusive mate. The male batterer is typically seen as possessing a dual personality. He can be either especially charming or extremely cruel. Selfishness and generosity are easily interchangeable parts of his personality, depending upon his mood. Jealousy and possessiveness are considered integral proponents in his violent disposition. The batterer's greatest fear is that the woman will leave him.

Based on a study conducted over a four-year period at New York's Abused Women's Aid in Crisis, Maria Roy, the founder and director of the organization which offers help to battered women, characterized the typical abusive male as:

- Between 26 and 35 years of age; followed by the 36 to 50 age group.
- Having a history of childhood abuse or an abusive family.
- Ninety percent do not have a criminal record, indicating that most offenders are not deviant outside the family.

Roy further found that:

- Most abuse occurs during the first 15 years of the relationship.
- Most battering begins almost immediately after the partnership develops.
- Most abuse is physical, without the use of weapons.
- Major changes in the family life (such as loss of income and death) increase the propensity or level of violence in relationships of long duration.[17]

SYMPTOMS OF BATTERING

Why do men physically abuse their spouses and lovers? What are the signs that abuse may be taking place? Research has shown that for many abusers sexual issues in the relationship are often symptomatic of the abuse.

Marital Rape

Rape is still often thought of in terms of strangers or casual acquaintances rather than committed by lovers or husbands. Indeed, up until the mid–1970s, in most states it was not a crime for a man to rape his wife. In 1975, South Dakota became the first state to make spousal rape a crime.

Just how many men rape their wives is impossible to establish since, for many victims, this continues to be a private matter which goes unreported and unprosecuted. There is some indication that the numbers may be high. Of completed rapes reported to the *National Crime Survey* for the years 1979 to 1987, 52 percent of the rapists were intimates.[18] Studies show that 1 in 10 wives has been sexually assaulted at least once by her spouse.[19]

There is a strong correlation between marital rape and battering. Lenore Walker found that 59 percent of her sample of battered women were forced to have sex with their spouses, compared to 7 percent of the nonbattered women.[20] Eighty-five percent of the battered women reported that the sex was unpleasant for the following reasons: (1) it was initiated to prevent abuse, (2) took place immediately after battering to calm the batterer, (3) occurred after the abusive spouse abused a child for fear he would continue, and (4) refusing sex meant the battered woman would not be given money for groceries or bills.

Other researchers support the relationship between battering and conjugal rape. K. Yllo held that forced sex was a form of violent power and control rather than a means for sexual gratification.[21] David Finkelhor, co-author of a book on marital rape, noted of rape by husbands: "These are brutal acts that are most often committed out of anger or power, with the idea to humiliate, demean or degrade the wife."[22]

In using a conservative definition of marital rape that included forced intercourse with penetration, Russell found that marital rape occurred more than twice as often as stranger perpetrated rape. This suggested that battered women stood a risk of being sexually assaulted at a rate 3 to 5 times that of nonbattered women.[23]

Currently at least 11 states have made marital rape a crime, with a number of states headed in the same direction.

Sexual Jealousy

Many battered women report that sexual problems such as frigidity, impotency, denial, and excessive demands lead to arguments and confrontations which erupt into physical violence.[24] In such cases, the abuser usually doubts his own virility and questions his wife's faithfulness, even at times questioning the paternity of his children. As a result, often the batterer forbids or severely curtails his wife's activities outside the home. Because of the brutality, many women feel alienated from their husbands and find sexual intimacy difficult—both of which only perpetuate the abuse.

The wife is also jealous of her husband at times, which may in turn trigger violent confrontations either borne out of denial or defense by the male.

Pregnancy and Battering

When women have cited pregnancy as a factor in wife abuse, the most common explanation has been the added strain put on the relationship. This has proven to be especially true when it is an unplanned pregnancy. Jealousy and resentment toward the unborn child are often precipitating factors in the abuse. When the relationship is already strained by other sexual problems, unemployment, etc., a pregnancy can add to the strain and increase the likelihood of violence. Walker[25] and Gelles[26] reported a high degree of battering during first, second and third pregnancies. In Walker's study, 50 percent of the batterers were said to be initially pleased with the pregnancy but it did not prevent the abuse.

Sexual Intimacy

Sex and intimacy appear to be related to wife battering in two ways. One is the relationship between battering and victim withdrawal from sexual intimacy as a consequence. According to Roy, this abuse and withdrawal often begin very early in the relationship.[27] The women she studied expressed feelings of worthlessness and alienation from their abusive husbands. This low self-esteem due to the battering made sexual intimacy difficult for the woman to achieve. Roy cited that accusations by the husband of infidelity and adultery by the wife contributed to the sexual problems and the battering.

A second correlation between sexual intimacy and battering exists in behavioral patterns of battered women and their inability to distinguish between sex and intimacy.[28] Following are reasons found why abused women have sexual relations with their abusive husbands:

- Seduction as an unrealistic sense of power.
- In order to keep the peace.
- Intense concentration on survival.
- Dependency upon an abusive though occasionally loving man.
- Joy from an intense intimate relationship.
- Knowledge of how to decrease the spouse's abusive behavior through a loving relationship.

Many such abused women may have been sexually abused during childhood. Walker advanced that "it is quite possible that early exposure to sexual abuse, with or without accompanying physical violence, creates a dependency upon the positive aspects of the intense intimacy experienced prior to the beginning of the battering behavior and continuing during the third phase of loving-kindness."[29]

PSYCHOLOGICAL ABUSE

Recent years have seen a greater emphasis placed on another form of woman battering that is just as detrimental to the woman's health and well being: psychological or emotional abuse.

In its broadest sense, psychological abuse can be defined as mistreatment in the form of threats, intimidation, isolation, degradation, mind games; and directing violence toward other family members or household objects (e.g., slamming doors). The first research project on psychological abuse in marriage in the United States was done by Patricia Hoffman, a psychologist at the St. Cloud State University Counseling Center in Minnesota. Hoffman defines this type of abuse as "behavior sufficiently threatening to a woman that she believes her capacity to work, to interact in the family or society, or to enjoy good physical or mental health, has been or might be endangered."[30]

Unfortunately there is no real way to measure the prevalence of psychological abuse of women, particularly when one takes into account the many women who remain silent, as well as those who may not even recognize that they are being psychologically violated. Notes Walker, as far back as the early 1970s when the number of refugees in England increased, "it became obvious that large numbers of women were seeking safety from psychological abuse."[31]

In a study of physical and psychological coerciveness, Walker found that both forms of abuse were present in assaultive couples and "cannot be separated, despite the difficulty in documentation."[32] Hoffman estimated, based on her study, that as many as 1 in 3 women may be involved in a psychologically abusive relationship.[33]

Marriage counselor Jeanne Weigum contends that psychological abuse of women is the underlying problem in the majority of dysfunctional relationships. "Women come in for counseling feeling unhappy," says Weigum. "But when they examine that unhappiness, it usually turns out that their husbands are practicing some form of psychological abuse."[34]

EXPLAINING ABUSIVE MEN

Much research has gone into trying to understand the abusive man and why he strikes out at the one perhaps closest to him — his wife or significant other. Psychologists have characterized batterers in terms of adhering to a traditional male role or having a weak, immature personality.

> Enactment of compulsive masculinity, often referred to as "machismo," is an effort to maintain complete dominance over his wife. On the other extreme, many batterers' personalities contain elements

of helplessness and dependency. The violent husband has been characterized as a "little boy wanting to be grown up and superior, as he'd been taught he should be."[35]

Batterers have been described as "intractable" or "treatable," depending upon their perception of the violent behavior. "The intractable abuser finds no fault in his abusive action, whereas the treatable husband experiences guilt and remorse after the violence. In the latter instance, it is possible that with counseling the offender can learn nonviolent means of coping."[36]

Abusive Backgrounds

Often both victims and abusers tend to come from violent backgrounds. Some studies have found that half the men who abuse women were themselves abused or witnessed family violence.[37] Batterers are more likely to come from abusive homes than battered women. Bonnie Carlson found that only one-third of the abused wives in her sample came from families where wife abuse had occurred.[38] J. Gayford's study found that 23 of 100 battered women had come from violent homes.[39]

Social Structure Theory

Social structure theory holds that male violence is a reflection of particular structural and situational stimuli.[40] In order for violence to occur, two conditions must be met: (1) situational or structural stress must be present, and (2) the potential batterer must have been socialized to view violence as an appropriate response to certain situations, such as frustration.

Murray Straus identifies nine ways in which the "male-dominant structure of the society and of the family create and maintain a high level of marital violence"[41]:

- The defense of male authority.
- Compulsive masculinity.
- Economic constraints and discrimination.
- Difficulties in child care.
- The preeminence for women of the wife role.

- The single-parent household myth.
- The woman's negative self-image.
- The conception of women as children.
- The male orientation of the criminal justice system.

Lee Bowker advanced that "these values and norms bind women into a position in which they are easily victimized at the same time that they encourage men to flex their muscles."[42]

WHY DO WOMEN REMAIN WITH AN ABUSIVE MATE?

The question of why physically or emotionally battered women tolerate this mistreatment has been probed perhaps more than any other question associated with wife abuse. On the surface it would seem to walk away from this anguish would be as simple as the front door. Some women do just that. And yet all too often, escaping an abusive spouse or boyfriend is far more difficult to do. There are a number of typical reasons ascribed for this, including:

- *Fear*—of the abuser, being humiliated, having others find out, being left alone.
- *Finances*—losing money, the house, standard of living.
- *Children*—losing financial support for them and a father.[43]
- *Social stigma*—shame, embarrassment, being labeled.
- *Guilt*—for bringing about the abuse or in believing that they are too needed by the abuser to leave.
- *Role expectations*—that abuse is a normal part of relationships; often based on learned experiences in childhood.

A cycle theory of violence has been developed by Lenore Walker as to why women remain in habitually abusive relationships.[44] The tension reduction theory advances that three specific phases exist in a recurring cycle of battering: (1) tension building, (2) the acute battering incident, and (3) loving contrition.

The tension stage consists of a series of minor or verbal attacks. The woman manages to cope with these episodes by minimizing their significance and/or severity and using anger reduction techniques. She seeks to appease the batterer by doing whatever is necessary to calm him down, in the process becoming even more submissive.

The second stage, the acute battering incident, is characterized by "the uncontrollable discharge of the tensions that have been built up during stage one." Typically the batterer unleashes both physical and verbal aggression upon the wife, which she is unable to prevent. It is in this phase of the cycle that most injuries, sometimes severe, take place.

The third stage is that of loving contrition or the "honeymoon period." The abuser becomes at once charming, loving, apologetic, kind, remorseful—in short, he takes a 180 degree turn and is willing to do anything to be forgiven. "Suddenly he's giving her gifts, good sex, pampering," says marriage and family counselor Laura Schlessinger. "She wants to believe he's really sorry and that he will change this time. In the glow of all this attention, she does believe it."[45] It is this contrition stage that provides the reinforcement for the woman remaining in the relationship. However, almost inevitably, stage one tension building resumes and a new cycle takes place.

SELF-DEFENSE FOR THE BATTERED WOMAN

For many battered women the only means of dealing with an abusive mate is to strike back violently. There are few statistics on male victims of spouse abuse, yet some researchers have found the incidence of female batterers to be significant. Robert Langley and Richard Levy estimated that 12 million men are physically abused by their wives in the United States during some point in their marriage.[46] Suzanne Steinmetz, author of an article titled "The Battered Husband Syndrome," estimated that 280,000 men in this country are battered each year.[47] Another study of spouse abuse findings approximated that 2 million husbands, compared to 1.8 million wives, had experienced at least one of the more serious forms of spouse abuse.[48]

This data notwithstanding, few believe that female batterers can measure up to male batterers in numbers or severity of violence. Rebecca Dobash and Russell Dobash found the ratio of male-to-female spouse abuse to be 66 to 1.[49]

Murders in Self-Defense

In relatively rare instances, the battered woman is driven to the ultimate measure of self-defense—killing her abusive mate. Recent studies show that wives constitute more than half of the murdered spouses annually, with husbands being 6 to 7 times more likely to kill than be killed.[50] Female perpetrators of spouse homicide have been documented. In a study of homicides and attempted homicides by females in Hungary, it was found that 40 percent of the victims were husbands, common-law husbands, and lovers.[51] A similar finding was made by J. Totman in a study of 120 female murders in the United States, where 40 percent of the women had killed husbands and lovers.[52] A study of females imprisoned for murder revealed that they were the sole perpetrators in 77 percent of the homicides, and in more than half of the homicides, the victim was an intimate or family member.[53] According to FBI figures, 4 percent of the male murder victims in the United States in 1992 were killed by a wife or girlfriend.[54]

Recent years have seen high profile cases of women killing their husbands or lovers with the motive often being self-defense after years of being the victim of spouse abuse. In a study of women charged with murder in Los Angeles County, Nancy Kaser-Boyd and Michael Maloney found that 42 percent of the women had killed a spouse or boyfriend.[55] Three-quarters of the women cited years of physical and psychological abuse at the hands of the victims. Another study of females imprisoned in a California penitentiary for murder found that 28 of the 30 women convicted of killing their spouses had been victims of wife battering.[56]

In *The Battered Woman Syndrome*, Walker gives a perspective on battered women turned murderers:

> Most women who killed their batterers have little memory of any cognitive processes other than an intense focus on their own survival.... Their description of the final incident indicates that they separate those angry feelings by the psychological process of a dissociative state.... This desperate attempt at remaining unaware of their own unacceptable feelings is a measure of just how dangerous they perceive their situation. They fear showing anger will cause their own death, and indeed it could as batterers cannot tolerate the woman's expression of anger.[57]

The battered woman who kills her abuser is often so consumed with hopelessness, helplessness, despair, and low self-esteem that she is unable to think beyond the desperation of the moment until the deed is done and the ramifications already set in motion as a consequence. In the article "Women and Homicide," writer Elissa Benedek speaks of the point of no return typical of many battered homicidal women:

"The battered wife has turned to social agencies, police, prosecutors, friends, ministers, and family, but they have not offered meaningful support or advice.... Abused women who have murdered their spouses reveal that they feel that homicide was the only alternative left to them."[58]

Sadly, battered women who kill their mates then become further victims as they often face murder charges, imprisonment, loss of their children, and lack of sympathy and understanding from the very social agencies that abandoned them in their hour of need.

BREAKING THE CYCLE
OF BATTERING

Short of killing their abusers, breaking the cycle of abusive treatment at the hands of husbands and lovers is perhaps the most difficult aspect of the battered woman's syndrome. Psychologist Ann McClenahan explains: "The longer a woman stays and the harder she works to make the marriage work, the harder it is to leave."[59]

Battered women's shelters have been established throughout the country as a first step in escaping the abuse and abuser. These shelters offer refuge, counseling and protection for battered women. More efforts are needed to get abused women to use such facilities for their safety and more shelters are sorely needed.

Criminal justice system agencies are better equipped in the nineties to deal with issues of family violence, and abusive men are more likely to serve time if charges are pressed. Nevertheless, law enforcement continues to fall short as an effective intervention to domestic violence, particularly wife abuse, which is often still looked upon as a private spousal matter. Most such cases fail to come to the attention of law enforcement, while laws are inconsistent from state to state. In fact, battered women must often take the initiative to escape the violence which, unfortunately, many victims are unable or unwilling to do.

PART V

The Sexploitation of Women

15. The Prostitution
of Women

Throughout history the victimization and exploitation of women have perhaps been most tragic in prostitution. Few other crimes reflect such a wide gender double standard as prostitution where women are far more likely than men to be recruited, abused, raped, killed, arrested, incarcerated, poor, and vulnerable to such diseases as AIDS. Many see prostitution as largely a victimless crime while others favor legalization of prostitution. Regrettably, such views further foster the victimization of women who prostitute themselves and increase the risks for all women with respect to sex crimes, sexual harassment, sexual diseases, and vulnerability.

DEFINING PROSTITUTION

Women's victimization through prostitution can be seen in the sexist definitions of prostitution over the years that made the term synonymous with women and promiscuity. In 1914 in the book *Prostitution in Europe*, Abraham Flexner defined prostitution as characterized

> by three elements variously combined: barter, promiscuity, and emotional indifference. The barter need not involve the passage of money. . . . Nor need promiscuity be utterly choiceless: a woman is not the less a prostitute because she is more or less selective in her association. Emotional indifference may be fairly inferred from barter and promiscuity.[1]

171

In *Prostitution in the United States*, Howard Woolston noted that prior to 1918 the only statutory definition of prostitution in the nation was in Section 2372 of the Indiana law, which read:

> Any female who frequents or lives in a house of ill-fame or associates with women of bad character for chastity, either in public or at a house which men of bad character frequent or visit, or who commits adultery or fornication for hire shall be deemed a prostitute.[2]

As recently as 1968, the Oregon Supreme Court defined the prostitute in terms of women when it ruled that "the feature which distinguishes a prostitute from other women who engage in illicit intercourse is the indiscrimination with which she offers herself to men for hire."[3]

In the 1970 book *Howard Street*, Nathan C. Heard wrote matter-of-factly, "A man is a natural pimp and a woman is a natural whore."[4]

In spite of these early, predominantly male, definitions of prostitution which many continue to subscribe to, prostitution today is generally recognized by criminologists as sex-for-hire by women, men, and children, and often involves sexual acts other than intercourse. Yet female prostitution remains the focus of most victimology and criminological studies of prostitution.

THE EXTENT OF
FEMALE PROSTITUTION

No one can be certain just how many women are in the prostitution business. However, with the broad and often discreet means for prostitutes to ply their trade (e.g., streetwalkers, call girls, massage parlors), it could well be in the millions. Official data may represent the best source for putting some perspective on the extent of prostitution. According to the *Uniform Crime Reports*, 56,244 females aged 18 and over were arrested for prostitution and commercialized vice in 1992.[5] This represented 99 percent of all females arrested for prostitution. Most female arrests for prostitution and commercialized vice came for women aged 25 to 34, followed by age 35 to 39. Experts believe that the actual number of female prostitutes is much higher—meaning the victimization which women as prostitutes must endure is that much greater.

DIFFERENTIAL ENFORCEMENT OF PROSTITUTION LAWS

Female prostitutes face discrimination at all stages of the criminal justice system compared to their male counterparts. Currently, prostitution is a crime in every state in the country, with the exception of Nevada where it is legal in most counties. "Thirty-eight states expressly prohibit payment for sexual acts; solicitation laws exist in forty-four states and the District of Columbia; and other states check prostitution through vagrancy and loitering statutes."[6]

Although most experts agree that there are as many male prostitutes as female, more women are subject to arrest for prostitution. For example, in 1992 nearly 2 women were arrested for prostitution or commercialized vice for every man.[7] This represented 2.5 percent of all female arrests compared to 0.3 percent of all male arrests.

Women are also more likely to be incarcerated than men for prostitution. Thirty percent of the women in jails at any given time in the United States were arrested for prostitution, while 70 percent of all women imprisoned for felonies were originally arrested for prostitution.[8]

There is a wide disparity between arrests of female prostitutes and their male johns. It is estimated that 20 percent of the male population solicits prostitutes at some point in their life, yet recent official figures show that only 2 customers are arrested for every 8 female prostitutes.[9] A report on female offenders in the District of Columbia in 1966 found that while 1,110 women were arrested for prostitution that year, only 4 men were charged with solicitation.[10]

Racism is also a reality of the discrimination poor and minority female prostitutes face in the criminal justice system. "Although the typical customers of prostitutes are middle-class men between the ages of 30 and 60, those most penalized by the law are poor black women who are 'forced onto the streets and into blatant solicitation where the risk of arrest is highest.'"[11] Black women are 7 times more likely to be arrested for prostitution than nonblack women, with the highest proportion of arrests occurring in inner cities where "living standards are low, the level of desperation high, and police prejudice endemic."[12]

TYPOLOGY OF FEMALE PROSTITUTES

A number of categories of female prostitutes have been established depending upon the circumstances in which in the woman prostitutes herself, payment, motivation, psychological profile, and other factors, including biases in differentiating prostitute "types." The victimization and exploitation of prostitutes may be equal in relative terms, but in actual terms certain classes of females are more prone to discrimination, violence, disease, and other hazards, such as streetwalkers, who must literally survive by selling themselves on the streets.

In *Prostitution and Morality*, Harry Benjamin and R. E. L. Masters divided prostitutes into two general categories: (1) voluntary, and (2) compulsive.[13] Voluntary prostitutes act rationally, freely choosing prostitution. Compulsive prostitutes are to some extent acting under compulsion by "psychoneurotic needs." The researchers acknowledged that in most instances prostitutes cannot be exclusively placed in either category.

Paul Goldstein described prostitutes in terms of occupational commitment and occupational milieu.[14] Occupational commitment refers to the frequency of a woman's participation in prostitution and is subcategorized into three types: (1) *temporary*—a discreet act of prostitution of not more than six months duration in a specific occupational milieu, (2) *occasional*—two or more discreet incidents of prostitution in a specific occupational milieu, each episode not longer than six months duration, and (3) *continual*—more than six months duration in a particular occupational milieu on a steady basis.

Occupational milieu refers to the specific types of prostitution in which the woman is involved. Goldstein divides these into seven categories:

- *Streetwalker.* A woman who overtly solicits males on the street and offers her sexual services for payment.
- *Massage Parlor Prostitute.* A woman who offers sexual favors in a massage parlor.
- *House Prostitute.* A woman who works in an establishment designed specifically for prostitution where male clients are serviced.
- *Call Girl.* A woman who works in a residence soliciting clients or is solicited over the telephone.
- *Madam.* A woman who supplies other prostitutes with clients for a percentage of the fee.
- *Mistress.* A woman who is primarily supported by one man at a time, or who sees only one man at a time for cash.
- *Barterer.* A woman who exchanges sexual favors for professional or other services, or for material goods such as drugs or clothes.

Three other types of prostitutes are noted in *Women and Criminality*:

- *Bar Girl*. A woman who works in a bar, lounge, or other entertainment establishment not specifically set up for prostitution, where male clients are solicited or the woman is willingly solicited by men for sexual services.
- *Sex Ring-Escort Prostitutes*. Women who are generally part of a large-scale phone referral operation for purposes of sexual favors for hire.
- *Referral Prostitute*. A woman who is referred to clients by others (such as other prostitutes). Unlike a madam, the referrer may have no financial stake in the referral.[15]

Prostitutes often move from one occupational milieu to another or engage in two or more types simultaneously, dependent upon their needs and circumstances. For example, a madam may double as a call girl.

EXPLAINING PROSTITUTION

Early attempts at explaining female prostitutes and prostitution were largely biased, unsound, and rejected. For instance, Cesare Lombroso, referred to by some as the father of criminology, believed prostitutes to be "born as such."[16] Another early theorist, William Thomas, proposed that women became prostitutes to satisfy their need for excitement and response.[17] It may have been Sigmund Freud's psychiatric hypothesis on prostitution that influenced much of the early thinking, which "inferred some inherent pathology among women who prostituted themselves."[18]

Modern sociological theories of prostitution examine it in terms of social structure, social pathology, and culture. Charles Winick and Paul Kinsie explained society's hostility toward prostitution by contending that the social structure is threatened by prostitution because "people tend to equate sexual activity with stable relationships, typified by the family."[19] Kingsley Davis' functionalist theory of prostitution advanced that

> the function served by prostitutes is the protection of the family unit, maintenance of the chastity and purity of the "respectable" citi-

zenry. . . . Morality is more potent than the financial benefits of prostitution, and . . . this societal system of morality creates prostitution by defining the sex drive in terms of a meaningful social relationship and denouncing prostitution as a meaningless sexual relationship.[20]

In the book *Social Pathology* Edwin Lemert described prostitution as a "formal extension of more generalized sexual pathology in our culture of which sexual promiscuity and thinly disguised commercial exploitation of sex in informal context play a large and important part."[21] Cultural transmission theorists explain prostitution as the result of a "weakening of family and neighborhood control and the persistence and transmission from person to person of traditional delinquent activities."[22]

Many experts reject the relationship between prostitution and ecological variables, finding that prostitution is present at all income and occupational levels because of "urban anonymity and the weakening of traditional moral values."[23] Theories of prostitution tend to remain gender-specific, thereby creating a built-in bias toward women as prostitutes and disregarding the male prostitute and predominantly male customer.

ECONOMICS AND WOMEN'S PROSTITUTION

Economic deprivation is believed by many social scientists to be the primary factor in female prostitution. Winick and Kinsie held that the decision to become a prostitute is based upon few employment opportunities and the recognition of the money to be made.[24] Lemert noted the inferior status women have with respect to "power and control over material gains" and believed prostitution to be the means for "balancing this differential in status."[25]

The most in-depth study of motivations for female entry into prostitution was conducted in the mid–1970s by anthropologist Jennifer James. She described five aspects of our socioeconomic structure that make prostitution alluring or a viable alternative to women:

- There are virtually no other occupations available to unskilled or low skilled women with an income comparable to prostitution.
- Virtually no other occupation exists for unskilled or low skilled women that provides the adventure or allows the independence of the prostitute lifestyle.

- The traditional "woman's role" is almost synonymous with the culturally defined female sex role, which emphasizes service, the woman's physical appearance, and her sexuality.
- The discrepancy between accepted male and female sex roles creates the "Madonna-whore" notion of female sexuality, such that women who are sexually active beyond the limits of their "normal" sex-role expectations are labeled deviant and lose social status.
- The cultural importance of wealth and material goods causes some women to desire "advantages to which [they are] not entitled by [their] position" in the socioeconomic stratification.[26]

The economic disadvantages of women in general are disproportionately evident among prostitutes, thereby furthering their victimization and susceptibility for exploitation.

PROSTITUTION AND SEXUAL ABUSE

Many researchers have documented a relationship between female prostitution and childhood sexual abuse, including incest and rape.[27] One study found that 90 percent of the female prostitutes had been sexually abused at some time in their lives.[28] Another study estimated that 9 out of 10 female prostitutes have been sexually assaulted during childhood.[29]

Female prostitutes are also the victims of a high rate of sexual assaults during the course of their profession. Rape is a common occurrence among many streetwalkers, largely due to their exposure and the high crime areas in which they typically operate.[30]

There is also a strong correlation between juvenile prostitution and adult prostitution, as well as other sex crimes and pornography, and sexually transmitted diseases.[31]

PROSTITUTION AND DRUG ABUSE

Many female prostitutes enter the profession as drug addicts, while others become addicted to drugs or alcohol after becoming prostitutes. A study of Baltimore street addicts found that 96 percent of those who used drugs daily supported their habit through such crimes as prostitution.[32] Several other studies cite a significant relationship between female prostitution and substance abuse.[33]

PROSTITUTION AND AIDS

The greatest risk female prostitutes face today is contracting AIDS (Acquired Immune Deficiency Syndrome). A number of studies illustrate the gravity of the risk as well as the bias against women who test positive for HIV (Human Immunodeficiency Virus), the forerunner to AIDS. A recent government study found that "many female prostitutes are carrying the AIDS virus and warned men to avoid prostitutes."[34] A Centers for Disease Control report found the rate of AIDS among prostitutes to be well above that of the general populations;[35] while a study of street prostitutes in Miami found that 41 percent of those tested were HIV-Positive.[36]

In a 1991 Gallup Poll on legalization of prostitution to help reduce AIDS, 6 of 10 women polled were against legalization, while nearly half the men polled felt prostitution should be legalized.[37] This gender disparity on the issue of legalization of prostitution underscores the nature of its existence and the problems of prostitution, particularly with respect to its most exploited group—women.

16. Pornography and Violence Against Women

Women have long been exploited through pornographic films, videos, photographs, and literature. Such materials often portray women as the sexual objects of men, in sexually explicit terms, in bondage, and, increasingly, in sadistic and violent pornography. The upsurge in the quantity and variety of pornography available in the United States in the last quarter of a century has left many psychologists and feminist groups associating pornography to a similar rise in rape, sexual assaults, battering, and other violent crimes against women. However, banning pornography in this country has proven to be an impossible task due to the complex issues associated with free-speech guarantees, censorship, and defining what constitutes pornography and obscenity. Antipornography statutes have been declared unconstitutional and it appears that pornography and its potential harmful effects with respect to women may be here to stay.

DEFINING PORNOGRAPHY

The word *pornography* derives from the Greek *pornographos*, which comes from *porne*, meaning prostitute or female captive, and *graphein*, which means to write; thus writings about prostitution.[1] In modern times, the definition of pornography has expanded to encompass the multitude of ways in which sexually explicit material can be produced, including writings, movies, photographs, videos, and computer pornography.

179

Nevertheless, there is no uniform definition of pornography, adding to the vagueness of the term and its implications on individuals and society as the following definitions indicate. The dictionary defines pornography as "writings, pictures, films, or other materials that are meant to stimulate erotic feelings by describing or portraying sexual activity." Philosopher Helen Longino's definition of pornography is "material that explicitly represents or describes degrading and abusive sexual behavior so as to endorse and/or recommend the behavior as described."[2] The Academic American Encyclopedia says "pornography, or obscenity, is any material, pictures, films, printed matter, or devices dealing with sexual poses or acts considered indecent by the public."

Pornography is often associated by definition with *obscenity*, which is generally defined as "something condemnatory, offensive, indecent, disgusting, or lewd to prevailing concepts of decency."[3] However, not everything that is obscene is pornographic, and vice versa. For the purposes of this chapter, an appropriate definition of pornography can be found in the book *Women and Criminality*:

> Any sexually explicit and/or titillating arousing written, photographic, pictorial (including moving pictures), or live depiction of women or children as objects for commercial exploitation, sexual abuse, degradation, regression, or humiliation that is offensive in its sexual content or acts to the population-at-large and that has a negative effect on certain elements of society.[4]

THE BUSINESS OF PORNOGRAPHY

By most accounts, pornography is an enormous business in the United States, taking in an estimated $6 billion annually.[5] The major players in the porn business include producers, distributors, advertisers, photographers, actors, and models. The sources for pornography are more diverse than ever before and include theaters, magazines, video stores, adult bookstores, cable television, and even network television where semi-nude women and violence against women have reached new levels, despite increased censorship and government regulations. Consequently, pornography consumers and viewers have an endless range of choices in the marketplace, meaning millions upon millions of dollars for the suppliers of pornographic materials, programming, live shows, etc.

By its very nature, pornography is an industry that has supported itself through "systematically eroticizing violence against women by producing and marketing images of men humiliating, battering, and murdering women for sexual pleasure. . . . Pornography is about power imbalances using sex as a weapon to subjugate women. In pornography the theme is assailant vs. victim."[6] The messages men receive from pornography's exploitation and victimization of women include the following:

- Women are passive, willing partners in their own victimization and exploitation.
- Women in pain are glamorous.
- Women are incapable of being independent or self-directed.
- It is appropriate that women's sexuality and behavior be defined by men.
- Men are entitled to frequent, unconditional use of women's bodies for men's pleasure.

Frances Patai, organizer of Women Against Pornography, argues that: "Pornography objectifies women by caricaturing and reducing them to a sum of their sexual parts and functions—devoid of sensibilities and intelligence."[7]

COMMISSION ON PORNOGRAPHY AND VIOLENCE AGAINST WOMEN

In 1985, the Attorney General's Commission on Pornography was established to "determine the nature, extent, and impact on society of pornography in the United States, and to make specific recommendations to the Attorney General concerning more effective ways in which the spread of pornography could be contained."[8] A government Commission on Obscenity and Pornography in 1970 had found no link between pornography and violent crime against women.[9]

The 11-member Attorney General's Commission concluded that there was a correlation between certain types of pornography and sexually violent and abusive crimes toward women, adding that exposure to even nonviolent sexually explicit material "bears some causal relationship to the level of sexual violence."[10] The Commission's report read:

> When clinical and experimental research has focused particularly on sexually violent material, the conclusions have been nearly unanimous. In both clinical and experimental settings, exposure to sexually violent materials has indicated an increase in the likelihood of aggression. More specifically, the research . . . shows a causal relationship between exposure to material of this type and aggressive behavior towards women. . . . The assumption that increased aggressive behavior towards women is causally related, for an aggregate population, to increased sexual violence is significantly supported by the clinical evidence, as well as by much of the less scientific evidence.[11]

The Commission called for a nationwide crackdown on the purveyors of hard-core pornography. Its key recommendations to Congress included:

- Amend the federal obscenity laws to eliminate the necessity of proving transportation to interstate commerce. A statute should be enacted only to require proof that distributing obscene material "affects" interstate commerce.
- Enact a forfeiture statute to reach the proceeds and instruments of any offense committed under the federal obscenity laws.
- Amend Title 18 of the United States Code to specifically proscribe obscene cable and satellite television programming.
- Enact legislation to make it an unfair business practice and an unfair labor practice for any employer to hire individuals to participate in commercial sexual performances.
- Enact legislation prohibiting the transmission of obscene material through the telephone or similar common carrier.[12]

Although the Attorney General's Commission on Pornography had its share of critics and criticism, the vast data used in the Commission's findings and recommendations "clearly justify the conclusion that there is at least some relationship between the pornography industry and the victimization of women."[13]

PORNOGRAPHY AND
BATTERED WOMEN

The link between pornography and woman battering has been increasingly established in the literature. In *Take Back the Night: Women on Pornography*, Laura Lederer asserts that "pornography is the ideology of a culture which promotes and condones rape, woman battering, and other crimes against women."[14] The following examples illustrate the association between pornography and the battering of women:

- In the movie *Swept Away*, an independent woman is systematically verbally and physically abused until being reduced to a passive sexual subordinate who desires further humiliation while loving her batterer.
- An album cover accentuates the crotch of a woman with the words: "Jump on It!"
- In the movie *Dressed to Kill*, women are portrayed as sex objects and are raped, tortured, and murdered, though the critics praised the film using such terms as "funny," "erotic," and "irresistible."[15]

The co-editor of *Rape and Child Abuse* describes the relationship between battered women and pornography:

> Woman battering objectifies women by reducing them to objects of possession. Both pornography and woman battering legitimize the pain inflicted on the woman by objectifying the woman. In addition, many women are raped and verbally assaulted while being battered.... Objectifying the sexual anatomy of women renders them inferior and nonhuman, thus providing the psychological foundation for committing violence against them.[16]

Studies of battered women have established a correlation to pornography. A study of 100 abused wives revealed that 15 percent of the women reported that their abusive spouses "seemed to experience sexual arousal from the violence—since the demand for sexual intercourse immediately followed the assault."[17]

Pornography and its effects on wife batterers is still being studied. The evidence seems to support the contention that "pornography (especially as it is legitimized in mainstream TV shows, ads, movies, fashion layouts, etc.) socializes some men into thinking that the maltreatment of women is erotic, sexually desirable, desired by women, and a necessary proof of virility."[18]

PORNOGRAPHY AND SEXUAL ASSAULTS

Researchers have shown significant relationship between pornography and sex crimes. In a study of rape victims, sociologist Pauline Bart noted:

> I didn't start out being against pornography; but if you're a rape researcher, it becomes clear that there is a direct link. Violent pornography is like an advertisement for rape.... Men are not born thinking women enjoy rape and torture.... They learn from pornography.[19]

In a study of mass-circulation sex magazines and the incidence of rape, Larry Baron and Murray Straus found that "rape increases in direct proportion to the readership of sex magazines."[20] Neil Malamuth, co-editor of *Pornography and Sexual Aggression*, warned that "in a culture that celebrates rape, the lives of millions of women will be affected."[21]

Law enforcement data further bolster the link between pornography and sexual assault of women. Michigan police recently analyzed more than two decades of sex crimes in the state and found

> numerous cases where the assailants had immersed themselves in pornographic films or pictures and then gone out and committed sex crimes. These crimes included rape, sodomy, and even the bizarre erotic crime of piquerism (piercing with a knife till blood flows, a kind of sexual torture). In some cases, the attacker admitted that the urge to rape or torture erotically came over him while reading an obscene picture magazine or attending a movie showing rape and erotic torture.[22]

The Los Angeles Police Department found a strong link between the clustering of adult entertainment establishments in Hollywood and an increase in the incidence of rape and other violent crimes.[23] Pornography is also often associated with female prostitution. A 1976 Task Force on Organized Crime found a tripartite relationship between pornography, prostitution, and substance abuse. "The young actors in pornographic films often perform for drugs rather than for money, then are forced into prostitution" to support drug habits.[24] The LAPD found that prostitution in the Hollywood adult entertainment district during a recent six-year period increased at a rate 15 times the city average.[25]

Prostitution and pornography have also been shown to be related to sexual assaults and physical violence against female prostitutes, including murder.[26]

PORNOGRAPHY AND
THE EXPLOITATION OF WOMEN

Perhaps the greatest victimization women must endure from pornography is the exploitation it inflicts on women inside and outside the industry. Women in pornographic materials and shows are typically nude or scantily clad, vacuous, abused, degraded, manipulated, paid less than their male counterparts, rarely in upper level production or directorial positions, and used at the whim of and largely for the entertainment of men. The residual effect is that pornography stereotypes, demeans, dehumanizes, and makes all women vulnerable to misinterpretations, imagination, lasciviousness, salaciousness, and violence.

In *The Seduction of Society*, William Stanmeyer addresses the exploitation of women by pornographers:

> Pornography feeds twisted male fantasies about women. Invariably the pornographic film or photo shows a beautiful woman vulnerable and available to be used, roughly, by the male with whom the viewer identifies.... The woman is made to appear no more than a function or an organ. The camera's focus and interest is solely genital: it is irrelevant who this person is; any woman would do, as long as her physical attributes are exaggerated. She has no value in herself, her only value and purpose is for the male. She is quite simply an object. She is a thing. This is true even if the pornography is not explicitly violent. Pornography that is not overtly violent is still implicitly violent because it objectifies and degrades women.[27]

The danger of pornography and its effects are not only to women but potentially to each of us, as the following passage from an article on pornography reveals:

> Pornography hurts all women by portraying them only as sexual objects. And it hurts men and boys as well, especially those who are exposed to pornography at an early age, by giving them a limited, leering view of women. In sum, pornography damages everyone in our society.[28]

17. Sexual Harassment and Stalking

The victimization of women has taken on broader meaning in recent years. Sexual harassment has come to the forefront of women's complaints about being victims of male sexual aggression in the workplace, thanks to some recent high profile allegations of sexual harassment. Anita Hill's accusations against then Supreme Court nominee Clarence Thomas helped fuel the drive toward greater recognition of sexual harassment and its potential effects on all parties involved.

A form of sexual harassment even more ominous to women that has been given increased attention in the last few years is stalking. Women are being targeted by stalkers in and outside the workplace with the results being fear, intimidation, nightmares, harassment, bodily injury, and in some instances death.

Legislators and law enforcement are taking steps to deal with sexual harassment; however, the problem is pervasive and victims still have much reason to fear and feel vulnerable to sexual harassers and stalkers.

WHAT IS SEXUAL HARASSMENT?

Defining sexual harassment is perhaps the biggest problem facing victims, perpetrators, and the legal system. What constitutes sexual harassment? For many, it is the slightest intrusion into their lives or livelihood with respect to sexual innuendos. Others may not consider an incident or situation to be sexual harassment unless it becomes physical aggression. Yet others may draw the line between normal behavior and sexual harassment only when it has a detrimental effect on the work environment, if not the job itself. In the broadest sense, sexual harassment has been defined as

> forms of unwanted sexual attention that occurs in working situations: visual (leering) or verbal (sexual teasing, jokes, comments or questions) behavior; unwanted touching or pinching; unwanted pressure for sexual favors with implied threats or retaliation for non-cooperation.[1]

The effects of sexual harassment on the victim can be devastating and are often compared to those felt by women victims of other forms of sexual victimization such as rape. In the book *Intimate Intrusions*, author Elizabeth Stanko talks about what sexual harassment means to women:

> Women are as likely to be distressed by persistent "low-level" harassment—leering, for instance—as they are by more blatant touching.... Harassed women report becoming nervous and irritable; they feel humiliated; they feel they cannot control the encounters with the harasser(s) and then feel threatened and helpless. Many develop techniques to protect themselves through, for example, avoidance.... These women describe the daily barrage of sexual interplay in the office as psychological rape. The day in and day out exposure to what many assume to be "harmless" behavior produces reactions similar to those of sexually assaulted women. In fact, rape crisis centers receive calls from sexually harassed women who report having similar feelings as raped women.[2]

Albeit the type and depth of sexual harassment may vary considerably from victim to victim, the effects can "represent a serious violation to the personal integrity of its victims. Such women are no longer regarded as employees or colleagues but sexual objects."[3]

THE EXTENT OF SEXUAL HARASSMENT

Many believe that the amount of sexual harassment that goes on daily in our society is so great that it is almost impossible to simplify by estimates. Nevertheless, several surveys have been conducted to put some perspective on the seriousness of the problem, including two in the mid–1970s by *Redbook*[4] and the Working Women United Institute.[5] However, the most comprehensive survey to date on sexual harassment was conducted in 1980 by the U.S. Merit Systems Protection Board (MSPB). It polled 23,000 federal employees on the nature and incidence of workplace sexual harassment and found that

> every form except actual or attempted rape or sexual assault was experienced by a sizeable percentage of women. The more ambiguous forms of sexual harassment—"sexual comments" and "suggestive looks"—were reported most often. These forms were more likely to be repeated.
>
> However, with the exception of actual or attempted rape or assault, most victims reported experiencing all forms of sexual harassment repeatedly. In addition, many reported experiencing more than one form of sexual harassment. We also found that the incidents of sexual harassment were not just passing events—most lasted more than a week, and many lasted more than six months. Thus not only did the sexual harassment occur repeatedly, it was of relatively long duration as well.[6]

The MSPB reached the following conclusions from the survey:

- Victims varied in age, race, ethnicity, and occupation.
- Sixty-seven percent of the women 16 to 19 years of age reported being harassed, compared to 33 percent of the women between the ages of 45 and 54.
- Fifty-three percent of the single women reported sexual harassment, compared to 37 percent of the married women.
- More highly educated women reported harassment than less educated women, possibly indicative of the former occupying nontraditional women's jobs or defining sexual harassment more broadly.
- One percent of the women reported being victims of actual or attempted rape or sexual assault.
- Six percent of the females reported being under pressure for sexual favors.

While no comparable study has been conducted in the private sector on sexual harassment, Patricia Mathis of the Office of Merit Systems Review and Studies concluded that the MSPB's finding "that people of all ages, salary levels, education backgrounds, and hometowns are potential victims—leads us to the observation that sexual harassment cannot be uniquely associated with Federal employment."[7]

The MSPB repeated the survey in 1987 and found the results to be fairly consistent with the first survey's.[8] A 1989 *National Law Journal* survey of 900 female attorneys found that "10 percent said that clients exerted unwanted pressure for dates; 9 percent complained of touching, cornering, or pinching; and 4 percent cited pressure for sex, sometimes as a prerequisite for getting the client's business."[9]

THE LEGAL RECOURSE AGAINST SEXUAL HARASSMENT

Notes Alan Deutschman, "The simplest and most effective way to put an end to harassment in most instances is to ask or tell the person to stop."[10] When this fails, as is the case for many sexual harassment victims, using the legal system may be their only recourse. Sexual harassment is a civil offense in which an employer may be liable for his/her or an employee's transgressions against another employee.

Much of the case law on sexual harassment is based on Title VII of the federal Civil Rights Act of 1964.[11] The act forbids employment discrimination based on sex, and authorized the creation of the Equal Employment Opportunity Commission (EEOC) which set guidelines defining sexual harassment. These included undesired physical or verbal sexual advances, requests for sexual favors, and other sexual misconduct when (1) an employee's submission is made an explicit or implicit condition of employment, (2) an employee's submission or rejection of is used with respect to employment decisions affecting the job status of the employee, or (3) such conduct has an adverse effect on the employee's job performance.

The legal definition of sexual harassment was expanded in the landmark 1986 Supreme Court decision *Meritor Savings Bank v. Vinson* to include "verbal or physical conduct that creates an intimidating, hostile, or offensive work environment or unreasonably interferes with an employee's job performance."[12] Hence the Court made "environmental abuse" a form of sexual harassment that women had a right against and now have a further legal avenue to pursue in the fight against sex discrimination and sexual harassment.

Despite these legal remedies, proving sexual harassment can be difficult and costly. Often the victim is the only witness to the allegations. An investigation may be long and detailed but inconclusive; usually a victory for the accused. In many instances, the victim of sexual harassment is left without credibility and a job—further victimization.

Some suggest that the victim's best weapon against sexual harassment may be the stability of their employer, as the following indicates:

> Sexual harassment tends to be less common in stable companies where employees feel some loyalty to the corporation and one another. They realize they must treat everyone with respect and sensitivity, if only because they are all going to be working together for a long time.[13]

STALKING

Sexual harassment has taken on a more terrifying form of victimization for many women, known as stalking. While the terminology is relatively new, the act of stalking is not. What is stalking? Most law enforcement departments define stalking as "the willful, malicious and repeated following or harassing of another person."[14] In most states where stalking is now illegal, stalking is defined as repeatedly following or harassing someone with a "credible threat of bodily harm."

Stalking has only been a recognized and serious issue for most of us since the 1980s with some highly publicized cases involving celebrities such as actress Rebecca Schaeffer who was fatally shot by an obsessed fan, and tennis star Monica Seles, stabbed by a man who had stalked her for a week. A typical example of stalking can be seen in a recent Senate Judiciary Committee hearing in which the wife of a Texas senator recounts her ordeal of being the victim of a stalker:

> Members of the 16-man, 2-woman Senate Judiciary Committee listened raptly as Kathleen Tobin Krueger, 34, wife of newly appointed Texas Senator Bob Krueger, delivered her tale of terror. Last summer, she said, she walked to the mailbox to find a note that read, "Look how close I can get to you. See, I could kill you right now if I wanted to."
>
> Krueger knew immediately who had written the note. For the past nine years, she and her husband and, from birth, their two daughters, have been stalked by a former employee who has rung their doorbell repeatedly, screamed obscenities over the telephone, and delivered countless death threats. When the Kruegers complained to the police, they were told that unless the harasser tried to harm them physically, there was nothing the authorities could do.[15]

Although it has taken such victims in the public eye to draw attention to stalking, the vast majority of victims are ordinary people who are stalked by ex-spouses, ex-lovers, co-workers, friends, and even strangers. Most victims tend to be female and most stalkers male.

Just how many stalkers there are in the United States is unknown, given the lack of crime data on this newly defined criminal act. The most significant study of stalking was conducted recently by Park Dietz, a forensic psychiatrist who estimated that there are 200,000 people in this country who are stalking someone.[16] Experts believe that many victims of stalkers are reflected in other crime statistics, such as amongst the 2 million cases of domestic violence reported annually. Almost one-third of the women murdered in the United States each year are killed by ex-spouses and ex-boyfriends. It is estimated that as many as 90 percent of the victims had been stalked.[17]

WHO ARE THE MEN WHO STALK AND WHY DO THEY DO IT?

There are basically two types of stalkers: (1) those who stalk ex-intimates or acquaintances, and (2) those who stalk strangers. Both types can be equally dangerous to the victim. Women who are stalked by casual acquaintances are often as puzzled as they are unnerved by the stalker's pursuit. "They often wonder if there were signs they should have looked for that would have told them that a fascination was deadly."[18]

Whether an ex-intimate, acquaintance or stranger, stalkers are and can be of any age, race, ethnicity, socioeconomic or educational background, and relationship to the person they choose to stalk. Most stalkers, however, share similar profiles. Nine out of 10 are believed to suffer from a mental disorder, including manic depression, schizophrenia, and paranoia. "Often, they delude themselves into believing that the victim has a romantic interest in them, a condition known as erotomania. Some of the people with these delusions are quite intelligent but they tend to be socially isolated. Many are withdrawn and lonely, never able to develop relationships. Most have had limited sexual experience."[19]

According to psychologist James Wulach, stalkers have trouble handling rejection and aggression.

> When some men suffer a blow to their self-esteem, as in unrequited love, they use aggression as a way to restore the equilibrium to their sense of self. . . . Men stalk to boost their self-esteem and restore a

sense of power. It's most likely to happen with men in their twenties and thirties who are often immature and need to prove themselves.[20]

Persistence is the characteristic most common to stalkers. "They will find out everything they need to know about the object of their desire — from where she lives and works to the most intimate details of her life."[21]

ANTISTALKING LAWS

Before 1990, victims had little defense against stalkers. Law enforcement largely viewed stalking as a domestic dispute. Furthermore, even if a complaint was taken seriously, there were no legal grounds for arresting a stalker unless the victim had been assaulted or another offense had taken place. Restraining orders were the main means a victim had for protecting herself—which generally offered little protection and less deterrence for the stalker.

Antistalking laws have given stalking victims their most important weapon to date against victimization. In 1990, California became the first state to make stalking a crime—this after five women in Orange County were murdered by stalkers in early 1990. Thirty-seven other states now have antistalking laws.[22] Stalking can be a felony or misdemeanor, depending on the state, repeated offenses, and/or violation of restraining orders—and can result in up to ten years in prison for an offender.

In early 1993, legislators introduced a bill in Congress that would make stalking a federal crime, with a maximum of 10 years incarceration should a stalker cross state lines or use the telephone or mail to deliver threats.

These important steps to protect victims of stalkers notwithstanding, the problem of stalking remains a serious one for many women throughout the country. "For the antistalking laws to have a real impact, courts must take them seriously and apply the new legal muscle they provide."[23]

PART VI

Protecting Women and Children from Violence and Exploitation

18. Responding to the Victimization and Sexual Exploitation of Children and Women

Recent years have seen important federal and state legislative efforts as well as community and law enforcement strides toward the prevention of children and women's victimization and exploitation. As a result, more and more victims are being identified, protected and treated, while more offenders are being identified, arrested, penalized and incarcerated. Nevertheless, it would be naive to suggest that violence towards women and children is under control or that sexual exploitation is on the wane. The truth is we have a long way to go in the fight against the victimization of children and women. However, we have also come a long way in terms of prevention, intervention, research, and, most of all, promise for the future.

ADDRESSING CHILDREN AT RISK, IN HARM'S WAY

Child Abuse Prevention and Treatment Act

In response to public concern about the increased numbers of abused, neglected and exploited children in the United States, the Child Abuse

Prevention and Treatment Act (P.L. 100-294) became law in 1974. The act defined child abuse and neglect and provided for

> (1) the establishment of a National Center on Child Abuse and Neglect, (2) increasing public awareness on child maltreatment, detection and reporting, (3) assisting states and local communities in developing more effective mechanisms for delivery of services to families, (4) providing training and technical assistance to state and local communities in dealing with the problems of child abuse and neglect, and (5) supporting research into causal and preventative measures in child victimization.[1]

In order to qualify for federal funds, states were required to meet a number of criteria, including: a comprehensive definition of child abuse and neglect, specifying child abuse reporting procedures, investigation of reports, and administrative procedures. Also required were the confidentiality of records and the appointment of guardians for child victims involved in abuse or neglect judicial proceedings.

The National Center on Child Abuse and Neglect

The National Center on Child Abuse and Neglect (NCCAN) was initially established by P.L. 93-247 in 1974 and reauthorized in 1988 under P.L. 100-294 (the Child Abuse Prevention, Adoption, and Family Services Act of 1988). As the federal agency responsible for child abuse and neglect matters, the NCCAN administers grants to states and territories, local agencies, and organizations nationwide for research, service programs, and assistance with respect to the identification, treatment, and prevention of child mistreatment in any form.

In 1991, NCCAN funded continuing and new projects including:

- Research on the impact of child abuse and neglect in neighborhoods.
- A longitudinal study to examine the antecedents and implications of neglect in a high-risk group of adolescents.
- Improving the services to substance abusing adolescents, parents and families.
- A project reviewing and synthesizing research on child maltreatment and recommending research needs for the future.
- Providing community-based public information and education models to address the relationship between substance abuse and child mistreatment.

- The National Resource Center on Child Abuse and Neglect in Englewood, Colorado.
- The National Resource Center on Child Sexual Abuse in Huntsville, Alabama.

Since 1975, NCCAN has funded more than 750 projects geared toward the protection of children from abuse and neglect.

Child Abuse, Domestic Violence, Adoption and Family Services Act

The Child Abuse, Domestic Violence, Adoption and Family Services Act of 1992 (P.L. 100–295) retained the mandates of the 1988 P.L. 294, including the requirement that NCCAN establish a national data collection and analysis program on child abuse and neglect, and further required that NCCAN reestablish a program which

> shall collect, compile, analyze and make available State child abuse and neglect reporting information which, to the extent practical, is universal and case specific, and integrated with other case-based foster care and adoption data collected by the Secretary.[2]

The National Child Abuse and Neglect Data System

The National Child Abuse and Neglect Data System (NCANDS) was founded by NCCAN in response to the legislation enacted in 1988.[3] Through voluntary reporting, NCANDS collects national data on child abuse and neglect from child protective services. It was designed to provide a comprehensive national database on the volume and nature of child maltreatment in order to assist policy makers and child welfare professionals.

In order to achieve the goals, NCANDS consists of two components:

- *Working Papers* — Summary Data Component (SDC) is a compilation of State child abuse and neglect statistics, including data on victims, perpetrators, and investigators.
- *Detailed Case Data Component (DCDC)* is a compilation of case-level data to provide more detailed analysis of State data.

Runaway and Homeless Youth Act

The Runaway and Homeless Youth Act (RHYA) was enacted in 1978.[4] Its purpose was to provide assistance to local organizations for operating temporary shelters for runaways. The act recognizes the severity of the problem of runaway children (e.g., abuse, delinquency, prostitution, substance abuse) in making grants available for the establishment and maintenance of runaway houses by states, localities, and nonprofit groups.

The 1980 amendment of the RHYA included the following provisions:

- Recognition that many "runaways" are actually "throwaways" and thus were forced to leave home.
- Clarification of the requirement that shelter services be made available to the families of homeless and runaway children.
- Program authorities for the development of model programs designed to help habitual runaways.

Protection of Children
Against Sexual Exploitation Act

The Sexual Exploitation Act of 1978 was meant to bridge the gaps existing in federal statutes aimed at protecting children from sexual exploitation. The law hoped to halt the production and dissemination of child pornography by prohibiting the transportation of children across state lines for purposes of sexual exploitation. Furthermore, the legislation extended the federal government's authority to prosecute producers and distributors of child pornography.

Specifically,

> the law provides punishment for persons who use, employ, or persuade minors (defined as any persons under 16) to become involved in the production of visual or print materials that depict sexually explicit conduct if the producers know or have reasons to know that the materials will be transported in interstate or foreign commerce or mailed. Punishment is also specifically provided for parents, legal guardians, or other persons having custody or control of minors and who knowingly permit a minor to participate in the production of such material.[5]

The act further provided for stiff monetary penalties against sexual exploiters of children.

In 1983, the U.S. Supreme Court upheld the constitutionality of a New York law prohibiting the dissemination of child pornography regardless of whether or not the material is judged to be legally obscene.[6] The ruling essentially upheld laws in 20 other states.

In November of 1993, President Clinton directed the Justice Department to draft new and stronger laws against child pornography — an indication of the country's continuing efforts to fight the mistreatment and exploitation of children.

Federal Parental Kidnapping Prevention Act

The Federal Parental Kidnapping Prevention Act was enacted in 1980, empowering the Federal Parental Locator Service to search for abducted children and kidnapping parents.[5] The act's purpose was to locate parent and child in order to determine custody rights, enforce such, and to prosecute parental child snatchers. A further intention of the legislation was to deter parental kidnapping and make child custody decrees uniform across the nation. While the act does not make child snatching by a parent a federal crime, it does enable the FBI to join in the search for abducted children.

Missing Children Act

Enacted in 1982, the Missing Children Act allowed for parents, guardians, or next-of-kin of missing children "confirmation" of an entry into the FBI's National Crime Information Center.[8] Many local police departments have access to the computer, assisting them in identifying and locating missing children. The act further allows for FBI intervention after proof that the child has been kidnapped.

Child Abuse Accountability Act

The Child Abuse Accountability Act was introduced in the House of Representatives in November 1993 by Representative Patricia Schroeder of Colorado. The bill would make child abusers accountable for their actions by allowing victims of physical child abuse access to a convicted abuser's Federal pension.

The act permits

> the garnishment of an annuity under the Civil Service Retirement System or the Federal Employee's Retirement System, if necessary to satisfy a judgment against an annuitant for physically abusing a child.[9]

Child Protective Services

Child Protective Services (CPS) is the agency that is primarily responsible for evaluation, intervention, prevention, protection, and treatment of child abuse and neglect cases in all states, ensuring that the services are first and foremost responsive to the needs and welfare of abused and neglected children.[10] The main role of CPS is to "ensure that children are protected from harm and the integrity of the family maintained."[11]

Child Protective Services is responsible for determining whether abuse or neglect has taken place or is likely to, and whether or not the child's health or life is in jeopardy. "If CPS concludes that a child's safety is threatened, it will make all efforts to keep the family together and, at the same time, ensure the child's safety."[12] When the two cannot be accomplished in tandem, CPS, through juvenile or family courts, removes the child from the parents to be put in foster care.

While treatment of abusive or neglectful families is emphasized by CPS in the hope of reestablishing family stability and a protective environment for the child, sometimes abusers are prosecuted in criminal court (usually involving sexual abuse or severe physical abuse) "to ensure that the abuser accepts and follows through with treatment and to ensure that a criminal act is appropriately deterred."[13]

In every state today there are child abuse reporting laws that mandate or require the reporting of suspected child abuse or neglect.

HELPING VICTIMIZED WOMEN HELP THEMSELVES

Female victims of violence and exploitation have received some financial justice since the mid–1980s through the 1984 Victims of Crime Act. It established a Crime Victims Fund with monies from federal offenders (i.e., fines, penalties, forfeited bail bonds, literary royalties).[14] The fund is used as part of state victim and compensation programs.

In 1990, the Office for Victims of Crime (OVC), through which the monies are obtained and dispensed, provided a record amount of $125 million to victims programs, including more than 1,600 programs specializing in assistance for victims of sexual assault crimes and domestic violence.[15]

Since 1986, the OVC has shown a commitment to assisting sexual assault victims in every state by supporting services including rape crisis hotlines and improved training for criminal justice practitioners and victim assistance professionals with respect to sexual assaults against women. Additionally, reimbursement by state compensation programs for counseling and medical expenses for victims rose 38 percent between fiscal years 1986 and 1989.[16]

Most states have enacted victims rights laws to protect women victims and improve their treatment within the criminal justice system. In 1990, a Federal Victims Bill of Rights became law, further supporting victims of crime and violence and their rights.

Battered Women's Shelters

Begun in England in 1972 when the first refuge was opened, battered women's shelters are now a staple throughout the United States as a means to protect women and children from the immediate threat or aftermath of domestic violence, wife and child abuse. Women's shelters or safe homes in the nineties come in all shapes and sizes, with trained volunteers and paid staff whose duties include advocacy, counseling, medical attention, and referral services.

Rape Crisis Centers

The first rape crisis centers in the United States opened in the early 1970s. Today there are over 100 across the nation; their philosophy basically the same: offer support and assistance to rape victims that are often unavailable anywhere else.

Rape crisis centers are staffed by trained volunteers and offer services to victims such as counseling, information regarding medical and legal aid, and support during trials. Many staff members live in the community or are themselves rape victims. The most important contribution rape crisis centers may make is in "helping the thousands of rape victims cope with what happened to them, educating members of their communities about rape and how to fight it."[17]

Protection from Sexual Harassment

Females are legally protected from sexual harassment on the job through Title VII of the federal Civil Rights Act of 1964, which makes it a civil offense to discriminate in employment on the basis of sex.[18] The act authorized the establishment of the Equal Employment Opportunity Commission (EEOC) which set guidelines defining inappropriate behavior, including unwanted sexual advances, physical or verbal, requests for sexual favors, and other conduct deemed sexual harassment as seen through the courts when (1) an employee's submission is made an explicit or implicit condition of employment, (2) an employee's submission or refusal of is used as the basis for employment decisions affecting the eployee's status, or (3) such conduct interferes with an employee's job performance.

In 1986, the U.S. Supreme Court ruled that a female bank teller had been made to feel economically vulnerable, adding the notion of environmental abuse to the Civil Rights Act and sex discrimination.[19]

Stalking Laws

Only in the past few years have women gained a legal recourse against stalkers. In 1990, California became the first state to pass an antistalking law, making it a felony to repeatedly follow or harass someone with a "credible threat to do bodily harm."[20] Since then, at least 37 other states have enacted antistalking legislation. In most states, a first stalking offense is a misdemeanor, punishable by up to a year in jail and a $1,000 fine; with felony charges and stiffer penalties being imposed for repeat or subsequent stalking convictions. In 1993, a bill was introduced to Congress that would make stalking a federal offense, punishable by up to ten years in prison.

Social Services Trends

Women in the nineties have other services available including self-help groups across the country, various social services agencies, 24-hour hotlines, toll free numbers to local and national networks, clearinghouses, referral services, civic organizations, and powerful political groups such as the National Organization for Women.

Notes

Chapter 1. Child Abuse and Neglect

1. C. Henry Kempe et al., "The Battered Child Syndrome," *Journal of the American Medical Association* 181 (1962): 17–24.

2. Vincent J. Fontana, *The Maltreated Child: The Maltreatment Syndrome in Children*, 2nd ed. (Springfield, Ill.: Charles C. Thomas, 1971).

3. L. Whiting, "Defining Emotional Neglect," *Children Today* 5 (1976): 2–5.

4. David A. Mrazek and Patricia Mrazek, "Psychosexual Development Within the Family," in Patricia Mrazek and C. Henry Kempe, eds., *Sexually Abused Children and Their Families* (New York: Pergamon Press, 1981), pp. 17–30.

5. Public Law 100-294.

6. Public Law 98-457.

7. National Association of Public Child Welfare Administrators, *Guidelines for the Development of a Model System of Protective Services for Abused and Neglected Children and Their Families* (Washington, D.C.: The American Public Welfare Association, March 18, 1987), p. 5.

8. *Child Abuse and Neglect Data: AHA Fact Sheet #1* (Englewood, CO: American Humane Association, 1994), p. 1.

9. U.S. Department of Health and Human Services, *National Child Abuse and Neglect Data System: Working Paper #2—1991 Summary Data Component* (Washington, D.C.: Government Printing Office, 1993), pp. 25–27.

10. Cited in Ronald Barri Flowers, *Children and Criminality: The Child as Victim and Perpetrator* (Westport, Conn.: Greenwood Press, 1986), p. 28. *See also* David G. Gil, *Violence Against Children: Physical Child Abuse in the United States* (Cambridge: Harvard University, 1970).

11. Murray A. Straus, Richard J. Gelles, and Suzanne K. Steinmetz, *Behind Closed Doors: Violence in the American Family* (New York: Doubleday, 1980), p. 146.

12. Ronald B. Flowers, *Demographics and Criminality: The Characteristics of Crime in America* (Westport, Conn.: Greenwood Press, 1989), Karen McCurdy and Deborah Daro, *Current Trends in Child Abuse Reporting and Fatalities: The Results of the 1992 Annual Fifty State Survey* (Chicago, Ill.: National Committee for Prevention of Child Abuse, 1993), pp. 2–23.

13. Cited in Flowers, *Children and Criminality*, p. 58.

14. D. T. Lunde, "Hot Blood's Record Month: Our Murder Boom," *Psychology Today* 9 (1975): 35–42.

15. James Garbarino and Deborah Sherman, "High-Risk Neighborhoods and High-Risk Families: The Human Ecology of Maltreatment," *Child Development* 51 (1980): 188–198.

16. Gil, *Violence Against Children*, p. 117.

17. Alene Russell and Cynthia Trainor, *Trends in Child Abuse and Neglect: A National Perspective* (Denver: American Humane Association, 1984), pp. 92–98.

18. Peggy Smith and Marvin Bohnstedt, *Child Victimization Study Highlights* (Sacramento: Social Research Center of the American Justice Institute, 1981).

19. Richard J. Gelles, "Violence Toward Children in the United States," *American Journal of Orthopsychiatry* 48, 4 (1978): 580–592.

20. Brandt F. Steele and C. Pollock, "A Psychiatric Study of Parents Who Abuse Infants and Small Children," in Ray E. Helfer and C. Henry Kempe, eds., *The Battered Child* (Chicago: University of Chicago Press, 1968), pp. 89–133.

21. Blair Justice and Rita Justice, *The Abusing Family* (New York: Human Sciences Press, 1976), p. 90.

22. Gil, *Violence Against Children*, p. 109.

23. Justice and Justice, *The Abusing Family*, p. 90.

24. Flowers, *Demographics and Criminality*, p. 152.

25. *Ibid.*

26. F. J. Bishop, "Children at Risk," *Medical Journal of Australia* 1 (1971): 623.

27. Steele and Pollock, "A Psychiatric Study of Parents," p. 128.

28. Gil, *Violence Against Children*, p. 110.

29. R. J. Light, "Abused and Neglected Children in America: A Study of Alternative Policies," *Harvard Educational Review* 143 (1973): 574.

30. Ray E. Helfer, *The Diagnostic Process and Treatment Programs* (Washington, D.C.: Office of Child Development, 1975).

31. Justice and Justice, *The Abusing Family*, p. 27.

32. J. Milowe and R. Lourie, "The Child's Role in the Battered Child Syndrome," *Journal of Pediatrics* 65 (1964): 1079–1081.

33. U.S. Department of Health and Human Services, Administration on Children, Youth and Families, *Child Abuse and Neglect: A Shared Community Concern* (Washington, D.C.: National Center on Child Abuse and Neglect, March 1992), p. 6.

34. Gelles, "Violence Toward Children," pp. 585–590.

35. R. Galdston, "Observations on Children Who Have Been Physically Abused and Their Parents," *American Journal of Psychiatry* 122, 4 (1965): 440–443.

36. P. Resnick, "Child Murder by Parents: A Psychiatric Review of Filicide," *American Journal of Psychiatry* 126, 3 (1969): 325–334.

37. Justice and Justice, *The Abusing Family*, p. 96.

38. Gil, *Violence Against Children*, p. 109.

39. *Child Abuse and Neglect: A Shared Concern*, p. 6.

40. Straus, Gelles, and Steinmetz, *Behind Closed Doors*, p. 26.

41. *Child Abuse and Neglect: A Shared Concern*, p. 6.

42. Flowers, *Children and Criminality*, pp. 66–67.

43. M. H. Lystad, "Violence at Home: A Review of the Literature," *American Journal of Orthopsychiatry* 45 (1975): 334.

44. *Child Abuse and Neglect: A Shared Concern*, p. 6.

45. E. Bennie and A. Sclare, "The Battered Child Syndrome," *American Journal of Psychiatry* 125, 7 (1969): 975–979.

46. Gil, *Violence Against Children*, p. 111.

47. Michael J. Martin and James Walters, "Familial Correlates of Selected Types of Child Abuse and Neglect," *Journal of Marriage and the Family* 5 (1982): 267–276.

48. D. H. Behling, "History of Alcohol Abuse in Child Abuse Cases Reported at Naval Regional Medical Center" (Paper presented at the National Child Abuse Forum, Long Beach, California, June 1971).

49. Brandt F. Steele, "Violence Within the Family," in Ray E. Helfer and C. Henry Kempe, eds., *Child Abuse and Neglect: The Family and the Community* (Cambridge: Ballinger, 1976), p. 12.

50. "Preventing Sexual Abuse of Children," *Parade Magazine* (May 26, 1985): 16.

51. Fontana, *The Maltreated Child*.

52. Christopher Ounsted, Rhonda Oppenheimer, and Janet Lindsay, "The Psychopathology and Psychotherapy of the Families, Aspects Bounding Failure," in A. Franklin, ed., *Concerning Child Abuse* (London: Churchill Livingston, 1975).

53. Cited in Flowers, *Children and Criminality*, pp. 101–, *See also* Norman A. Polansky, Christine De Saix, and Shlomo A. Sharlin, *Child Neglect: Understanding and Reaching the Parents* (New York: Child Welfare League of America, 1972).

54. Martin R. Haskell and Lewis Yablonsky, *Crime and Delinquency*, 2nd ed. (Chicago: Rand McNally, 1974).

55. Steele, "Violence Within the Family."

56. H. E. Simmons, *Protective Services for Children*, 2nd ed. (Sacramento: Citadel Press, 1970).

57. D. E. Adams, H. A. Ishizuka, and K. S. Ishizuka, *The Child Abuse Delinquent: An Exploratory/Descriptive Study* (Unpublished MSW thesis, University of South Carolina, South Carolina, 1977).

58. Jeanne Cyriaque, "The Chronic Serious Offender: How Illinois Juveniles 'Match Up'," Illinois Department of Corrections, *Illinois* (February 1982): 4–5.

59. See, for example, E. Y. Deykin, "Life Functioning in Families of Delinquent Boys: An Assessment Model," *Social Services Review* 46, 1 (1971): 90–91; M. F. Shore, "Psychological Theories of the Causes of Antisocial Behavior," *Crime and Delinquency* 17, 4 (1971): 456–458.

60. Flowers, *Children and Criminality*, pp. 3–12.

61. *Ibid.*, p. 5.

62. Mason P. Thomas, Jr., "Child Abuse and Neglect, Part I: Historical Overview, Legal Matrix and Social Perspectives," *North Carolina Law Review* 50 (1972): 293–349.

63. Flowers, *Children and Criminality*, pp. 3–12.

64. *Ibid.*, p. 43.

65. E. J. Merrill, "Physical Abuse of Children: An Agency Study," in V. De Francis, ed., *Protecting the Battered Child* (Denver: American Humane Association, 1962).

66. Flowers, *Children and Criminality*, p. 44.

67. M. L. Blumberg, "Psychopathology of the Abusing Parent," *American Journal of Psychotherapy* 28 (1974): 21–29.

68. Flowers, *Children and Criminality*, pp. 97–101.

69. *Ibid.*

70. *Ibid.*; Ann Buchanan and J. E. Oliver, "Abuse and Neglect as a Cause of Mental Retardation: A Study of 140 Children Admitted to Subnormality Hospitals in Wiltshire," in Gertrude J. Williams and John Money, eds., *Traumatic Abuse and Neglect of Children at Home* (Baltimore, Md.: Johns Hopkins University Press, 1980), pp. 311–312.

71. Flowers, *Children and Criminality*, p. 98.

72. J. Roberts, M. M. Lynch, and P. Duff, "Abused Children and Their Siblings—A Teacher's View," *Therapeutic Education* 6 (1978): 25–31.

Chapter 2. Domestic Violence

1. J. Boudouries, "Homicide and the Family," *Journal of Marriage and the Family* 33, 4 (1971).

2. Richard J. Gelles, *The Violent Home* (Beverly Hills: Sage Publications, 1987); Del Martin, *Battered Wives* (San Francisco: Glide Publications, 1976).

3. Martin, *Battered Wives*; Ronald B. Flowers, *Demographics and Criminality: The Characteristics of Crime in America* (Westport, Conn.: Greenwood Press, 1989), pp. 151–158.

4. Flowers, *Demographics and Criminality*; U.S. Federal Bureau of Investigation, *Crime in the United States: Uniform Crime Reports 1992* (Washington, D.C.: Government Printing Office, 1993), p. 151.

5. U.S. Federal Bureau of Investigation, *Crime in the United States: Uniform Crime Reports 1992* (Washington, D.C.: Government Printing Office, 1993), p. 221.

6. *Ibid.*, p. 17.

7. U.S. Department of Justice, Bureau of Justice Statistics Special Report, *Family Violence* (Washington, D.C.: Government Printing Office, 1984), p. 1; U.S. Department of Justice, Bureau of Justice Statistics, *Criminal Victimization in the United States, 1991: A National Crime Victimization Survey Report* (Washington, D.C.: Government Printing Office, 1992).

8. *Family Violence*, p. 3.

9. U.S. Department of Justice, Bureau of Justice Statistics, *Female Victims of Violent Crime* (Washington, D.C.: Government Printing Office, 1991), p. 1.

10. *Criminal Victimization*, 1991, p. 65.

11. *Family Violence*, pp. 1–4.

12. *Uniform Crime Reports 1992*, p. 13.

13. Cited in Glenn Collins, "The Violent Child: Some Patterns Emerge," *New York Times* (September 27, 1982), B3.

14. L. Bender and F. J. Curran, "Children and Adolescents Who Kill," *Journal of Criminal Psychopathology* 1, 4 (1940): 297.

15. B. M. Cormier et al., "Adolescents Who Kill a Member of the Family," in John M. Eekelaar and Sanford N. Katz, eds., *Family Violence: An International and Interdisciplinary Study* (Toronto: Butterworths, 1978), p. 468.

16. D. Sargeant, "Children Who Kill—A Family Conspiracy?" in J. Howells, ed., *Theory and Practice of Family Psychiatry* (New York: Brunner-Magel, 1971).

17. W. M. Easson and R. M. Steinhilber, "Murderous Aggression by Children and Adolescents," *Archives of General Psychiatry* 4 (1961): 1–9.

18. Cited in Jeanne Thornton, "Family Violence Emerges from the Shadows," *U.S. News & World Report* (January 23, 1984), p. 66.

19. Gelles, *The Violent Home*.

20. R. Chester and J. Streather, "Cruelty in English Divorce: Some Empirical Findings," *Journal of Marriage and the Family* 34, 4 (1972): 706–710.

21. Flowers, *Demographics and Criminality*, p. 154.

22. Cited in Frances Patai, "Pornography and Women Battering: Dynamic Similarities," in Maria Roy, ed., *The Abusive Partner: An Analysis of Domestic Battering* (New York: Van Nostrand Reinhold, 1982); Murray Straus, "Wife-Beating: How Common and Why?" *Victimology* 2 (1978): 443–458.

23. R. Whitehurst, "Violently Jealous Husbands," *Sexual Behavior* 1, 4 (1971): 32–38, 40–41.

24. Robert Langley and Richard C. Levy, *Wife Beating: The Silent Crisis* (New York: E. P. Dutton, 1977).

25. Suzanne K. Steinmetz, "The Battered Husband Syndrome," *Victimology* 2 (1978): 507.

26. *Ibid.*

27. D. A. Gaquin, "Spouse Abuse: Data from the National Crime Survey," *Victimology* 2 (1977–1978): 632–643.

28. G. Levinger, "Sources of Marital Dissatisfaction Among Applicants for Divorce," *American Journal of Orthopsychiatry* 36, 5 (1966): 803–807.

29. Linda S. King, "Responding to Spouse Abuse: The Mental Health Profession," *In Response to Family Violence* 4, 5 (1981): 7–9.

30. Ronald B. Flowers, *Children and Criminality: The Child as Victim and Perpetrator* (Westport, Conn.: Greenwood Press, 1986), p. 52.

31. Suzanne K. Steinmetz, "The Use of Force for Resolving Family Conflicts: The Training Ground for Abuse," *Family Coordinator* 26 (1977): 19.

32. Murray A. Straus, Richard J. Gelles, and Suzanne K. Steinmetz, *Behind Closed Doors: Violence in the American Family* (Garden City, NY: Doubleday/Anchor, 1979).

33. *Ibid.*

34. Cited in "Parental Abuse," *USA Today* (March 18, 1983), p. 1D.

35. Karen S. Peterson, "The Nightmare of a Battered Parent," *USA Today* (March 18, 1983), p. A6.

36. Straus, Gelles, and Steinmetz, *Behind Closed Doors*.

37. Carol A. Warren, "Parent Batterers: Adolescent Violence and the Family," Pacific Sociological Association, Anaheim, Calif., April 1978, pp. 3–5.

38. P. Hellsten and O. Katila, "Murder and Other Homicide by Children Under 15 in Finland," *Psychiatric Quarterly Supplement* 39, 1 (1965): 54–74.

39. Cited in Cliff Yudell, "I'm Afraid of My Own Children," *Reader's Digest* (August 1983), p. 79.

40. Rudolf Dreikurs and Vicki Saltz, *Children: The Challenge* (New York: Hawthorne Books, 1964), p. 201.

41. M. A. Freeman, *Violence in the Home* (Farnborough, England: Saxon House, 1979), p. 239.

42. W. Goode, "Violence Among Intimates," *Crimes and Violence* 13 (1969): 941–977.

43. S. Zalba, "The Abused Child: A Survey of the Problem," *Social Work* 11, 4 (1966): 3–16.

44. See, for example, L. Eron, "Symposium: The Application of Role and Learning Theories to the Study of the Development of Aggression in Children," *Proceedings of the Rip Van Winkle Clinic* 10 (1959): 3–61.

45. F. Ilfeld, Jr., "Environmental Theories of Violence," in D. Danield, M.

Gilula, and F. Ochberg, eds., *Violence and the Struggle for Existence* (Boston: Little, Brown, 1970).

46. Murray A. Straus, "A General System Theory Approach to a Theory of Violence Between Family Members," *Social Science Information* 12, 3 (1973): 101–125.

47. David G. Gil, *Violence Against Children: Physical Child Abuse in the United States* (Cambridge: Harvard University Press, 1970).

48. D. Abrahamsen, *Our Violent Society* (New York: Funk and Wagnalls, 1970).

49. Flowers, *Demographics and Criminality*, p. 159.

50. R. Graves, *Greek Myths* (New York: Penguin, 1962).

51. *Oliver Twist* and *North and South* are two such examples. See also F. Basch, *Relative Creatures* (London: Allen Lane, 1974).

52. Freeman, *Violence in the Home*, p. 6.

53. Richard J. Gelles and Murray A. Straus, "Violence in the American Family," *Journal of Social Issues* 35, 2 (1979): 15–39.

Chapter 3. Runaways and Throwaways

1. Carolyn Males and Julie Raskin, "The Children Nobody Wants," *Reader's Digest* (January 1984), pp. 63–66; Michael Satchell, "Kids for Sale," *Parade Magazine* (July 20, 1986), p. 4.

2. Cited in Patricia Hersch, "Coming of Age on City Streets," *Psychology Today* (January 1988), p. 34.

3. *Ibid.*, p. 31.

4. U.S. Federal Bureau of Investigation, *Crime in the United States: Uniform Crime Reports 1992* (Washington, D.C.: Government Printing Office, 1993), p. 227.

5. *Ibid.*, pp. 229, 231.

6. J. A. Bechtel, "Statement Before the Senate Subcommittee to Investigate Juvenile Delinquency," Washington, D.C., January 14, 1973.

7. Ronald B. Flowers, *Demographics and Criminality: The Characteristics of Crime in America* (Westport, Conn.: Greenwood Press, 1989), pp. 90–97.

8. James A. Hildebrand, "Why Runaways Leave Home," *Police Science* 54 (1963): 211–216.

9. Louise Homer, "Criminality-Based Resource for Runaway Girls," *Social Casework* 10 (1973): 474.

10. Robert Shellow, "Suburban Runaways of the 1960s," *Monographs of the Society for Research in Child Development* 32 (1967): 17.

11. Cited in Hersch, "Coming of Age," p. 31.

12. Hildebrand, "Why Runaways Leave Home," pp. 211–216.

13. C. J. English, "Leaving Home: A Typology of Runaways," *Society* 10 (1973): 22–24.

14. Ronald B. Flowers, *Children and Criminality: The Child as Victim and Perpetrator* (Westport, Conn.: Greenwood Press, 1986), p. 133.

15. Mary Barbera-Hogan, "Teen Sex for Sale," *Teen* 31 (January 1987), p. 22.

16. Cited in Males and Raskin, "The Children Nobody Wants," p. 63.

17. Cited in "'Runaways', 'Throwaways,' 'Bag Kids'—An Army of Drifter Teens," *U.S. News & World Report* (March 11, 1985), p. 53.

18. Males and Raskin, "The Children Nobody Wants," p. 63.

19. K. C. Brown as quoted in *ibid.*

20. "'Rat Pack' Youth: Teenage Rebels in Suburbia," *U.S. News & World Report* (March 11, 1985), p. 51.

21. *Ibid.*, p. 54.

22. June Bucy as quoted in Dotson Rader, "I Want to Die So I Won't Hurt No More," *Parade Magazine* (August 18, 1985), p. 4.

23. Cited in Hersch, "Coming of Age," pp. 31–32.

24. *Ibid.*, p. 32.

25. Cited in John Zaccaro, Jr., "Children of the Night," *Woman's Day* (March 29, 1988), p. 138.

26. *Ibid.*, p. 137.

27. Hersch, "Coming of Age," p. 35.

28. *Ibid.*, p. 34.

29. Cited in Zaccaro, Jr., "Children of the Night," p. 137.

30. Hersch, "Coming of Age," p. 37.

31. The Runaway and Homeless Youth Act, 42 U.S.C. §5701–5702 Supp. II (1978).

32. P.L. No. 96-509; 42 U.S.C. §5711 Supp. (1981).

Chapter 4. Missing and Abducted Children

1. Sally Abrahams, "Parental Kidnapping Is the Agony of the '80s," *USA Today* (July 16, 1983), p. 4D; Gary Turbak, "The City That Finds Its Missing Children," *Reader's Digest* (April 1984), p. 135.

2. Cited in Abrahams, "Parental Kidnapping," p. 40.

3. Ronald B. Flowers, *Children and Criminality: The Child as Victim and Perpetrator* (Westport, Conn.: Greenwood Press, 1986), p. 86.

4. "Vaccines for the Epidemic of Missing Children," *Psychology Today* 17, 5 (1983): 76.

5. Flowers, *Children and Criminality*, pp. 86–87; J. Densen-Gerber and S. F. Hutchinson, "Medical-Legal and Societal Problems Involving Children—Child Prostitution, Child Pornography and Drug-Related Abuse: Recommended Legislation," in Selwyn M. Smith, ed., *The Maltreatment of Children* (Baltimore, Md.: University Park Press, 1978), pp. 317–350.

6. *Ibid.*

7. 18 U.S.C. §1073 (1980).

8. 128 Cong. Rec. 8, 566 (1982).

9. Flowers, *Children and Criminality*, pp. 191–192.

Chapter 5. The Sexual Abuse and Exploitation of Children

1. See, for example, Gerald M. Caplan, "Sexual Exploitation of Children: The Conspiracy of Silence," *Police Magazine* 5, 1 (1982): 46–51; David Finkelhor, *Sexually Victimized Children* (New York: Free Press, 1979).

2. Leroy C. Schultz, "The Child as a Sex Victim: Socio-Legal Perspectives," in Israel Drapkin and Emilo Viano, eds., *Victimology: A New Focus*, Vol. 5 (Toronto: D. C. Heath, 1975), p. 178.

3. Ronald B. Flowers, *Children and Criminality: The Child as Victim and Perpetrator* (Westport, Conn.: Greenwood Press, 1986), p. 75.

4. Reay Tannahill, *Sex in History* (New York: Stein and Day, 1980), p. 370.

5. Pamela D. Mayhall and Katherine E. Norgard, *Child Abuse and Neglect: Sharing Responsibility* (Toronto: John Wiley and Sons, 1983), p. 11.

6. Tannahill, *Sex in History*, p. 374.

7. *Ibid.*, p. 372.

8. Flowers, *Children and Criminality*, p. 7.

9. Jeanne M. Giovannoni and Rosina M. Becerra, *Defining Child Abuse* (New York: Free Press, 1979), p. 242.

10. Public Law 100-294.

11. *Child Abuse and Neglect Reporting and Investigation: Policy Guidelines for Decision-Making* (Washington, D.C.: American Bar Association, 1987), p. 7.

12. *Protecting the Child Victim of Sex Crimes* (Denver: American Humane Association, 1966), p. 2.

13. *Child Victims of Incest* (Denver: American Humane Association, 1968), p. 5.

14. *Sexual Abuse of Children: Implications for Casework* (Denver: American Humane Association, 1967), p. 10.

15. Schultz, "The Child as a Sex Victim," p. 177.

16. Karen McCurdy and Deborah Daro, *Current Trends in Child Abuse Reporting and Fatalities: The Results of the 1992 Annual Fifty State Survey* (Chicago, Ill.: National Committee for Prevention of Child Abuse, 1993), p. 10.

17. David Finkelhor, "How Widespread Is Child Sexual Abuse?" *Perspectives on Child Maltreatment in the Mid '80s* (Washington, D.C.: National Center on Child Abuse and Neglect Information, 1984).

18. U.S. Department of Health and Human Services, *National Child Abuse and Neglect Data System: Working Paper 2—1991 Summary Data Component* (Washington, D.C.: National Center on Child Abuse and Neglect, 1993), p. 29.

19. *American Association for Protecting Children, Highlights of Official Child Neglect and Abuse Reporting 1984* (Denver: American Humane Association, 1985).

20. Cited in Mayhall and Norgard, *Child Abuse and Neglect*, p. 100.

21. Peggy Smith and Marvin Bohnstedt, *Child Victimization Study Highlights* (Sacramento: Social Research Center of the American Justice Institute, 1981), p. 2.

22. B. G. Braun, "The Role of the Family in the Development of Multiple Personality," *International Journal of Family Psychiatry* 5, 4 (1984): 303–313.

23. Phil M. Coons, "Psychiatric Problems Associated with Child Abuse: A Review," in J. J. Jacobsen, *Psychiatric Sequelae of Child Abuse* (Springfield, Ill.: Charles C. Thomas, 1986); Diane E. Russell, *Intrafamilial Child Sexual Abuse: A San Francisco Survey* (Berkeley, Calif.: Wright Institute, 1983).

24. National Center on Child Abuse and Neglect, *Research Symposium on Child Sexual Abuse* (Washington, D.C.: Department of Health and Human Services, 1988), pp. 3–4.

25. *Ibid.*, p. 4; B. G. Braun, "The Transgenerational Incidence of Dissociation and Multiple Personality Disorder: A Preliminary Report," in R. P. Kluft, ed., *Childhood Antecedents of Multiple Personality* (Washington, D.C.: American Psychiatric Press, 1985).

26. P. H. Gebhard, J. H. Gagnon, W. B. Pomeroy, and C. V. Christenson, *Sex Offenders* (New York: Harper & Row, 1965); Harold J. Vetter and Ira J. Silverman, *The Nature of Crime* (Philadelphia: W. B. Saunders, 1978).

27. D. Abrahamsen, *The Psychology of Crime* (New York: Columbia University Press, 1960); B. Karpman, *The Sex Offender and His Offenses* (New York: Julian Press, 1962).

28. *Ibid.*

29. *Ibid.*; Flowers, *Children and Criminality*, pp. 76–83.

30. David Finkelhor, Sharon Araji, Larry Baron, Angela Browne, Stephanie Peters, and Gail Wyatt, *A Sourcebook on Child Sexual Abuse* (Beverly Hills: Sage Publications, 1986), p. 201.

31. John E. Henderson, Diana J. English, and Ward R. MacKenzie, "Family Centered Casework Practice with Sexually Aggressive Children," *Journal of Social Work and Human Sexuality* 7, 2 (1988).

32. The National Adolescent Perpetrator Network, "Preliminary Report from the National Task Force on Juvenile Sexual Offending 1988," *Juvenile & Family Court Journal* 39, 2 (1988): 5.

33. Flowers, *Children and Criminality*, p. 96.

34. *Ibid.*, p. 97.

35. *Ibid.*

36. Mimi H. Silbert, "Delancey Street Study: Prostitution and Sexual Assault," Summary of results, San Francisco, Delancey Street Foundation, 1982, p. 3; Jeanne Cyriaque, "The Chronic Serious Offender: How Illinois Juveniles 'Match Up'," Illinois Department of Corrections, *Illinois* (February 1982), pp. 4–5.

Chapter 6. Incest and Child Molestation

1. Patricia Beezley Mrazek, "Definition and Recognition of Child Sexual Abuse: Historical and Cultural Perspectives," in Patricia Beezley Mrazek and C. Henry Kempe, eds., *Sexually Abused Children and Their Families* (New York: Pergamon Press, 1981), p. 7.

2. M. Sidler, *On the Universality of the Incest Taboo* (Stuttgart: Enke, 1971).

3. H. D. Jubainville, *La Familie Celtique: Etude de Droit Compare* (Paris: Librarie Emile Bouillon, 1905); Edward Westermarch, *The History of Human Marriage*, 5th ed. (New York: Macmillan, 1921).

4. Theodore Schroeder, "Incest in Mormanism," *American Journal of Urology and Sexology* 11 (1915): 409–416.

5. Cited in Jean Renvoize, *Incest: A Family Pattern* (London: Routledge & Kegan Paul, 1982), p. 51.

6. Quoted in Marshall D. Schechter and Leo Roberge, "Sexual Exploitation," in Ray E. Helfer and C. Henry Kempe, eds., *Child Abuse and Neglect: The Family and the Community* (Cambridge, Mass.: Ballinger Publishing Co., 1976), p. 129.

7. Ronald B. Flowers, *Women and Criminality: The Woman as Victim, Offender, and Practitioner* (Westport, Conn.: Greenwood Press, 1987), pp. 61–62.

8. Cited in Carol L. Mithers, "Incest: The Crime That's All in the Family," *Mademoiselle* 96 (June 1984), p. 127.

9. Cited in Kathy McCoy, "Incest: The Most Painful Family Problem," *Seventeen* 43 (June 1984), p. 18.

10. Cited in Anita Manning, "Victims Must Face the Hurt," *USA Today* (January 10, 1984), p. 5D.

11. Judie Howard, "Incest: Victims Speak Out," *Teen* (July 1985), p. 30.

12. Cited in *ibid.*, p. 31.

13. *Ibid.*

14. Flowers, *Women and Criminality*, p. 61.

15. H. Stoenner, *Child Sexual Abuse Seen Growing in the United States* (Denver: American Humane Association, 1972).

16. S. Kirson Weinberg, *Incest Behavior* (New York: Citadel Press, 1966), pp. 34–40.

17. Quoted in Howard, "Incest: Victims Speak Out," p. 31. See also Susan Forward and C. Buck, *Betrayal of Innocence: Incest and Its Devastation* (Los Angeles: J. P. Tarcher, Inc., 1978).

18. Adele Mayer, *Incest: A Treatment Manual for Therapy with Victims, Spouses, and Offenders* (Holmes Beach, Fla.: Learning Publications, 1983), p. 22.

19. Cited in Heidi Vanderbilt, "Incest: A Chilling Report," *Lears* (February 1992), pp. 60–62.

20. Herbert L. Packer, *The Limits of the Criminal Sanction* (Stanford, Calif.: Stanford University Press, 1968), pp. 296–316.

21. Cited in Vanderbilt, "Incest: A Chilling Report," p. 62.

22. *Ibid.*, pp. 62–63.

23. *Ibid.*

24. Weinberg, *Incest Behavior.*

25. R. Medlicott, "Parent-Child Incest," *Australian Journal of Psychiatry* 1 (1967): 180.

26. R. Lidz and T. Lidz, "Homosexual Tendencies in Mothers of Schizophrenic Women," *Journal of Nervous Mental Disorders* 149 (1969): 229.

27. See, for example, P. Machotka, F. S. Pittman, and K. Flomenhaft, "Incest as a Family Affair," *Family Process* 6 (1967): 98.

28. See, for example, A. C. Kinsey, W. B. Pomeroy, and C. E. Martin, *Sexual Behavior in the Human Male* (Philadelphia: W. B. Saunders, 1948).

29. Quoted in Vanderbilt, "Incest: A Chilling Report," p. 63.

30. Forward and Buck, *Betrayal of Innocence.*

31. Jean Goodwinn, Lawrence Cormier, and John Owen, "Grandfather-Granddaughter Incest: A Trigenerational View," *Child Abuse and Neglect* 7 (1983): 163–170.

32. *Ibid.*

33. K. C. Meiselman, *Incest: A Psychological Study of Causes and Effects with Treatment Recommendations* (San Francisco: Jossey-Bass, 1978).

34. L. Bender and A. Blau, "The Reactions of Children to Sexual Problems with Adults," *American Journal of Orthopsychiatry* 8, 4 (1937): 500–518.

35. Mayer, *Incest: A Treatment Manual,* p. 13.

36. Schechter and Roberge, "Sexual Exploitation," p. 131.

37. David Finkelhor, *Sexually Victimized Children* (New York: Free Press, 1979); L. Burton, *Vulnerable Children* (New York: Schocken Books, 1968).

38. Susan Forward as quoted in Howard, "Incest: Victims Speak Out," p. 80.

39. Flowers, *Women and Criminality,* pp. 62–63; Vanderbilt, "Incest: A Chilling Report," p. 54.

40. Joel Greenberg, "Incest Out of Hiding," *Science News* 117, 4 (1980): 218–220; "Incest, Teen Prostitution Linked," *USA Today* (January 10, 1984), p. 5D.

41. Flowers, *Women and Criminality;* Ronald B. Flowers, *Children and Criminality: The Child as Victim and Perpetrator* (Westport, Conn.: Greenwood Press, 1986), pp. 3–12.

42. Quoted in Mithers, "Incest: The Crime," p. 216.

43. Sandy Rovner, "Healthtalk: Facing the Aftermath of Incest," *Washington Post* (January 6, 1984), p. D5.

44. Vanderbilt, "Incest: A Chilling Report," p. 74.

45. Quoted in Howard, "Incest: Victims Speak Out," p. 32.

Chapter 7. Statutory Rape and Other Sex Crimes

1. Caroline Wolf Harlow, *Female Victims of Violent Crime* (Washington, D.C.: U.S. Department of Justice), p. 9.

2. Pamela Hersch, "Coming of Age on City Streets," *Psychology Today* (January 1988), p. 35.

3. H. Gagnon, "Female Child Victims of Sex Offenses," *Social Problems* 13 (1965): 191.

4. L. Radzinowicz, *Sexual Offenses* (New York: Macmillan, 1957), p. 83.

5. P. H. Gebhard, *Sex Offenders: An Analysis of Types* (New York: Bantam, 1969), p. 747.

6. J. Weiss, "A Study of Girl Sex Victims," *Psychiatric Quarterly* 29 (1955): 1.

7. Israel Drapkin and Emilo Viano, *Victimology: A New Focus*, Vol. V (Toronto: D. C. Heath, 1975), pp. 177–178.

8. Gagnon, "Female Child Victims."

9. *Ibid.*, p. 183.

10. Drapkin and Viano, *Victimology: A New Focus*.

11. P. H. Gebhard, J. H. Gagnon, W. B. Pomeroy, and C. V. Christenson, *Sex Offenders* (New York: Harper and Row, 1965).

12. E. P. Sarafino, "An Estimate of the Nationwide Incidence of Sexual Offenses Against Children," *Child Welfare* 58, 2 (1979): 127–134.

13. Susan Brownmiller, *Against Our Will: Men, Women, and Rape* (New York: Simon and Schuster, 1975), pp. 278–279.

14. J. M. Reinhardt, *Sex Perversions and Sex Crimes* (Springfield, Ill.: Charles C. Thomas, 1957).

15. Albert K. Cohen, "The Sociology of the Deviant Act: Aromie Theory and Beyond," *American Sociological Review* 2 (1965): 5–14.

16. Johan W. Mohr, R. Edward Turner, and M. B. Jerry, *Pedophilia and Exhibitionism* (Toronto: University of Toronto Press, 1964).

17. J. M. MacDonald, *Rape Offenders and Their Victims* (Springfield, Ill.: Charles C. Thomas, 1971); J. L. Mathis, *Clear Thinking About Sexual Deviations* (Chicago: Nelson-Hall, 1972).

18. Ronald B. Flowers, *Children and Criminality: The Child as Victim and Perpetrator* (Westport, Conn.: Greenwood Press, 1986), p. 76.

19. *Ibid.*, p. 77.

20. Mathis, *Clear Thinking About Sexual Deviations*, p. 37.

21. Gebhard, Gagnon, Pomeroy, and Christenson, *Sex Offenders*.

22. J. C. Coleman, *Abnormal Psychology and Modern Life* (Glenview, Ill.: Scott, Foresman and Co., 1972).

23. Flowers, *Children and Criminality*, p. 80.

24. Quoted in Harold J. Vetter and Ira J. Silverman, *The Nature of Crime* (Philadelphia: W. B. Saunders Co., 1978), p. 115.

25. Flowers, *Children and Criminality*, p. 80.

26. Robert H. Morneau and Robert R. Rockwell, *Sex, Motivation and the Criminal Offender* (Springfield, Ill.: Charles C. Thomas, 1980), p. 73.

27. Gebhard, Gagnon, Pomeroy, and Christenson, *Sex Offenders*.

28. Richard von Krafft-Ebing, *Psychopathia Sexualis* (New York: Stein & Day, 1965).

29. Morneau and Rockwell, *Sex, Motivation and the Criminal Offender*, pp. 87–89.

30. *Ibid.*

31. Reinhardt, *Sex Perversions and Sex Crimes*; Clifford Allen, *The Sexual Perversions and Abnormalities* (London: Oxford University Press, 1949).

32. Morneau and Rockwell, *Sex, Motivation and the Criminal Offender*, p. 142.

33. Magnus Hirschfield, *Sexual Anomalies: The Origins, Nature and Treatment of Sexual Disorders* (New York: Emerson, 1956).

34. Morneau and Rockwell, *Sex, Motivation and the Criminal Offender*, p. 145.

35. David Finkelhor, Linda Meyer Williams, Nanci Burns, and Michael Kalinowski, *Sexual Abuse in Day Care: A National Study Executive Summary* (Durham: University of New Hampshire, 1988).

36. National Center on Child Abuse and Neglect *Research Symposium on Child Sexual Abuse: May 17–19, 1988* (Washington, D.C.: U.S. Department of Health and Human Services, 1988), p. 3.

Chapter 8. The Prostitution of Children

1. Ronald B. Flowers, *Children and Criminality: The Child as Victim and Perpetrator* (Westport, Conn.: Greenwood Press, 1986), p. 7.

2. Henry Benjamin and R. E. L. Masters, *Prostitution and Morality* (New York: Julian Press, 1964), p. 161.

3. *Ibid.*, p. 162.

4. Flowers, *Children and Criminality*, p. 7; Reay Tannahill, *Sex in History* (New York: Stein and Day, 1980), p. 374.

5. Judianne Densen-Gerber and S. F. Hutchinson, "Medical-Legal and Societal Problems Involving Children, Child Prostitution, Child Pornography and Drug-Related Abuse; Recommended Legislation," in Selwyn M. Smith, ed., *The Maltreatment of Children* (Baltimore, Md.: University Park Press, 1978), p. 318.

6. *Ibid.*

7. Sam Meddis, "Teen Prostitution Rising, Study Says," *USA Today* (April 23, 1984), p. 3A.

8. Robin Lloyd, *For Money or Love: Boy Prostitution in America* (New York: Ballantine, 1976), pp. 58–72.

9. Flowers, *Children and Criminality*, p. 82.

10. Mimi H. Silbert, *Sexual Assault of Prostitutes: Phase One* (Washington, D.C.: National Institute of Mental Health, 1980), p. 15.

11. Ellen Hale, "Center Studies Causes of Juvenile Prostitution," *Gannett News Service* (May 21, 1981).

12. Jennifer James, *Entrance into Juvenile Prostitution* (Washington, D.C.: National Institute of Mental Health, 1980), p. 18.

13. Paul H. Hahn, *The Juvenile Offender and the Law*, 3rd ed. (Cincinnati: Anderson, 1984), p. 125.

14. R. Barri Flowers, *The Adolescent Criminal: An Examination of Today's Juvenile Offender* (Jefferson, N.C.: McFarland and Co., Inc., 1990), pp. 54–64.

15. U.S. Federal Bureau of Investigation, *Crime in the United States: Uniform Crime Reports 1992* (Washington, D.C.: Government Printing Office, 1993), pp. 229, 231.

16. James, *Entrance into Juvenile Prostitution*, p. 17.

17. *Uniform Crime Reports*, p. 231.

18. James, *Entrance into Juvenile Prostitution*, p. 29; D. Kelly Weisberg, *Children of the Night: A Study of Adolescent Prostitution* (Lexington, Mass.: Lexington Books, 1985), p. 94.

19. Sparky Harlan, Luanne L. Rodgers, and Brian Slattery, *Male and Female Adolescent Prostitution: Huckleberry House Sexual Minority Youth Services Project* (Washington, D.C.: Department of Health and Human Services, 1981), p. 7.

20. Enablers, *Juvenile Prostitution in Minnesota: The Report of a Research Project* (St. Paul: The Enablers, 1978), p. 18.

21. James, *Entrance into Juvenile Prostitution*, p. 19.

22. *Ibid.*, p. 19; Enablers, *Juvenile Prostitution*, p. 18.

23. Silbert, *Sexual Assault*, p. 10.

24. Maura G. Crowley, "Female Runaway Behavior and Its Relationship to Prostitution," Masters thesis, Sam Houston State University, Institute of Contemporary Corrections and Behavioral Sciences, 1977, p. 63.

25. Harlan, Rodgers, and Slattery, *Male and Female Adolescent Prostitution*, p. 14.

26. *Ibid.*, p. 21.

27. Mimi H. Silbert, "Delancey Street Study: Prostitution and Sexual Assault," Summary of results (San Francisco: Delancey Street Foundation, 1982), p. 3.

28. Flowers, *The Adolescent Criminal*, p. 57; Crowley, "Female Runaway Behavior," p. 63.

29. Flowers, *The Adolescent Criminal*, p. 57.

30. *Ibid.*; James, *Entrance into Juvenile Prostitution*, p. 68; Dorothy H. Bracey, *"Baby-Pros": Preliminary Profiles of Juvenile Prostitutes* (New York: John Jay Press, 1979), p. 23.

31. Flowers, *The Adolescent Criminal*, p. 58.

32. John G. Hubbell, "Child Prostitution: How It Can Be Stopped," *Reader's Digest* (June 1984), pp. 202, 205.

33. *Ibid.*; Flowers, *Children and Criminality*, pp. 81–83.

34. James, *Entrance into Juvenile Prostitution*, p. 68.

35. Flowers, *The Adolescent Criminal*, p. 58.

36. Lloyd, *For Love or Money*, p. 211.

37. Hilary Abramson, "Sociologists Try to Reach Young Hustlers," *Sacramento Bee* (September 3, 1984), p. A8.

38. Tamar Stieber, "The Boys Who Sell Sex to Men in San Francisco," *Sacramento Bee* (March 4, 1984), p. A22.

39. Weisberg, *Children of the Night*, p. 61.

40. Alfred Danna, "Juvenile Male Prostitution: How Can We Reduce the Problem?" *USA Today* 113 (May 1988): 87.

41. *Ibid.*, p. 88.

42. Cited in Stieber, "The Boys Who Sell Sex to Men," p. A22. See also Flowers, *The Adolescent Criminal*, p. 62; Weisberg, *Children of the Night*, pp. 124–128.

43. Weisberg, *Children of the Night*, p. 75.

44. *Ibid.*, pp. 117–119; Enablers, *Juvenile Prostitution*, p. 89.

45. Weisberg, *Children of the Night*, p. 118; Crowley, "Female Runaway Behavior," p. 80; Harlan, Rodgers, and Slattery, *Male and Female Adolescent Prostitution*, pp. 22–23.

46. Harlan, Rodgers, and Slattery, *Male and Female Adolescent Prostitution*, p. 22.

47. Donald M. Allen, "Young Male Prostitutes: A Psychosocial Study," *Archives of Sexual Behavior* 9, 5 (1980).

48. Flowers, *Children and Criminality*, p. 97.

49. John Zaccaro, Jr., "Children of the Night," *Woman's Day* (March 29, 1988), p. 137.

50. Patricia Hersch, "Coming of Age on City Streets," *Psychology Today* (January 1988), p. 32.

51. *Ibid.*

52. *Ibid.*, p. 31.

53. *Ibid.*, p. 37.

54. Cited in Flowers, *The Adolescent Criminal*, p. 63.

55. Quoted in Hersch, "Coming of Age," p. 37.

Chapter 9. Child Pornography

1. Rita Rooney, "Children for Sale: Pornography's Dark New World," *Reader's Digest* (July 1983), p. 53.

2. Reay Tannahill, *Sex in History* (New York: Stein and Day Publishers, 1980), p. 320.

3. Ronald B. Flowers, *Children and Criminality: The Child as Victim and Perpetrator* (Westport, Conn.: Greenwood Press, 1986), p. 82.

4. Judianne Densen-Gerber and S. F. Hutchinson, "Medical-Legal and Societal Problems Involving Children—Child Prostitution, Child Pornography and Drug-Related Abuse; Recommended Legislation," in Selwyn M. Smith, ed., *The Maltreatment of Children* (Baltimore, Md.: University Park Press, 1978), p. 322.

5. *Ibid.*, p. 321.

6. Rooney, "Children for Sale," p. 55.

7. Ann Burgess, "The Use of Children in Pornography and Sex Rings," *Legal Response: Child Advocacy and Protection* 2, 4 (1981): 1–10.

8. Flowers, *Children and Criminality*, pp. 82–83.

9. "Child Pornography on the Rise Despite Tougher Laws," *Sacramento Union* (April 7, 1984), p. E6.

10. *Ibid.*

11. *Ibid.*

12. 18 U.S.C. §§2251, 2253-2254 (1978).

13. Linda Greenwood, "Justices Uphold Law Barring Child Pornography," *New York Times* (July 3, 1982), p. 1.

14. Rooney, "Children for Sale," pp. 54–55.

15. Flowers, *Children and Criminality*, pp. 82–83.

16. *Ibid.*, p. 83.

Chapter 10. Violent Crimes Against Children

1. U.S. Department of Justice, *Criminal Victimization in the United States, 1991: A National Crime Victimization Survey Report* (Washington, D.C.: Government Printing Office, 1992), pp. 60, 65.

2. U.S. Federal Bureau of Investigation, *Crime in the United States: Uniform Crime Reports, 1992* (Washington, D.C.: Government Printing Office, 1993), p. 16. See also *Uniform Crime Reports* for 1991 and 1983.

3. Ibid., pp. 18–20; Ronald B. Flowers, *Children and Criminality: The Child as Victim and Perpetrator* (Westport, Conn.: Greenwood Press, 1986).

4. Caroline Harlow, *Female Victims of Violent Crime* (Washington, D.C.: U.S. Department of Justice, 1991), p. 9.

5. *Ibid.*

6. *National Crime Victimization Survey*, p. 23.

7. Harlow, *Female Victims*, p. 8.

8. *Ibid.*

9. *Ibid.*, p. 7; *National Crime Victimization Survey*, p. 75; U.S. Department of Justice, *Teenage Victims: A National Crime Survey Report* (Washington, D.C.: Government Printing Office, 1986), p. 8.

10. Ronald B. Flowers, *Demographics and Criminality: The Characteristics of Crime in America* (Westport, Conn.: Greenwood Press, 1989), pp. 99–102.

11. *Uniform Crime Reports*, p. 17.

12. Harlow, *Female Victims*, p. 11.

13. *Teenage Victims*, pp. 2–4.

14. *National Crime Victimization Survey*, p. 106.

15. *Teenage Victims*, p. 4.

Chapter 11. School Violence and Victimization

1. Associated Press, January 6, 1994.

2. *See* R. Barri Flowers, *The Adolescent Criminal: An Examination of Today's Juvenile Offender* (Jefferson, N.C.: McFarland and Co., Inc., 1990), pp. 83–97; U.S. Department of Justice, Office of Justice Programs, *Drugs & Crime Data* (Washington, D.C.: Government Printing Office, 1992); Ken Barun, "How to Help Your Children Stay Off Drugs," *Parade Magazine* (May 1, 1988), p. 15.

3. U.S. Department of Justice, *School Crime: A National Crime Victimization Survey Report* (Washington, D.C.: Government Printing Office, 1991), p. 3.

4. Walter B. Miller, *Violence by Youth Gangs and Youth Groups as a Crime Problem in Major American Cities* (Washington, D.C.: Government Printing Office, 1975); Walter B. Miller, "Gangs, Groups and Serious Youth Crime," in David Schichor and Delos H. Kelly, eds., *Critical Issues in Juvenile Delinquency* (Lexington, Mass.: Lexington Books, 1980).

5. Flowers, *The Adolescent Criminal*, p. 103.

6. *Ibid.*, p. 100.

7. U.S. Department of Justice, *Highlights from 20 Years of Surveying Crime Victims* (Washington, D.C.: Government Printing Office, 1993), p. 27.

8. *School Crime*, pp. 12–13.

Chapter 12. Violent Crimes Against Women

1. U.S. Department of Justice, *Violence Against Women: A National Crime Victimization Survey Report* (Washington, D.C.: Government Printing Office, 1994), p. 2.

2. Ronald B. Flowers, *Demographics and Criminality: The Characteristics of Crime in America* (Westport, Conn.: Greenwood Press, 1989), pp. 99–102.

3. U.S. Federal Bureau of Investigation, *Crime in the United States: Uniform Crime Reports 1992* (Washington, D.C.: Government Printing Office, 1993), p. 16.

4. *Crime Victimization in the United States: 1970–90 Trends*, p. 19.

5. U.S. Department of Justice, Bureau of Justice Statistics, *Highlights from 20 Years of Surveying Crime Victims* (Washington, D.C.: Government Printing Office, 1993), p. 9.

6. *Violence Against Women*, p. 2.

7. Caroline Harlow, *Female Victims of Violent Crime* (Washington, D.C.: U.S. Department of Justice, 1991), p. 7.

8. U.S. Department of Justice, *Criminal Victimization in the United States, 1992: A National Crime Victimization Survey Report* (Washington, D.C.: Government Printing Office, 1994), p. 22.

9. U.S. Department of Justice, *Criminal Victimization in the United States, 1991: A National Crime Victimization Survey Report* (Washington, D.C.: Government Printing Office, 1992), p. 56.

10. *Violence Against Women*, pp. 6–8.

11. *Ibid.*, p. 6.

12. *National Crime Victimization Survey*, p. 86.

13. *Ibid.*, pp. 108–109.

14. *Ibid.*, pp. 110–111.

15. Cited from the Gallup Organization, Inc., in U.S. Department of Justice, *Sourcebook of Criminal Justice Statistics— 1992* (Washington, D.C.: Government Printing Office, 1993), p. 186.

16. George Gallup, Jr., *The Gallup Poll Monthly*, No. 318 (Princeton, N.J.: The Gallup Poll, 1992), p. 53.

17. *Ibid.*

18. Cited from the Roper Organization, Inc., in *Sourcebook of Criminal Justice Statistics*, p. 194.

19. Gallup, Jr., *The Gallup Poll Monthly*, p. 5.

20. Cited from the Gallup Organization, Inc., in *Sourcebook of Criminal Justice Statistics*, p. 211.

Chapter 13. Rape and Sexual Assault of Women

1. Estimate is based on consistent trends through the 1980s until 1993.

2. Carol V. Horos, *Rape* (New Canaan, Conn.: Tobey Publishing Co., 1974), p. 3.

3. Susan Brownmiller, *Against Our Will: Men, Women and Rape* (New York: Simon and Schuster, 1975).

4. U.S. Federal Bureau of Investigation, *Crime in the United States: Uniform Crime Reports 1992* (Washington, D.C.: Government Printing Office, 1993), p. 23.

5. U.S. Department of Justice, Bureau of Justice Statistics, *Highlights from 20 Years of Surveying Crime Victims* (Washington, D.C.: Government Printing Office, 1993), p. 9.

6. U.S. Department of Justice, *Violence Against Women: A National Crime Victimization Survey Report* (Washington, D.C.: Government Printing Office, 1994), p. 2.

7. Diana E. Russell, *Sexual Exploitation: Rape, Child Abuse, and Workplace Harassment* (Beverly Hills: Sage Publications, 1984), pp. 46–47.

8. Brownmiller, *Against Our Will*, p. 190; Nancy Gager and Cathleen Schurr, *Sexual Assault: Confronting Rape in America* (New York: Grosset and Dunlap, 1976), p. 91.

9. Ronald B. Flowers, *Women and Criminality: The Woman as Victim, Offender, and Practitioner* (Westport, Conn.: Greenwood Press, 1987), pp. 27–43.

10. Barbara J. Rodabaugh and Melanie Austin, *Sexual Assault: A Guide for Community Action* (New York: Garland STPM Press, 1981), pp. 24–25.

11. National Commission on the Causes and Prevention of Violence, *Crimes of Violence: A Staff Report,* Vol. 2 (Washington, D.C.: Government Printing Office, 1969).

12. Menachem Amir, *Patterns in Forcible Rape* (Chicago: University of Chicago Press, 1971), p. 261.

13. U.S. Department of Justice, *Criminal Victimization in the United States, 1991: A National Crime Victimization Survey Report* (Washington, D.C.: Government Printing Office, 1992), p. 56.

14. Harlow, *Female Victims,* p. 7.

15. *Ibid.*

16. *National Crime Victimization Survey,* p. 103.

17. "The Date Who Rapes," *Newsweek* (April 9, 1984), p. 91.

18. *Ibid.*

19. Cited in Ellen Sweet, "Date Rape," *Ms/Campus Times* (October 1985), p. 58.

20. "Marital Rape: Drive for Tougher Laws Is Pressed," *New York Times* (May 15, 1987), p. A16.

21. Flowers, *Women and Criminality,* pp. 36–37.

22. A. Nicholas Groth, Ann W. Burgess, and Lynda L. Holmstrom, "Rape: Power, Anger, and Sexuality," *American Journal of Psychiatry* 34 (1977): 1239–1243.

23. Paul H. Gebhard, John H. Gagnon, Wardell B. Pomeroy, and Cornelia V. Christenson, *Sex Offenders: An Analysis of Types* (New York: Harper & Row, 1965), pp. 198–204; Richard T. Rada, *Clinical Aspects of the Rapist* (New York: Grune and Stratton, 1978), pp. 122–130.

24. Julia R. Schwendinger and Herman Schwendinger, *Rape and Inequality* (Beverly Hills: Sage Publications, 1983), p. 65.

25. *Ibid.,* p. 71; Flowers, *Women and Criminality,* p. 40.

26. Lorenne M. Clark and Debra J. Lewis, *Rape: The Price of Coercive Sexuality* (Toronto: Canadian Women's Educational Press, 1977), pp. 128–131.

27. Brownmiller, *Against Our Will,* pp. 13–14.

Chapter 14. Battered Women

1. Caroline Harlow, *Female Victims of Violent Crime* (Washington, D.C.: Office of Justice Programs, 1991), p. 1.

2. Terry Davidson, "Wifebeating: A Recurring Phenomenon Throughout History," as cited in Maria Roy, *The Abusive Partner: An Analysis of Domestic Battering* (New York: Van Nostrand Reinhold, 1982), p. 12.

3. Friedrich Engels, *The Origin of Family Private Property and the State* (Moscow: Progress Publishers, 1948), pp. 53–58.

4. Ronald B. Flowers, *Women and Criminality: The Woman as Victim, Offender, and Practitioner* (Westport, Conn.: Greenwood Press, 1987), p. 15.

5. Flowers, *Women and Criminality,* p. 15; R. Calvert, "Criminal and Civil Liability in Husband-Wife Assaults," in Suzanne K. Steinmetz and Murray Straus, eds., *Violence in the Family* (New York: Dodd, Mead, 1975), p. 89.

6. Mildred D. Pagelow, *Woman Battering: Victims and Their Experiences* (Beverly Hills: Sage Publications, 1981), p. 33.

7. Ronald B. Flowers, *Demographics and Criminality: The Characteristics of Crime in America* (Westport, Conn.: Greenwood Press, 1989), pp. 151–160.

8. Suzanne K. Steinmetz, *The Cycle of Violence: Assertive, Aggressive, and Abusive Family Interaction* (New York: Praeger Publishers, 1977).

9. Lenore E. Walker, "Treatment Alternatives for Battered Women," in Jane R. Chapman and Margaret Gates, eds., *The Victimization of Women* (Beverly Hills: Sage Publications, 1978), p. 144.

10. Diana E. Russell, *Rape in Marriage* (New York: Macmillan, 1982).

11. Cited in Judith Levine, "Crimes Against Women Are Growing and So Are Our Fears," *Glamour* (February 1986), p. 210.

12. Frances Patai, "Pornography and Woman Battering: Dynamic Similarities," in Maria Roy, ed., *The Abusive Partner*, p. 92.

13. *Ibid.*

14. U.S. Federal Bureau of Investigation, *Crime in the United States: Uniform Crime Reports 1992* (Washington, D.C.: Government Printing Office, 1993), p. 17.

15. Flowers, *Women and Criminality*, pp. 15–16.

16. Terry Davidson, *Conjugal Crime: Understanding and Changing the Wife-Beating Pattern* (New York: Hawthorne, 1979).

17. Maria Roy, "Four Thousand Partners in Violence: A Trend Analysis," in Maria Roy, ed., *The Abusive Partner*, pp. 34–35.

18. Harlow, *Female Victims*, p. 7.

19. "Marital Rape: Drive for Tougher Laws Is Pressed," *New York Times* (May 13, 1987), p. A16.

20. Lenore E. Walker, *The Battered Woman Syndrome* (New York: Springer, 1984), pp. 48–49.

21. K. Yllo, *Types of Marital Rape: Three Case Studies,* presented at the National Conference for Family Violence Researchers, University of New Hampshire, Durham, July 1981.

22. Cited in "Marital Rape," p. A16.

23. Russell, *Rape in Marriage.*

24. Roy, "Four Thousand Partners," pp. 31–32.

25. Walker, *The Battered Woman Syndrome*, p. 51.

26. Richard J. Gelles, "Violence and Pregnancy: A Note on the Extent of the Problem and Needed Services," *Family Coordinator* 24 (1975): 81–86.

27. Roy, "Four Thousand Partners," p. 32.

28. Flowers, *Women and Criminality*, pp. 19–20.

29. Walker, *The Battered Woman Syndrome*, p. 55.

30. Quoted in Cheryll Ostrom, "The Battle Scars of Emotional Abuse," *Sacramento Bee* (October 29, 1986), p. B1.

31. Walker, *The Battered Woman Syndrome.*

32. *Ibid.*

33. Cited in Ostrom, "The Battle Scars," p. B1.

34. *Ibid.*

35. Flowers, *Women and Criminality*, p. 20; Kathleen H. Hofeller, *Social, Psychological and Situational Factors in Wife Abuse* (Palo Alto, Calif.: R & E Research Associates, 1982), p. 39.

36. Flowers, *Women and Criminality*, p. 20; Davidson, *Conjugal Crime*, p. 23.

37. Hofeller, *Social, Psychological, and Situational Factors*, p. 43.

38. Bonnie E. Carlson, "Battered Women and Their Assailants," *Social Work* 22, 6 (1977): 456.

39. J. Gayford, "Wife Battering: A Preliminary Survey of 100 Cases," *British Medical Journal* 1 (1975): 194–197.

40. Richard J. Gelles, *The Violent Home: A Study of the Physical Aggression Between Husbands and Wives* (Beverly Hills: Sage Publications, 1972).

41. Murray A. Straus, "Sexual Inequality, Cultural Norms, and Wife-Beating," *Victimology* 1 (1976): 62–66.

42. Lee H. Bowker, *Women, Crime, and the Criminal Justice System* (Lexington, Mass.: Lexington Books, 1978), p. 128.

43. Studies show that only around 1 in 3 fathers totally complies with court ordered child support during the first year after divorce. By the 10th year of divorce, only 13 percent of the fathers pay full child support, while nearly 8 out of 10 fathers pay no child support at all after 10 years.

44. Walker, *The Battered Woman Syndrome*.

45. Cited in Nancy Baker, "Why Women Stay with Men Who Beat Them," *Glamour* (August 1983), p. 366.

46. Robert Langley and Richard C. Levy, *Wife Beating: The Silent Crisis* (New York: E. P. Dutton, 1977).

47. Suzanne K. Steinmetz, "The Battered Husband Syndrome," *Victimology* 2 (1978): 507.

48. Richard J. Gelles, "The Myth of Battered Husbands," *MS* (October 1979): 65–72.

49. Rebecca Dobash and Russell Dobash, *Violence Against Wives* (New York: Free Press, 1979).

50. K. Yllo and Murray A. Straus, "Interpersonal Violence Among Married and Cohabiting Couples," paper presented at the annual meeting of the National Council on Family Relations, Philadelphia, 1978.

51. G. Rasko, "The Victim of the Female Killer," *Victimology* 1 (1976): 396–402.

52. J. Totman, *The Murderess: A Psychological Study of the Process* (Ann Arbor: University Microfilms, 1971).

53. D. Ward, M. Jackson, and R. Ward, "Crimes of Violence by Women," in D. Mulvihill, M. M. Tamin, and L. A. Curtis, eds., *Crimes of Violence* (Washington, D.C.: Government Printing Office, 1969).

54. *Uniform Crime Reports*, p. 17.

55. Cited in Sandy Nelson, "Women Who Kill," *Sacramento Bee* (December 30, 1986), p. B9.

56. Cited in Nick Jordan, "Till Murder Us Do Part," *Psychology Today* (July 1985), p. 7.

57. Walker, *The Battered Woman Syndrome*, p. 40.

58. Cited in Glen Collins, "A Study Assesses Traits of Women Who Kill," *New York Times* (July 7, 1986), p. C18.

59. Quoted in Ostrom, "The Battle Scars of Emotional Abuse," p. B1.

Chapter 15. The Prostitution of Women

1. Abraham Flexner, *Prostitution in Europe* (New York: Century Co., 1914), p. 11.

2. Howard B. Woolston, *Prostitution in the United States* (New York: Century Co., 1921), p. 35.

3. *State v. Perry*, 249 Oregon 76, 81, 436 p. 2d 252, 255 (1968).

4. Nathan C. Heard, *Howard Street* (New York: Dial Press, 1970), p. 86.

5. U.S. Federal Bureau of Investigation, *Crime in the United States: Uniform Crime Reports 1992* (Washington, D.C.: Government Printing Office, 1993), pp. 231–232.

6. Ronald B. Flowers, *Women and Criminality: The Woman as Victim, Offender, and Practitioner* (Westport, Conn.: Greenwood Press, 1987), p. 120.

7. *Uniform Crime Reports*, p. 226.

8. Marilyn G. Haft, "Hustling for Rights," in Laura Crites, ed., *The Female Offender* (Lexington, Mass.: Lexington Books, 1976), pp. 212–213.

9. Jennifer James, "The Prostitute as Victim," in Jane R. Chapman and Margaret Gates, eds., *The Victimization of Women* (Beverly Hills: Sage Publications, 1978), p. 176.

10. "Offenders in the District of Columbia," *Report of the D.C. Commission on the Status of Women* (Washington, D.C.: Government Printing Office, 1972), p. 18.

11. Flowers, *Women and Criminality*, p. 129.

12. Haft, "Hustling for Rights," p. 212.

13. Harry Benjamin and R. E. L. Masters, *Prostitution and Morality* (New York: Julian Press, 1964).

14. Paul J. Goldstein, *Prostitution and Drugs* (Lexington, Mass.: Lexington Books, 1979), pp. 34–37.

15. Flowers, *Women and Criminality*, p. 124.

16. Cesare Lombroso and William Ferraro, *The Female Offender* (New York: Appleton, 1900).

17. William I. Thomas, *The Unadjusted Girl: With Cases and Standpoint for Behavior Analysis* (New York: Harper and Row, 1923).

18. Flowers, *Women and Criminality*, p. 121; Sigmund Freud, *New Introductory Lectures on Psychoanalysis* (New York: W. W. Norton, 1933).

19. Charles Winick and Paul M. Kinsie, *The Lively Commerce* (Chicago: Quadrangle Books, 1971).

20. Flowers, *Women and Criminality*, pp. 121–122; Kingsley Davis, "The Sociology of Prostitution," *American Sociological Review* 2 (1937): 744–755.

21. Edwin M. Lemert, *Social Pathology* (New York: McGraw-Hill, 1951), p. 237.

22. Robert E. Faris, *Social Disorganization* (New York: Ronald Press, 1955), p. 271.

23. Jennifer James, "Motivations for Entrance into Prostitution," in Laura Crites, ed., *The Female Offender* (Lexington, Mass.: Lexington Books, 1976), p. 186; Norman Jackson, Richard O'Toole, and Gilbert Geis, "The Self-Image of the Prostitute," in John H. Gagnon and William Simon, eds., *Sexual Deviance* (New York: Harper and Row, 1967), p. 46.

24. Winick and Kinsie, *The Lively Commerce*, p. 271.

25. Flowers, *Women and Criminality*, p. 122; Lemert, *Social Pathology*.

26. James, "Motivations for Entrance into Prostitution," p. 194.

27. Flowers, *Women and Criminality*; Mimi H. Silbert, "Delancey Street Study: Prostitution and Sexual Assault," Summary of results (San Francisco: Delancey Street Foundation, 1982), p. 3.

28. Sparky Harlan, Luanne L. Rodgers, and Brian Slattery, *Male and Female Adolescent Prostitution: Huckleberry House Sexual Minority Youth Services Project* (Washington, D.C.: Government Printing Office, 1981), p. 21.

29. Harlan, Rodgers, and Slattery, *Male and Female Adolescent Prostitution*, p. 21.

30. Flowers, *Women and Criminality*; Silbert, "Prostitution and Sexual Assault," p. 62.

31. Flowers, *Women and Criminality*; U.S. Department of Justice, *Attorney General's Commission on Pornography: Final Report*, Vol. 1 (Washington, D.C.: Government Printing Office, 1986); R. Barri Flowers, *The Adolescent Criminal: An Examination of Today's Juvenile Offender* (Jefferson, N.C.: McFarland and Co., Inc., 1990).

32. William E. McAuliffe and Robert A. Gordon, "A Test of Lindesmith's Theory of Addiction: The Frequency of Euphoria Among Long-Term Addicts," *American Journal of Sociology* 79 (1974): 795–840.

33. See Flowers, *Women and Criminality*; James A. Inciardi, "Women, Heroin and Property Crime," in Susan K. Datesman and Frank R. Scarpitti, eds., *Women, Crime, and Justice* (New York: Oxford University Press, 1980).

34. Flowers, *Women and Criminality*, p. 128. Margaret Engel, "Many Prostitutes Found to Be AIDS Carriers," *Washington Post* (September 20, 1985), p. A1.

35. Cited in Ronald B. Flowers, "Violent Women: Are They Catching Up to Violent Men or Have They Surpassed Them?" (Unpublished article, June 1988).

36. *Ibid.*

37. George Gallup, Jr., *The Gallup Poll Monthly*, No. 313 (Princeton, N.J.: The Gallup Poll, October 1991), p. 73.

Chapter 16. Pornography and Violence Against Women

1. Ronald B. Flowers, *Women and Criminality: The Woman as Victim, Offender, and Practitioner* (Westport, Conn.: Greenwood Press, 1987), pp. 47–48.

2. Helen E. Longino, "Pornography, Oppression, and Freedom: A Closer Look," in Laura Lederer, ed., *Take Back the Night: Women on Pornography* (New York: William Morrow, 1980), p. 44.

3. Flowers, *Women and Criminality*, p. 48.

4. *Ibid.*

5. *Ibid.*

6. Frances Patai, "Pornography and Woman Battering: Dynamic Similarities," in Maria Roy, ed., *The Abusive Partner: An Analysis of Domestic Battering* (New York: Van Nostrand Reinhold, 1982), pp. 91–92.

7. *Ibid.*, p. 93.

8. U.S. Department of Justice, *Attorney General's Commission on Pornography: Final Report*, Vol. 1 (Washington, D.C.: Government Printing Office, 1986), p. 215.

9. Commission on Obscenity and Pornography, *Technical Report of the Commission on Obscenity and Pornography: Legal Analysis*, Vol. 2 (Washington, D.C.: Government Printing Office, 1971).

10. *Attorney General's Commission on Pornography*, p. 326.

11. *Ibid.*, pp. 324–325.

12. *Ibid.*, pp. 465–490.

13. Flowers, *Women and Criminality*, p. 53.

14. Lederer, *Take Back the Night*, pp. 19–20.

15. Patai, "Pornography and Woman Battering," p. 93.

16. *Ibid.*, pp. 93–94.

17. Kathleen Barry, *Female Sexual Slavery* (Englewood Cliffs, N.J.: Prentice-Hall, 1979), p. 145.

18. Patai, "Pornography and Woman Battering," p. 96.

19. Cited in Hillary Johnson, "Violence Against Women—Is Porn to Blame?" *Vogue* 175 (September 1985), p. 678.

20. Larry Baron and Murray A. Straus, "Sexual Stratification, Pornography, and Rape in the United States," in Neil M. Malamuth and Edward Donnerstein, eds., *Pornography and Sexual Aggression* (Orlando, Fla.: Academic Press, 1984), p. 206.

21. Cited in Johnson, "Violence Against Women," p. 678.

22. William A. Stanmeyer, *The Seduction of Society* (Ann Arbor, Mich.: Servant Books, 1984), pp. 29–30.

23. *Ibid.*, p. 49.

24. *Ibid.*, p. 42; Flowers, *Women and Criminality*, p. 54.

25. Stanmeyer, *The Seduction of Society*, p. 49.

26. Flowers, *Women and Criminality*, pp. 51–56.

27. Stanmeyer, *The Seduction of Society*, pp. 67–68.

28. Linda T. Sanford and Mary E. Donovan, "What Women Should Know About Pornography," *Family Circle* (February 1981), p. 12.

Chapter 17. Sexual Harassment and Stalking

1. Elizabeth A. Stanko, *Intimate Intrusions: Women's Experience on Male Violence* (London: Routledge and Kegan Paul, 1985), p. 60.

2. *Ibid.*, pp. 60–61.

3. Ronald B. Flowers, *Women and Criminality: The Woman as Victim, Offender, and Practitioner* (Westport, Conn.: Greenwood Press, 1987), p. 66.

4. "Questionnaire: How Do You Handle Sex on the Job?" *Redbook* (January 1976).

5. Laura J. Evans, "Sexual Harassment: Women's Hidden Occupational Hazard," in Jane Roberts Chapman and Margaret Gates, eds., *The Victimization of Women* (Beverly Hills: Sage Publications, 1978), pp. 203–222.

6. U.S. Merit Systems Protection Board, Office of Merit Systems Review and Studies, *Sexual Harassment in the Federal Workplace: Is It a Problem?* (Washington, D.C.: Government Printing Office, 1978), p. 5.

7. *Ibid.*, p. V.

8. Alan Deutschman, "Dealing with Sexual Harassment," *Fortune* 124 (November 4, 1991), p. 145.

9. *Ibid.*, pp. 145, 148.

10. *Ibid.*, p. 148.

11. See Title VII of the 1964 Civil Rights Act.

12. Deutschman, "Dealing With Sexual Harassment," p. 148.

13. *Ibid.*

14. Claire Serant, "Stalked: Any Woman Can Become a Victim of This Heinous Crime," *Essence* (October 1993), p. 73.

15. "Nowhere to Hide," *People* (May 17, 1993), p. 63.

16. *Ibid.*

17. "Murderous Obsession: Can New Laws Deter Spurned Lovers and Fans From 'Stalking' or Worse?" *Newsweek* 120 (July 13, 1992), p. 61.

18. Serant, "Stalked," p. 76.

19. Shirley Streshinsky, "The Stalker and Her Prey," *Glamour* (August 1992), p. 238.

20. Quoted in Serant, "Stalked," p. 73.

21. *Ibid.*, p. 76.

22. "Nowhere to Hide," p. 63.

23. "Murderous Obsession," p. 61.

Chapter 18. Responding to the Victimization and Sexual Exploitation of Children and Women

1. 42 U.S.C. §5101-5106 (1974); as amended by Child Abuse Prevention and Treatment and Adoption Reform Act of 1978, P.L. No. 95-266, 92 Stat. 205 (1978).

2. The Child Abuse, Domestic Violence, Adoption and Family Act of 1992, P.L. 100–295.

3. U.S. Department of Health and Human Services, *National Child Abuse and Neglect Data System: Working Paper #2—1991 Summary Data Component* (Washington, D.C.: National Center on Child Abuse and Neglect, 1993), pp. 1, 6.

4. The Runaway and Homeless Youth Act, 42 U.S.C. §5701-5702 (Supp. II, 1978).

5. 18 U.S.C. §2251, 2253–2254 (1978).

6. Cited in Linda Greenwood, "Justices Uphold Law Barring Child Pornography," *New York Times* (July 3, 1983), p. 1.

7. 18 U.S.C. §1073 (1980).

8. 128 Cong. Rec. 8, 566 (1982).

9. H.R. 3694 (1993).

10. James L. Jenkins, Marsha K. Salus, and Gretchen L. Schultze, *Child Protective Services: A Guide for Workers* (Washington, D.C.: Government Printing Office, 1979).

11. *Child Abuse and Neglect: A Shared Community Concern* (Washington, D.C.: National Center on Child Abuse and Neglect, 1992), p. 10.

12. *Ibid.*

13. *Ibid.*

14. Caroline Harlow, *Female Victims of Violent Crime* (Washington, D.C.: Office of Justice Programs, 1991), p. 111.

15. *Ibid.*

16. *Ibid.*

17. Ronald B. Flowers, *Women and Criminality: The Woman as Victim, Offender, and Practitioner* (Westport, Conn.: Greenwood Press, 1987), p. 191.

18. Title VII of the 1964 Civil Rights Act.

19. See *Meritor Savings Bank v. Vinson* (1986).

20. "Nowhere to Hide," *People* (May 17, 1993), p. 63.

Bibliography

Barry, Kathleen. *Female Sexual Slavery.* Englewood Cliffs, N.J.: Prentice-Hall, 1979.

Bart, Pauline B. *Stopping Rape: Successful Survival Strategies.* New York: Pergamon Press, 1985.

Blume, E. Sue. *Secret Survivors: Uncovering Incest and Its Aftereffects in Women.* New York: John Wiley & Sons, Inc., 1990.

Boyle, Patrick. *Scout's Honor: Sexual Abuse in America's Most Trusted Institution.* Rocklin, Calif.: Prima Building, 1994.

Bravo, Ellen and Ellen Cassedy. *The 9 to 5 Guide to Combating Sexual Harassment.* New York, NY: John Wiley & Sons, 1993.

Brownmiller, Susan. *Against Our Will: Men, Women and Rape.* New York: Simon and Schuster, 1975.

Buchwald, Emilie, Pamela R. Fletcher and Martha Roth. *Transforming a Rape Culture.* Minneapolis, Minn: Milkweed Editions, 1993.

Burgess, A. W., C. R. Hartman, M. P. McCausland, P. Power. "Response Patterns in Children and Adolescents Exploited Through Sex Rings and Pornography." *American Journal of Psychiatry* 141, 5 (1984): 656–662.

_____ and Christine A. Grant. *Children Traumatized in Sex Rings.* Washington, D.C.: National Center for Missing and Exploited Children, 1988.

Danna, Alfred. "Juvenile Male Prostitution: How Can We Reduce the Problem?" *USA Today* 113 (May 1985): 86–88.

Davidson, Terry. *Conjugal Crime: Understanding and Changing the Wife-Beating Pattern.* New York: Hawthorne Books, 1979.

Earle, Alice M. *Child Life in Colonial Days.* New York: Macmillan, 1926.

Edwards, Susan S. *Policing Domestic Violence: Women, the Law and the State.* Newbury Park, Calif.: Sage Publications, 1989.

Evans, Patricia. *The Verbally Abusive Relationship.* Holbrook, Mass.: Bob Evans, Inc. Publishers, 1992.

Faller, Kathleen C. *Understanding Child Sexual Maltreatment.* Newbury Park, Calif.: Sage Publications, 1990.

Faludi, Susan. *Backlash: The Undeclared War Against American Women.* New York: Crown, 1991.

Finkelhor, David. *Sexually Victimized Children.* New York: Free Press, 1979.

Flowers, Ronald Barri. *Children and Criminality: The Child as Victim and Perpetrator.* Westport, Conn.: Greenwood Press, 1986.
_____. *Women and Criminality: The Woman as Victim, Offender, and Practitioner.* Westport, Conn.: Greenwood Press, 1987.
Fontana, Vincent J. *The Maltreated Child: The Maltreatment Syndrome in Children,* 2nd ed. Springfield, Ill.: Charles C Thomas, 1971.
Gager, Nancy and Cathleen Schurr. *Sexual Assault: Confronting Rape in America.* New York: Grosset and Dunlap, 1976.
Gelles, Richard J. *The Violent Home.* Beverly Hills: Sage Publications, 1987.
Gil, David G. *Violence Against Children: Physical Child Abuse in the United States.* Cambridge: Harvard University Press, 1970.
Harlan, Sparky, Luanne L. Rodgers, and Brian Slattery. *Male and Female Adolescent Prostitution: Huckelberry House Sexual Minority Youth Services Project.* Washington, D.C.: Department of Health and Human Services, 1981.
Harlow, Caroline W. *Female Victims of Violent Crime.* Washington, D.C.: Office of Justice Programs, 1991.
Hersch, Patricia. "Coming of Age on City Streets." *Psychology Today* (January 1988): pp. 28–37.
James, Jennifer. *Entrance into Juvenile Prostitution.* Washington, D.C.: National Institute of Mental Health, 1980.
Jones, Ann. *Next Time, She'll Be Dead: Battering & How To Stop It.* Boston, Mass.: Beacon Press, 1994.
Katz, Sedelle, and Mary A. Mazur. *Understanding the Rape Victim: A Synthesis of Research Findings.* New York: John Wiley and Sons, 1979.
Langelan, Martha J. *Back Off!: How to Confront and Stop Sexual Harassment and Harassers.* New York, NY: Fireside, 1993.
Langley, Robert and Richard C. Levy. *Wife Beating: The Silent Crisis.* New York: E. P. Dutton, 1977.
Leach, Penelope. *Children First: What Our Society Must Do—And Is Not Doing for Our Children Today.* New York: Alfred A. Knopf, 1994.
Lederer, Laura, ed. *Take Back the Night: Women on Pornography.* New York: William Morrow, 1980.
Lloyd, Robin. *For Money or Love: Boy Prostitution in America.* New York: Ballantine, 1976.
McCurdy, Karen and Deborah Daro. *Current Trends in Child Abuse Reporting and Fatalities: The Results of the 1992 Annual Fifty State Survey.* Chicago, Ill.: National Committee for Prevention of Child Abuse, 1993.
Malamuth, Neil M., and Edward Donnerstein. *Pornography and Sexual Aggression.* Orlando, Fla.: Academic Press, 1984.
Martin, Del. *Battered Wives.* San Francisco: Glide Publications, 1976.
Morneau, Robert H. and Robert R. Rockwell. *Sex, Motivation and the Criminal Offender.* Springfield, Ill.: Charles C Thomas, 1980.
National Center on Child Abuse and Neglect. *National Child Abuse and Neglect Data System: Working Paper #2—1991 Summary Data Component.* Washington, D.C.: Government Printing Office, 1993.
O'Brien, Shirley. *Child Pornography.* Dubuque, Iowa: Kendall/Hunt, 1983.
Okun, Lewis. *Woman Abuse: Facts Replacing Myths.* New York: University of New York Press, 1986.
Oliver, J. E. "The Epidemiology of Child Abuse." In Selwyn M. Smith, ed. *The Maltreatment of Children.* Baltimore, Md.: University Park Press, 1978.

Pagelow, Mildred D. *Woman-Battering: Victims and Their Experiences.* Beverly Hills: Sage Publications, 1981.

Parrish, Dee A. *Abused: A Guide to Recovery for Adult Survivors of Emotional/ Physical Child Abuse.* Barrytown, NY: Station Hill Press, Inc., 1990.

Paymar, Michael. *Violent No More: Helping Men End Domestic Abuse.* Alameda, Calif.: Hunter House, Inc., 1993.

Radbill, Samuel X. "A History of Child Abuse and Infanticide." In Ray E. Helfer and C. Henry Kempe, eds. *The Battered Child,* 2nd ed. Chicago: University of Chicago Press, 1974.

Reinhardt, J. M. *Sex Perversions and Sex Crimes.* Springfield, Ill.: Charles C. Thomas, 1957.

Renvoize, Jean. *Incest: A Family Pattern.* London: Routledge and Kegan Paul, 1982.

Roberts, Cathy. *Women and Rape.* New York, NY: New York University Press, 1989.

Rooney, Rita. "Children for Sale: Pornography's Dark New World." *Reader's Digest* (July 1983): 53–55.

Roy, Maria, ed. *The Abusive Partner: An Analysis of Domestic Battering.* New York: Van Nostrand Reinhold, 1982.

Russell, Diana E. H. *Intrafamilial Child Sexual Abuse: A San Francisco Survey.* Berkeley, Calif.: Wright Institute, 1983.

————. *Rape in Marriage.* New York: Macmillan, 1982.

————. *Sexual Exploitation: Rape, Child Sexual Abuse, and Workplace Harassment.* Beverly Hills: Sage Publications, 1983.

Satchell, Michael. "Kids for Sale: A Shocking Report on Child Prostitution Across America." *Parade Magazine* (July 20, 1986): pp. 4–6.

Shoop, Robert J. and Jack W. Hayhow, Jr. *Sexual Harassment in Our Schools.* Needham Heights, Mass.: Allyn and Bacon, 1994.

Solomon, Theo. "History and Demography of Child Abuse." *Pediatrics* 51, 4 (1973): 773–776.

Stanko, Elizabeth, A. *Intimate Intrusions: Women's Experiences of Male Violence.* London: Routledge and Kegan Paul, 1985.

Steinmetz, Suzanne. *The Cycle of Violence: Assertive, Aggressive and Abusive Family Interaction.* New York: Praeger, 1977.

Straus, Murray A., Richard J. Gelles, Suzanne K. Steinmetz. *Behind Closed Doors: Violence in the American Family.* New York: Doubleday, 1980.

Tannahill, Reay. *Sex in History.* New York: Stein and Day Publishers, 1980.

Tifft, Larry L. *Battering of Women.* Boulder, CO: Westview Press, Inc., 1993.

U.S. Department of Health and Human Services. *Child Abuse and Neglect: A Shared Community Concern.* Washington, D.C.: Government Printing Office, 1992.

U.S. Department of Health and Human Services. *Research Symposium on Child Sexual Abuse.* Washington, D.C.: Office of Human Development Services, 1988.

U.S. Department of Justice. *Attorney General's Commission on Pornography: Final Report,* Vol. 1. Washington, D.C.: Government Printing Office, 1986.

U.S. Department of Justice. Bureau of Justice Statistics. *Highlights from 20 Years of Surveying Crime Victims: The National Crime Victimization Survey, 1973–92.* Washington, D.C.: Government Printing Office, 1993.

U.S. Department of Justice. Bureau of Justice Statistics Special Report. *Family Violence.* Washington, D.C.: Government Printing Office, 1984.

U.S. Department of Justice. *Criminal Victimization in the United States: 1973–90 Trends.* Washington, D.C.: Government Printing Office, 1992.

U.S. Department of Justice. *Criminal Victimization in the United States, 1991: A National Crime Victimization Survey Report.* Washington, D.C.: Government Printing Office, 1992.

U.S. Department of Justice. *Criminal Victimization in the United States, 1992: A National Crime Victimization Survey Report.* Washington, D.C.: Government Printing Office, 1994.

U.S. Department of Justice. *School Crime: A National Crime Victimization Survey Report.* Washington, D.C.: Government Printing Office, 1991.

U.S. Department of Justice. *Sourcebook of Criminal Justice Statistics—1992.* Washington, D.C.: Government Printing Office, 1993.

U.S. Department of Justice. *Teenage Victims: A National Crime Survey Report.* Washington, D.C.: Government Printing Office, 1986.

U.S. Department of Justice. *Violence Against Women: A National Crime Victimization Survey Report.* Washington, D.C.: Government Printing Office, 1994.

U.S. Federal Bureau of Investigation. *Crime in the United States: Uniform Crime Reports 1992.* Washington, D.C. Government Printing Office, 1993.

U.S. Merit Systems Protection Board, Office of Merit Systems Review and Statutes. *Sexual Harassment in the Federal Workplace: Is it a Problem?* Washington, D.C.: Government Printing Office, 1981.

Vanderbilt, Heidi. "Incest: A Chilling Report." *Lears* (February 1992): pp. 60–74.

Walker, Lenore E. *The Battered Woman Syndrome.* New York: Springer Publishing Co., 1984.

————. *Terrifying Love: Why Battered Women Kill and How Society Responds.* New York, NY: Harper & Row, 1989.

Weisberg, D. Kelly. *Children of the Night: A Study of Adolescent Prostitution.* Lexington, Mass.: Lexington Books, 1985.

Wiehe, Vernon R. and Teresa Herring. *Perilous Rivalry: When Siblings Become Abusive.* Lexington, Mass.: Lexington Books, 1991.

Williams, Gertrude J., and John Money, eds. *Traumatic Abuse and Neglect of Children at Home.* Baltimore, Md.: Johns Hopkins University Press, 1980.

Index

abandonment 7, 10, 17, 20

abducted children 1, 45–49; *see also* missing children

Abrahamsen, D. 34

abuse 5, 47, 90, 171; causes of 19–22; cycle of 17, 19; and delinquency 19; and missing children 47; and neglect 5–22; *see also* under specific abuse

Abused Women's Aid in Crisis 159

Academic American Encyclopedia 180

acquaintance rape 143, 149–150; *see also* date rape; domestic violence; marital rape; rape

Adams, D.E. 19

The Admirable Discourses of the Plain Girl 90

Against Our Will: Men, Women and Rape (Brownmiller) 144, 154

aggravated assault 29, 105, 142

AIDS (Acquired Immune Deficiency Syndrome) 36, 44–45, 85, 88–89, 171, 178

alcohol abuse 17, 32, 43, 44, 88, 118

American Bar Association (ABA) 46, 55

American Enterprise Institute 55

American Humane Association (AHA) 13, 49, 56

American Journal of Psychiatry 29

American Public Welfare Association 55

Amir, Menachem 147

Aristotle 20

assault(s) 1, 23, 25, 29, 64, 87, 93, 97, 103, 105, 110, 111, 113, 116, 118, 123, 127, 134, 137, 140, 142, 143, 145, 177, 183; aggravated 29, 105, 142; sexual 26, 54, 56, 78, 134, 143–153, 160, 179, 183–184, 188

Assaultive crimes 103, 105

Attorney General's Commission on Pornography 181–182

Baron, Larry 184

Bart, Pauline 183

battered child syndrome 1; *see also* child abuse; child neglect

"battered husband syndrome" 166

"battered parent syndrome" 32

"battered woman syndrome" 157

The Battered Woman Syndrome (Walker) 167

battered women 156–168; and abusive backgrounds 164; the batterers of 159–160, 163–164; breaking the cycle of 168; characteristics of 158–159; defining the 157, 163; extent of 157–158; history of 156–157 and marital rape 160–161; and pornography 182–183; and psychological abuse 162–163; self-

231